TEACHING ENGLISH SOUTH-EAST ASIA

Nuala O'Sullivan

PASSPORT BOOKS
a division of *NTC/Contemporary Publishing Company*
Lincolnwood, Illinois USA

Published by Passport Books
a division of NTC/Contemporary Publishing Company
4255 West Touhy Avenue
Lincolnwood (Chicago), Illinois
60646-1975

ISBN 0-8442-0877-9
Library of Congress Catalog Card Number: on file

First published by In Print Publishing Ltd.
9 Beaufort Terrace
Brighton BN2 2SU
UK

Typeset by MC Typeset
Printed in the U.K. by Bell & Bain

In memory of
James Gildea O'Sullivan (1915–1995)

Acknowledgments

Thanks to: Colin Bell, Conor Boyle, Natalie Burwell, Jane Butterworth, Sarah Christie, Duncan Fyfe, Alastair Dingwall, Áine Doody, John Edmondson, Anthony Green, Anna Groom, Niki Meehan, Catherine Nightingale, Francis O'Brien, Jerry O'Sullivan, Denley Pike, Emma Robinson, Maja Sanchez, Heather Swabey, Pascale Taylor, Rachel Wijaksono and Simon Winetroube.

I would especially like to thank Natalie Burwell and Sarah Christie. Natalie co-wrote Chapters 1–6, and helped enormously with proof-reading and editing, and Sarah co-wrote chapter 4 (Thailand).

About the author

Nuala O'Sullivan has spent the last seven years teaching English in South-east Asia. She has taught in Singapore, Indonesia and Thailand and has travelled extensively throughout the region. She is currently a teacher-trainer in ECC (Thailand), Bangkok and an English language presenter on Keng, Keng, Keng, a weekly Thai children's TV programme.

The advice given in *Teaching English in South-east Asia* is based mainly on first-hand experience.

International House

International House (IH) began in 1953, when John and Brita Haycraft opened a language school in Cordoba, Spain. It has since developed into the largest independent British-based organization for teaching English, with over 100 000 students, 2 000 teachers, and some 90 schools around the world.

The home of the organization is International House in London, a non-profit-making educational charity whose aim is to raise the standard of English teaching worldwide. Trustees include prominent academics, as well as representatives of the British Council, ARELS/FELCO and BBC English by Radio and Television.

International House in London, based at 106 Piccadilly, operates one of the principal schools of English in the UK, as well as International House Teacher Training. The latter offers a variety of courses leading to the Cambridge/RSA CELTA and the Cambridge/RSA DTEFLA Diploma, and courses for foreign teachers of English. It also offers specialized training courses - Teaching Business English, Development Course in Teacher Training, Director of Studies Training Course, etc. As well as being responsible for over half of the Cambridge/RSA CELTA training in the world, International House Teacher Training is the sole body authorized to offer a Distance Training Programme leading to the Cambridge/RSA DTEFLA.

International House in London is also the home of the Central Department, headquarters of the IH World Organization. This is an association of independent language schools and teacher training institutes which are affiliated to, but not owned by, the International House Trust. The Central Department supplies the affiliated schools with materials and advice on a wide range of educational and administrative matters, organizes annual conferences, and monitors standards. Through its Staffing Unit, IH recruits teachers and senior staff for the affiliated schools and other approved institutes.

The opinions expressed in this book are not necessarily those of IH, and, while every care has been taken to ensure accuracy, IH cannot accept responsibility for any errors or omissions.

Table of contents

CHAPTER 4
THAILAND

CHAPTER 5
LAOS

CHAPTER 6
CAMBODIA

CHAPTER 7
VIETNAM

CHAPTER 8
MALAYSIA

CHAPTER 9
SINGAPORE

CHAPTER 10
BRUNEI

CHAPTER 11
INDONESIA

CHAPTER 12
THE PHILIPPINES

Figure 1. South-east Asia.

Introduction

My aim in writing this book has been to provide a much-needed and easily accessible resource book for people who are interested in teaching and living in South-east Asia.

Chapters 1–3 provide an overview of living and teaching in South-east Asia and **Chapters 4–12** give detailed guides to nine of the countries in the region.

In **Chapter 1** the similarities between countries in the region are highlighted; similar customs, traditions and religions in the region are considered. Also in this chapter I look at health-care in South-east Asia, as well as the Asian attitude to women, gays and lesbians and physically challenged people.

Chapter 2 tells you how to be trained as an EFL (English as a foreign language) teacher and how to find a job in South-east Asia. There is advice on training courses in Australia, New Zealand, the UK, Ireland, the USA and Canada, as well as on courses available in South-east Asia. There are tips on how to find a job, either before or after you arrive in South-east Asia, in both the voluntary and private sectors. There are also ten vital questions to ask at an interview, whether you are being interviewed at home or in South-east Asia.

Chapter 3 analyses difficulties students in the region have with English and aims to sensitize teachers to cultural considerations in the South-east Asian classroom. I look at how South-east Asian students are culturally different from Western students and suggest ways of teaching them that will increase your chances of being a successful teacher while in South-east Asia. I also look at some of the common problems South-east Asian students have in the areas of grammar, pronunciation and listening.

Teaching Asians to speak English is often a very difficult task. Although many students in South-east Asia have studied English for five years or more, they often still find it almost impossible to speak with any degree of fluency. *Teaching English in South-east Asia* helps you to understand Asian students, and will be a source of ideas for unlocking their capabilities. It contains, for example, 20 ways of helping Asian students to relax – which are key in creating a non-threatening classroom and a place where students feel safe enough to attempt fluency. The book is full of practical ideas which you can put to immediate use in the classroom, whether you are already a practising teacher, or a complete novice to teaching.

Chapters 4–12 provide a country-by-country living and teaching guide for nine countries in South-east Asia: Thailand, Laos, Cambodia, Vietnam, Malaysia, Singapore, Brunei, Indonesia and the Philippines. Here you will find information on visa requirements, how to find long-term accommodation, useful addresses of schools, places to stay, and names and addresses of likely pubs and bars in which to find other teachers or expats.

Some country chapters are much shorter than others, and this is a reflection of the amount of teaching work available in those countries. For example, in Brunei and the Philippines many local people speak English, so there is not much demand for EFL teachers. Some country chapters may seem long considering the amount of EFL work available there. However, as countries like Laos, Vietnam and Cambodia continue to open up to capitalism, the private EFL market will almost certainly expand. The chapters on Laos, Vietnam and Cambodia reflect this potential. Burma is not included is this book because of the lack of teaching opportunities at present. A small British Council Direct Teaching Operation (DTO) has opened up recently in Rangoon, but other than that paid EFL posts are minimal. It is also the case the Aung San Suu Kyi, the leader of the National League for Democracy and a Nobel Peace Prize recipient, has asked that tourists and business people stay away from Burma until full human rights and a democratic government have been restored there.

I have made every effort to make this book user-friendly. In addition to laying out the information as clearly as possible, I have tried to make it easy to find a topic or piece of information. There is an extensive table of contents, as well as an index. In addition I have included up to six appendices in each of the country chapters covering areas such as case histories of teachers or volunteers who have worked there, public holidays, and useful words and phrases.

Teaching English in South-east Asia deals with the practicalities of living in the region. The needs of a long-term visitor are different from those of a traveller and this book includes valuable information to help you settle comfortably in South-east Asia. To make the most of your time abroad you might need to know how to interpret a Thai address or how to avoid cultural misunderstanding in Muslim Brunei – and this book will help you do it.

Who goes to South-east Asia?

People who teach English in South-east Asia fall into four main categories. First, there are qualified EFL teachers who go to teach

English professionally. These teachers usually enjoy a higher standard of living than would be possible on the same salary in the West. Second, there are those who want to contribute to development in the region, usually through volunteer work. (See below for details of aid organizations working in South-east Asia.) These volunteers often use their EFL skills in government schools, teacher-training colleges, or refugee camps and they are usually paid a small living allowance. Third, there are those who go to South-east Asia to study a particular aspect of Asian culture – for example, to learn to play *gamelan* music in Indonesia, to subject themselves to a Thai kickboxing regimen, or to practise Buddhist meditation in Vietnam. Finally, there are those who are travelling in South-east Asia and find that a month or two is just not long enough to see all there is to see. People in these last two groups often try to supplement their savings with EFL work. Although this is beginning to change, there are still opportunities for unqualified teachers to earn some extra cash teaching English either privately or through less reputable schools in the region.

Telephone and fax numbers

Telephone and fax number are given with their city code in brackets, eg Bangkok numbers are prefaced by (02), Kuala Lumpur numbers by (03), London numbers by (0171), etc. When calling from outside the country you should dial your country's code for international calls, followed by the national code and the city code without the 0, eg to phone Bangkok from the UK you should dial 00 66 2 and then the number.

National codes for countries included in this book are:

Australia	61	New Zealand	64
Brunei	673	The Philippines	63
Cambodia	855	Singapore	65
Canada	1	Thailand	66
Indonesia	62	UK	44
Ireland	353	USA	1
Laos	856	Vietnam	84
Malaysia	60		

1

Living in South-east Asia

There are many similarities between the countries of South-east Asia, and further similarities between groups of countries in the region. For example, the Chinese influence is still very strong in countries such as Singapore, and parts of Thailand, Vietnam and Indonesia. Islamic culture and religion is strong in Malaysia, Brunei and Indonesia, while Buddhism is the main religion in Thailand, Laos, Cambodia and Vietnam. There are economic similarities among the countries in the region; those which are developed (Singapore and Brunei), those which are developing (Thailand, Indonesia, Malaysia and the Philippines), and those which are under-developed (Vietnam, Laos and Cambodia). There are also similarities in the languages spoken in the region: Malay is spoken in Malaysia and Brunei, and is very similar to Indonesian (Filipino Tagalog is also based on Malay); Thai is similar to Lao; and both Hokkien and Mandarin are spoken by the ethnic Chinese in South-east Asia. Four languages are written with a different script from Roman languages (Vietnamese, Lao, Thai and Khmer), and three are tonal (Vietnamese, Lao and Thai).

CULTURAL CONSIDERATIONS

In South-east Asia there are many similarities between countries about what is and what is not considered acceptable behaviour. **Chapters 4–12** contain specific information about customs unique to each country. The following basic guidelines apply to all.

Showing anger

Any display of anger is considered impolite in Asia. Showing anger is interpreted simply as a lack of self-control, never as a show of strength.

In the puppet theatre in Indonesia, the characters with smooth, calm faces are the heroes and heroines, while the red-faced, coarser-featured puppets – the ones who are always shouting and losing their tempers – are considered uncouth and rude.

If you feel like shouting and screaming at the immigration official in front of you because you just cannot understand why it takes so long to get your work visa processed, DON'T! No matter how difficult it seems at the time, shouting will get you nowhere fast in Asia. Take a deep breath, count to ten, and then count to ten again in the local language. The person who loses control loses any moral force in the situation and is easily discounted from then on. (This is connected with *losing face*, see below.)

Smiling

South-east Asians are famous for their smiles and their friendliness. However, an Asian smile can convey a multitude of emotions including embarrassment, anger, fear or sadness. Do not be too disconcerted when a student tells you a tale of family death and then smiles. The death of a loved one is no more funny in Asia than anywhere else but smiling is considered more appropriate and dignified than crying in public. (This, again, is connected with *losing face*, see below.)

Being alone

Most South-east Asians are family and group orientated. A person alone is often viewed with pity, or suspicion. If you live or travel alone, most Asians will think you odd, sad, a little bit mad, or very brave, and you will often be asked 'But why are you alone?' Solitary pastimes are uncommon in South-east Asia. Much more usual is for a whole extended family to sit together in the evening and talk, while watching TV.

So if you like to sit outside quietly, reading a book by yourself, be ready for plenty of interruptions and inquiries from neighbours and curious passers by.

Losing and saving face

'Face' is a combination of personal, family, group, work-place, neighbourhood and national pride. It is about maintaining an unruffled, respectable, appropriate image. It can be difficult to pin it down, but it is an everyday fact of life in South-east Asia.

Part of maintaining face is the Asian desire to avoid conflict at all costs. If you ask an Asian to do something they don't want to do, or that might even be impossible, the usual answer to your request will be a polite, 'Yes'. This does not actually mean that your request will be carried out.

It is considered polite not to deliver bad news. To any question you ask, you will almost always get some kind of charming answer, but it will seldom be one an Asian thinks might disappoint you. It is unlikely that Asians will answer 'I don't know', as this would be seen as a loss of face. Thus, even if they are not sure of their answer, Asians will often tell you something – anything – rather than admit that they don't know and therefore, disappoint you. (Interestingly in Indonesian *Kurang tahu* can be translated as 'I don't know', but translates literally as 'I less than know'.) As you can imagine, this makes asking a stranger for directions in South-east Asia potentially fraught with difficulties for both of you.

Yes/no questions are notoriously easy for Asians to answer, and difficult for Westerners with different assumptions, to understand. The answer is always 'Yes'.

Part of the face-saving culture is trying to avoid ruffling feathers. Thus, direct criticisms make people lose face, as can pointing out mistakes to someone who is in some way superior to you (for example, someone older than you, your parents, teacher or boss). What actually goes on behind the scenes in someone's personal life, or in a corrupt government ministry, for example, is not relevant to their social 'face', and mentioning such things is simply considered rude. Well-known examples of injustice or hypocrisy are usually alluded to obliquely in conversation, if at all.

Criticizing your host country can make the people of that country – and you, for your insensitivity – lose face. So, those politically-charged lessons that work so well in the West ('If you became President in a bloodless coup, how would you restructure the whole damn country?' or 'What are the ten things that you hate most about your government?'), will go down like a lead balloon, and you will find your students refusing to be drawn into an issue that might prove embarrassing. To use a different metaphor, Asians often see political discussions as opening a can of worms that wise people should leave alone. Awareness of the social, political and economic forces that could tear their society apart, and perhaps have done so in recent history, is one of the reasons behind this reticence. Another reason is not wanting to criticize the government, as this would be seen as a loss of face for those people in authority who should be, at least openly, respected by ordinary citizens.

Dressing modestly and conservatively

In Asia, initial impressions count for a lot. Connected to the idea of maintaining and losing face, Asians will, for example, go into huge debt for their child's wedding. They might not be able to afford it, but the bride must look beautiful, and if the dress costs thousands of dollars, so be it.

As a teacher you will be awarded a lot of respect simply because of your profession. But although Asians traditionally look up to their teachers, if you are not dressed the part, they will find it hard to respect you. Road-workers or trishaw-drivers wear shorts and flip-flops because they cannot afford more expensive clothes. As a teacher, even if you think these are the most comfortable clothes you could wear, you are expected to dress like a teacher, and that means no to scruffy jeans or your favourite old T-shirt. Such clothes are not considered 'orderly' (*riap-roi* in Thai), a concept that carries a lot of cultural weight.

Increasingly Asian students are beginning to realize that not all EFL teachers are qualified. They know that there are people travelling through their country who pick up casual English teaching work, and this realization does not endear such teachers to them. If this describes you, dress well and you won't meet as much resistance from your students as you will if you are unqualified and dressed scruffily.

Another cultural note on dress: quite often, local products that you think look really smart when you first arrive have 'hippy traveller' connotations for the local people. This holds true, unfortunately, for most clothes bought in the market. So that breezy floral sundress or pair of drawstring batik trousers might not give the impression you want to give when you are first trying to establish yourself as a teacher in a new school.

Using chopsticks

Chopsticks are common in all countries of the region. However, in Brunei, Malaysia and Indonesia people tend to eat with the right hand and/or use a spoon and fork.

To hold chopsticks, place one chopstick between your thumb and forefinger and hold it firmly against the first joint of your middle or ring finger. This chopstick should not move. Hold the other one like a pen, opening and closing it against the lower one.

Do not leave chopsticks stuck upright in a bowl of rice. This looks similar to incense sticks which are burned at a funeral and is considered very bad luck in Chinese-influenced countries.

Beckoning people

Signalling with your index figure is considered rude, and in some countries (Indonesia, for example) it is the way that you would call a dog to you. Instead, beckon by using your whole hand, palm turned down and repeatedly moving your four fingers in towards your palm and out again.

Bargaining

Although shopping centres and supermarkets are now common, especially in the larger cities, the majority of people in South-east Asia do most of their shopping at the market and in small, local shops. Asians bargain over everything, so supermarkets or large shops which have fixed prices take all the fun out of shopping for Asians. Department stores and supermarkets also tend to have higher rents and, therefore, much higher prices than shops where you can haggle. Unfortunately, bargaining is hard work and most Westerners find the novelty of bargaining every day over the price of half a dozen eggs a bit wearing. Many are happy to pay higher prices in fixed-price shops. However, if you do bargain, you will gain more respect from your local shop-owner and you will feel as if you are really participating in life in South-east Asia. Here are a few tips to help you in your early days:

- Get a rough idea of the going price before you start bargaining; either by looking around in fixed-price shops or by asking other foreigners or locals.
- Once you start bargaining you are committed to buying, so don't start haggling unless you are ready to buy.
- Ask the price, and when you hear the first price, go way over the top in head-shaking and looks of amazement. If in doubt, watch Asians bargaining, and you will see a potential Oscar winner in every performance. Then simply ask for a discount, say it's too expensive, and/or offer a lower price. When the shop-owner offers the second price, go back to looks of astonishment, etc, etc. If the shop-keeper shows you the price on a calculator, it's often an indication that you can take the calculator, punch in your suggested price and you can banter back and forth with the calculator, each of you offering prices until you come to an agreement. This is also very useful if you have not yet mastered the numbers in the country you are in. If only there had been a calculator the time I very successfully bargained for a wicker basket in Indonesia and managed to haggle from 6 000 rupiah *up* to 8 000 rupiah, not only to the delight of the shop-owner, but to the amusement of all the customers.
- You can haggle over other things besides the cost: getting batteries included, free delivery, or a discount if you buy more than you originally asked for.
- Remember that shop-owners have had years more experience of bargaining than you have and they will usually get the better of customers brought up in fixed-price cultures. Face-saving is a very important part of Asian culture and shop-owners would see it as a loss of face if either the customer got the last word in, or a foreigner beat them at their own game.

- Remember too, that the amount of money you are haggling over is probably very small to you, in relation to your pay, but that for the shop-owners it is a much larger percentage of their income.
- At all times keep it light-hearted. One purchase is not the end of the world. Showing anger or shouting is very bad form and will endear you to no-one.
- When in doubt, smile.

Hiring household help

For many Westerners in South-east Asia, the idea of paying someone to wash their clothes, cook their meals and tidy their house smacks of colonialism and exploitation, and so the whole issue of hiring someone to help in your house is fraught with emotional, economic and political considerations. You may want to bear in mind, however, that you are not doing the poor Asian woman who comes to your door asking for work any favours by doing your own washing, cleaning and housekeeping, and that spreading some of your wealth around the local community is one of the best ways of integrating yourself into your new neighbourhood.

> I didn't want to hire a pembantu (in Indonesian, literally a person who helps) as I disapproved of paying someone else to do my housework when I was perfectly capable of doing it myself. I thought a washing machine was essential, but although my Indonesian partner and I spent a long time window-shopping for a machine, there always seemed to be a reason to put off the actual purchase. Eventually, I found out that Heri thought that the amount of money we planned to spend on a washing machine was criminal when I could have used the money to employ someone for a year to do my washing by hand. The compromise we ended up with was a washing machine *and* a pembantu.
>
> *Pascale Taylor, England*

The best rule in South-east Asia, as in any foreign country, is to watch what a local does, and then follow suit if the custom causes no great ethical and moral trauma for you. Obviously, if you think a local custom is wrong, follow your own conscience and don't feel compelled into thinking that a practice cannot really be wrong simply because it has been done that way there for years.

The bathroom and toilet

In South-east Asia, bathrooms and toilets are not usually in separate rooms. The bathroom floor is tiled and slightly sloped towards a drain in the middle of the floor. Where there is no shower, bathing is done by scooping water from a filled bath and washing yourself while you stand *outside* the bath. The toilet is either a conventional Western-styled one, or a squat-kind. Toilet paper is becoming more common, but if you care for the environment or want to live more like the locals do, then simply use the small water scoop that you use for having a bath to wash yourself after using the toilet.

Asking and answering personal questions

For most Westerners, questions about their salary, why they are not married and, if they are married, why they do not have any children seem very personal; but for most Asians these are merely friendly inquiries. In some South-east Asian countries you will be asked 'Where are you going?' (In Indonesian and Malay, for example, *Mau ke mana?*) Although at times it can get wearing, and 'It's none of your business' might occasionally spring to mind, no offence is intended in this question, and none should be taken. Any answer, such as 'To the shops', or '*Jalan, jalan*', ('Walking, walking' in Indonesia and Malaysia) is quite acceptable. Asians do not want to know in great detail the ins and outs of your secret rendezvous, but ask 'Where are you going?' in the same way that Westerners ask 'How are you?', without actually expecting a detailed run-down of your every illness.

If you are embarrassed by answering questions on how much your salary is, how much your rent is, how much you paid for your last holiday flight, answers of 'Enough' or 'Expensive' are quite acceptable face-savers.

Women

South-east Asia is a very safe place for women to live and work in – you will probably be a lot safer walking down a street at night in Jakarta or Bangkok than you would be in London or New York.

Asians might think you a bit strange if you are over 20 and not married, or if you are married and do not have any children. You may find it irritating to be constantly questioned about why you are not married, or, if you are married, questioned about why you do not have any children – or even about the kind of birth control you use. However, you should bear in mind that these questions are not considered rude or intrusive in Asian culture.

You may feel some social pressure to be rather 'feminine' in South-east Asia. Asian women are much more likely to be demure, quiet, and self-effacing than their Western counterparts tend to be. Of course, in the larger cities this is changing, and women are now involved in politics and business; the idea of a woman working outside the home is not quite as absurd as it seemed 10 or 15 years ago. Be that as it may, most Asian women still defer to men and their husbands, at least in public, particularly in the Muslim countries.

As a foreigner, you are already considered strange, by virtue of the fact that you left your home country by choice, and so acting as demurely as an Asian women is not considered essential for foreign women. On the other hand, dressing 'appropriately' is essential for success in your dealings with South-east Asians. Asians are fairly conservative in the way they dress, and knees and shoulders are usually covered up. In most schools women are expected to wear a dress, skirt or a very smart pair of trousers. Even if the school you are working in does not have a strict formal dress code, you will be doing yourself a favour if you dress as smartly as possible when you go to work. Asians do judge a book by its cover, and once your wardrobe has lost you respect, especially from your older students, it can be difficult to regain it.

Gays and lesbians

In most of South-east Asia homosexuality is tolerated, but not accepted as a viable life-choice for Asians by their families and community. In many countries in this region, the age of consent is the same for heterosexuals as homosexuals, and there are few if any laws regarding homosexual behavior. (The exception is Singapore, where homosexuality is still illegal.) This is because government and religious institutions have traditionally not intruded into what is considered a purely private realm. Sexual practices will not be commented on as long as they are not reflected in the public *face* of the person. (For example, it is heavily made-up transvestites, who publicly challenge mainstream gender roles, or gays who act very 'effeminately' who bear the brunt of criticism and sometimes even assault.)

Asian lesbians and gays in Asia are very rarely out of the closet, and they are usually pressured by their families to marry and 'get a real life'. In a way, all Asians are 'passing' all the time – maintaining 'face', hiding anger, cultivating respect despite what they might feel inside – so the cultural impetus for homosexuals to bring public and private lives into line with each other by being 'out' is simply not present here as in the West.

In all countries the Chinese, with their Confucian emphasis on the family, are less tolerant of homosexuality than other South-east Asian cultures. Buddhists tend to see homosexuality as bad luck or bad karma, and there are social sanctions against it, but they do not view it as a sin or moral failing. They think that if you have a choice, straight is better, but if you're already gay, enjoy it and be happy.

As for attitudes to homosexual foreigners, the worst you will probably have to face in Asia is smiling confidence that heterosexual marriage and child-rearing represent Ultimate Reality, and same-sex liaisons are 'just practice', or a matter of sowing wild oats.

Homophobia in Buddhist-influenced cultures is rare and 'queer bashing' of foreigners is practically unheard of in the region. South-east Asia is in many ways a congenial place for lesbians and gays.

You should be a bit careful about public displays of affection, but not because you would be in any kind of danger. It's simply that most Asians of whatever sexual orientation consider PDA inappropriate and rude. By this, however, they mean clearly *sexualized* touching. You'll see same-sex couples or groups holding hands in public all the time, but this is not (usually) a sign of homosexuality – rather it's a sign that in the public mind, sexuality is reserved for male/female pairings. Same sex friends in Asia usually display wonderful camaraderie, and touching is not at all taboo.

In each country in the region there is usually at least one pub, disco, or café where you can meet other gays or lesbians and find out more information about what is happening. Some addresses for the larger countries are given below:

Thailand

Utopia, 116/1 Sukhumvit Soi 23, Bangkok. South-east Asia's only multi-purpose lesbian and gay venue. Useful for current information on the (rapidly changing) scenes in other cities in the region. (Tel: 259 9619).

Silom Road Soi 3 is an exclusively gay area with bars and discos.

Vietnam

The Gold Cock, 5 Bao Khanh, Hanoi.

Malaysia

Boom-Boom Room (upstairs) Leboh Ampang, Kuala Lumpur.

Singapore

Velvet Underground (gay-friendly), Jiak Kim Street, Singapore.

Indonesia

Moonlight, Jalan Hayam Wuruk, Jakarta.

Physically challenged people

In much of South-east Asia, traditional, superstitious views of physically challenged people still hold sway. It is still very common for non able-bodied children (as well as children with learning difficulties) to be confined to home, for fear of bringing shame on their parents, or exposing the bad luck/bad karma they're afflicted with. So the 'invisibility' of a segment of the population starts early, and is reinforced by major obstacles to mobility. In the 18 months I worked in Singapore I never once saw a person in a wheelchair, and this was probably due in part to the lack of wheelchair access in public buildings. A telling indictment of Thailand's neglect (similar to that in all South-east Asian countries) is related by Sunan Willcox of Assist, a Chiang Mai-based project for the physically challenged: 'Even the

Disabled Passport Registration Office in this town is located at the top of a very long flight of stairs. I think that sums up the problem in a nutshell.' ('Meek No More', *The Nation*, 18 January 1996). In many parts of South-east Asia as yet there is simply no public recognition that the physically challenged have rights too.

Most able-bodied Asians feel that the kinds of jobs non-able-bodied people currently do (eg giving massages, selling lottery tickets on the street, or working in sweat shops) are quite 'appropriate for their station in life', and preferable to begging. The concept of *dis*ability is so far-reaching that, for example, a special school for children in the north of Thailand, one of only a handful in the country, refuses to let even one physically challenged adult onto its management committee.

In Thailand and Singapore the most visible group of physically challenged people are the deaf. For example, regular informal meetings are held in McDonald's beside the YMCA on Sundays in Singapore and in Mah Boon Krong shopping centre in Bangkok on Sundays. However in general, most physically challenged people keep a very low profile, or are made to keep a very low profile by a combination of their families, communities and lack of adequate facilities.

If you are going to South-east Asia as a paid EFL teacher, you will probably see very few disabled people, but if you are going to South-east Asia as an aid worker you are more likely to meet and work with physically challenged people. For example, VSO runs a programme in the north of Thailand teaching blind people, and in Cambodia foreign aid organizations such as the Halo Trust are training amputees to do the skilled work of de-mining the countryside.

If you are physically challenged you will probably find many people in South-east Asia unsympathetic and even unhelpful. You will be considered more of a marvel than foreigners already are, an attitude that could keep you at a distance from the culture. Daily life in Asia could be very difficult as infrastructural support simply does not exist.

Transport

P. J. O'Rourke has some 'Third World Driving Hints' that certainly apply to most of the countries in South-east Asia (see over). He talks about using the horn, but for this region, read 'using the horn and dipping your headlights'.

Traffic jams and exhaust fumes are a part of life in the huge cities of Jakarta and Bangkok, and increasingly so in the smaller cities such as Hanoi and Phnom Penh. In the congested cities in the region travelling takes up much more time than is does in the West and is much more frustrating.

Singapore is the exception when talking about traffic jams and exhaust fumes. The government has gone to great lengths to control

> There is a precise and complicated etiquette of horn use. Honk your horn only under the following circumstances:
> 1) When anything blocks the road
> 2) When anything doesn't
> 3) When anything might
> 4) At red lights
> 5) At green lights
> 6) At all other times
>
> *P. J. O'Rourke, Holidays in Hell, Picador, 1988*

both the number of cars and the pollution levels allowed in this city state. One way the government has done this is by implementing a restricted zone around the city centre. If you want to drive in the restricted zone during particular hours you have to pay a fee. The result is that there are far fewer cars going into the city centre every day and therefore, few traffic jams. When a similar initiative was introduced in Jakarta, unfortunately, the results weren't quite what the government hoped for. A three-in-one (three people in one car) system was introduced recently to relieve peak-hour congestion in the main business areas. It resulted in enterprising young people offering themselves for rent and just as many cars with one legitimate passenger continuing to congest Jakarta's main streets during the rush hours.

Although it might seem that there is no rhyme or reason to South-east Asian driving, there are some basic rules you can follow.

(1) See above on the use of the horn and dipped head-lights.
(2) Remember that nobody has the right of way.
(3) In an accident the hitter is always wrong, so don't concern yourself too much with what's behind you, just concentrate on what's in front of you.

If you are involved in an accident and responsible for it, you will have to pay any medical and car-repair expenses. If possible, DO NOT get the police involved, as this will usually mean endless paper work and cost you a lost of money (a fee to report the accident, a fee to write up the report, a fee to retrieve your car, a fee if you want the 'express' service, etc, etc, etc).

Hitch-hiking

Hitching is very uncommon in South-east Asia since there is almost always some form of public transport available. Singapore is too small to make hitching worthwhile and, in the other countries in the region if you hitch you should offer the driver some money, either by paying for the petrol or buying food, which might defeat the object of hitching. In countries where so many people are poor, a foreigner expecting to have a free ride would be ludicrous to most South-east Asians.

MAJOR RELIGIONS IN SOUTH-EAST ASIA

The two major religions in the region are Islam and Buddhism. Although there are other religions, notably Catholicism in the Philippines and Confucianism and Taoism in Singapore, Muslims and Buddhists account for most of the population of South-east Asia and it is also these two major religions that could present cultural misunderstandings for you, if you are not already familiar with them.

Islam (Brunei, Indonesia, Malaysia and Singapore)

If you are living and teaching in Brunei, Indonesia, Malaysia or Singapore you will have a lot of contact with Muslims. Indonesia is the biggest Muslim country in the world with 80% of Indonesians declaring themselves Muslim. In Indonesia, Malaysia and Brunei, Islam is the majority religion, while in Singapore the largest minority, the Malays, who make up 14% of the population, are Muslims.

History of Islam

Muhammad ibn Abdallah, a member of the Quraysh tribe, was born in 571 AD. He was a merchant in the city of Mecca and in about 610 AD he took his family to Mount Hira for a spiritual retreat during the month of *Ramadan*. *Ramadan* was a sacred period when the Arabs distributed food and alms to the poor, and spent time praying to the High God of the Arabs. On the 17th night of *Ramadan* on Mount Hira Muhammad was awakened by an overwhelming divine presence. Explaining this later he said that an angel had appeared to him and commanded him *'Iqra'* ('Recite'). Muhammad refused three times, but finally, the first words of the new scripture emerged from him:

> 'Recite in the name of thy Sustainer, who has created – created man out of a germ-cell! Recite – for thy Sustainer is the Most Bountiful, One who has taught man the use of the pen – taught him what he did not know! (Quran 96:1 translated by Muhammad Asad).

The scripture was revealed to Muhammad over a period of 23 years in a very painful process – 'Never once did I receive a revelation without feeling that my soul was being torn away from me' he said in later years. The scripture was called *al-qur'an* – which means 'the Recitation'.

The Quraysh tribe, Muhammad's first audience, already believed in *Allah* so Muhammad saw himself as reminding them or calling them back to their best selves, away from presumption *(yatqa),* egotism and greed. The Quran reminded the Quraysh to thank Allah and not themselves for their growing financial success. They were to look for signs *(ayat)* of God's benevolence in the natural world and reproduce this goodness in their own society. Muhammad introduced *salat,* bowing down in ritual prayer twice a day, which horrified the Quraysh who saw it as the posture of a slave.

In time Muhammad's religion would be known as *islām* which means 'submission or surrender to God'; a *Muslīm* was a person who had surrendered fully to God. Almost 600 years after Muhammad, Islam was brought to Indonesia by peaceful Gujerati merchants from India who introduced a strand of Islam that had incorporated Persian and Indian philosophies. In Malaysia the earliest recorded evidence of Islam is an inscription dating from 1303 which stated the penalties for those who did not observe the moral codes of Islam.

Islamic law and custom

There are five Islamic laws which every Muslim must abide by. The following terms are written in Indonesian and Malay.

- *Syahadat/Shahada:* confessing belief in Allah as the only God and Muhammad as his prophet.
- *Sholat/Salat:* praying five times a day facing Mecca.
- *Zakat:* giving alms (food or money) to the poor at the end of *Ramadan* – the fasting month.
- *Puasa/Saum:* fasting from sunrise to sunset during *Ramadan.*
- *Hajj/Haj:* making the pilgrimage to Mecca, if it is safe to go there and you are healthy and wealthy enough.

While you are living and teaching in a Muslim country the following guidelines may help you:

Using your right hand. Muslims consider the left hand to be unclean, so to avoid offending Muslims, you should never offer them anything with your left hand. It is also considered impolite to eat with your left hand, or to offer food to someone with your left hand. Of course, if your right hand if full, it is acceptable to use your left hand, but you should also apologize as you do so.

The role of women. Women are not vocal in Islamic countries, and when they are out in public they tend to be more covered-up than other Asian or Western women (especially in Malaysia). If you are a woman living in a Muslim country it is unlikely that you will be required to wear a headscarf or *jelbab,* but you should take care to cover the tops of your arms and shoulders and, if you are wearing a skirt, make sure that it covers most of your legs.

Sex segregation. In the mosque the sexes are strictly segregated and this segregation can also be seen at parties, in schools, or in any group activity. Do not be surprised if this happens in your classroom and a pair-work activity falls flat when you put a mixed-sex Muslim pair together.

Alcohol. In Islamic Malaysia and Indonesia, alcohol is readily available. However, if you have Muslim guests to your house, you should remember to have some soft drinks on hand. If you are invited to a Muslim party, wedding or circumcision, it would be considered impolite if you brought alcohol with you, or asked for it.

In Brunei, Muslims are forbidden by law to buy or receive alcohol. Non-Muslims may bring their duty-free alcohol allowance into the country, but are not able to buy any alcohol legally while in Brunei.

Haram (forbidden) food. Pork is forbidden for Muslims. Chicken and meat must be slaughtered by a Muslim to make it *halal,* suitable for Muslims to eat. If you have Muslim friends to your house, you should serve only *halal* meat. Any supermarket in the region will have meat that is very clearly marked *halal* – or you can also recognize it by the green crescent and star symbol printed on the packet.

Friday closing. Friday is the main day for visiting the mosque. Many government buildings are closed on Friday afternoons, or have longer lunch times than they do during the rest of the week.

Musholla (Praying room). In Muslim houses, there is usually a *musholla,* with a prayer mat, and a sign to indicate the direction of Mecca. Most public buildings, including language schools in Muslim countries, also provide a *musholla.* Particularly during the fasting month of *Ramadan,* if you are teaching an early evening class, when the sun sets, students may ask to leave your class to go and pray in the *musholla,* and also to break their fast briefly, with coffee and small cakes which the school will usually provide for Muslims who are fasting.

Dogs. Muslims are not allowed to come into contact with a dog's saliva, wet nose, tongue or hair. If you have Muslim friends to your house and you have a dog, if possible you should try to keep your dog outside when your guests are in the house.

Respect for Islam. While you are living in a South-east Asian Islamic country it is important to respect the Muslim religion. Although the prayers being chanted from your local mosque through a loud-speaker might constitute noise pollution to you, it would be considered very offensive if you actually complained.

Visiting a mosque. Non-Muslims can visit most mosques, but you should check first, before you enter. Some mosques do not allow visitors into the main prayer hall and some do not allow visitors during prayer time. You should take off your shoes before you go into a mosque and should be dressed appropriately (for women this means covering your head, shoulders and legs, for men covering your legs and for both sexes clean, smart clothes). Muslim women are not allowed to go into a mosque when they are having their period; Western women are requested to abide by this rule. While in the mosque you should not walk in front of a person praying and you should never touch the Quran.

When they visit a mosque, Muslim women usually wear a white, floor-length robe, over their own clothes, and cover their heads with a white veil. Usually Muslim men wear a *songkok (*a black velvet hat) and a sarong over their trousers. Men who have made the Haj pilgrimage to Mecca wear a small white skull cap.

Ramadan (The fasting month). Ramadan is in the ninth month of the Islamic year. During this month Muslims get up before sun-rise, eat breakfast and then fast until sunset. Muslims also refrain from drinking, having sex, smoking or thinking impure thoughts from sunrise to sunset. Muslims use this month as a special time for worship, prayer and contemplation. Although Muslims are instructed to go about their daily working lives as normal during *Ramadan,* it is still difficult for them, especially in the heat of the South-east Asian tropics. As a teacher you should go easy on your students during Ramadan as it can be difficult for students to concentrate on their lessons when they are hungry and thirsty. You should also try to be understanding if your students are less lively or hard-working than usual in the classroom during *Ramadan.*

Most schools provide some snacks for students to break their fast with when the mosques call out at sunset (around 6 pm) that the day's fasting is over.

Idul Fitri/Hari Raya. Idul Fitri (Indonesia)/*Hari Raya* (Malaysia, Brunei and Singapore) is the day or days of celebration to mark the end of the fasting month. Everyone dresses in new clothes and visits their family home where the younger members beg forgiveness from the older members for wrong-doings in the previous year. In Indonesia, for example, the front pages of the newspapers often carry a photo of President Suharto kneeling before his mother and asking for her forgiveness.

During this period the whole of Indonesia, Malaysia and Brunei seems to be on the move, with everyone desperately trying to get back to their home town for the celebrations. As this is likely to be a time when your school is closed, make sure you book your flight, train or bus in advance if you can, especially if you are thinking of getting out of Jakarta, or Kuala Lumpur.

If you employ a *pembantu* (household help) remember that employers usually give their staff a double salary for *Idul Fitri/Hari Raya*. Unfortunately, if you are not a Muslim, you do not get a double salary from your boss.

Buddhism (Cambodia, Laos, Thailand and Vietnam)

If you are living and teaching in Cambodia, Laos, Thailand and Vietnam most of your students will be Buddhists. Buddhism is the majority religion in these four countries, and in Thailand, for example, more than 90% of the people declare themselves Buddhists.

History of Buddhism

Therevada Buddhism was first introduced into the region in the early part of the 12th century by Burmese monks who came across it in Ceylon (now Sri Lanka), and spread it among the common people. By the 15th century, Therevada Buddhism was the dominant religion in Burma, Thailand, Laos, and Cambodia. In Laos, King Setthathirat, who ruled from 1547 to 1571, tried to make Vientiane the country's Buddhist centre and by the late 17th century, Buddhism was being taught in Lao schools. In Cambodia, Buddhism was introduced between the 13th and 14th centuries and was the state religion until 1975.

The Buddha was an Indian prince who lived in North India or present-day Nepal from 563 to 483 BC. His personal name (in Sanskrit) was Siddhartha, and his family name, Gautama. He was married at the age of 16, and lived in great luxury with Princess Yasodhara. At 29, he rejected his courtly life and started a search for truth, wandering the valleys of the Ganges for six ascetic years – meditating, fasting, and learning the disciplines espoused by different religious teachers. Finding these systems and methods unconvincing and inadequate, Gautama went his own way. Then one evening, sitting under a tree that was later called the Bodhi- or Bo-tree, the Tree of Wisdom, he attained Enlightenment. Henceforth he would be known as the Buddha: the Enlightened One, or the One Who Has Woken Up. In South-east Asia, he is often called *Sakyamuni,* or the Sage of the Sakyas, the name of the Nepalese tribe he was prince of. Gautama arrived at four noble truths which he said had the power to liberate anyone who could realize them and put them into practice. He preached his first sermon immediately, and then spent the next 45 years teaching his Way of liberation from spiritual bondage to whoever would listen, regardless of their caste or sex.

The four noble truths that Buddha realized under the Bo-tree were:

- *The truth of dukkha:* All forms of existence are subject to *dukkha* – suffering or conflict.
- *The truth of the cause of dukkha*: Dukkha is caused by *tanha* – thirst or desire, which arises in a 12-stage cycle called the *Paṭicca-samuppāda.*
- *The truth of the cessation of dukkha:* Elimination of the causes of *dukkha* and *dukkha* will cease to arise. This cessation of *dukkha* is *Nirvāṇa.*
- *The truth of the path:* The Eightfold Way, also known as the Middle Path, is the way to extinguish *dukkha.* The Eightfold Way consists of:

  Wisdom – Paññā
  Right Understanding
  Right Thought
  Ethical Conduct – Sīla
  Right Speech
  Right Action
  Right Livelihood
  Mental Discipline – Samādhi
  Right Effort
  Right Mindfulness
  Right Concentration

According to the late Buddhadasa Bhikku, a highly respected Thai monk, 'The Buddha intended us to see that there is no person, there is no individual; there are only *dhammas,* natural phenomena. Therefore, we should not hold the belief that there is this religion and that religion. The label, 'Buddhism', was attached only afterwards, and this is the same with Christianity, Islam, and every religion' (from a 1989 lecture entitled 'No Religion!'). Although Gautama did not intend to found a religious system, Buddhism is certainly a religion today. Its practices have evolved through history, and may bear little resemblance to the Buddha's original teachings, at least in terms of lay understanding. For example, in Thailand today, it is popularly believed that only ordained monks can attain *nirvana,* and if a layman – it would have to be a man – were somehow able to reach enlightenment and become an *arahant,* a saint, he would have to take the vows to enter the brotherhood of monks *within seven days,* or he would die!

Soon after the Buddha began teaching, the community of monks, the *Sangha,* was established. The *Sangha* in India eventually arrived at a new interpretation of the Buddha's life based on the original Pali Canon of accepted teachings and stories, but also stressing later Sanskrit texts. This offshoot, which came to believe that the Buddha was a transcendent being among other such beings, became known as Mahayana Buddhism. The branch based on the original texts is known as Therevada Buddhism (or Hinayana Buddhism). Therevadin Buddhism is often called the 'southern' school because it spread from India to the south, into Burma, Thailand, Laos, and Cambodia. Mahayana Buddhism, spread north to Nepal, Tibet, China, Korea, Mongolia, Vietnam and Japan. But even in mainly Therevadin South-east Asia, you will come across Mahayanic practices and shrines, especially among the Chinese community.

Buddhist customs

The following are some tips for being respectful among Buddhists.

Buddhist monks. Buddhist monks are treated with great respect by all Asians. Any man who is not a criminal can become a Buddhist monk. In Thailand, Laos, Cambodia and Vietnam, it is common for young men to become monks for at least a short period. After leaving school and before going to university or starting work, young men often join a *wat* for anything from three weeks to three months. A monk's whole family gains merit when a son or brother becomes a monk.

Monks are allowed to own an alms bowl, three pieces of clothing, a belt, a razor, a needle and a water filter. They should not murder, steal, tell lies, have sex, eat after noon, drink alcohol, wear ornaments, sleep in a comfortable bed, or eat anything other than what is given to them when they collect alms in the morning.

Monks are not allowed to touch women, so if you want to give something to a monk, either food, alms or a donation if you are in a temple, you should first put your offering on a ceremonial cloth that the monk will slide towards him so as to avoid actually coming into contact with you. This view of women as having a spiritually polluting influence (walking under a clothesline with women's underwear on it can undo the magic influence of amulets and charms, according to a current Thai superstition!) although not backed up by Buddhist scripture, is certainly a strongly held belief in Buddhist cultures. Protest on this issue will get you absolutely nowhere.

The Wat. The *wat,* or Buddhist temple is sacred. If you visit a *wat* you should dress appropriately, (no shorts, flip-flops, beach clothes or old or dirty clothes), and be careful about what and who you photograph. It is always better to ask someone if you can go ahead and take a picture without causing offence. You should take off your shoes before entering a temple and you should never touch a Buddha image, or climb on top of one, not even to pose briefly for that perfect shot. Do your best to be respectful.

The head. The head is the most important part of the body in Buddhist culture, so if you are talking to a monk, try to be sure that your head is lower than his. This is also true if you are talking to a superior, or someone older than you. Your should never touch someone on the head; either adult or child.

The feet. In Buddhist culture, the feet are the 'lowest' part of the body, not just physically, but morally. They are considered inherently dirty, so never point at someone with your feet. Putting your feet up on tables and chairs is considered offensive. If you are sitting on the floor, it is best to tuck your feet under your body, as crossing your legs means that your feet are pointing at somebody. When teaching, do not sit on a table or desk, as this is supposed to draw attention to your feet, and is considered unseemly for teachers.

THE CHINESE

There is a significant minority of people of Chinese origin in all South-east Asian countries, and in Singapore they are in the majority. In countries where they do not make up the majority, the ethnic-Chinese community and indigenous people often come into conflict. This is certainly the case in Indonesia and Malaysia, where the fact that the majority are Muslim and the Chinese are usually Buddhist or Christian may contribute to tensions.

After Singapore, the country in the region where the Chinese are most integrated is Thailand. Perhaps this is because the country as a whole is more economically developed, and the distribution of wealth at the top end of the scale is fairly evenly divided between the Thais and the ethnic Chinese, or perhaps it is because both the Thais and Chinese are mainly Buddhists.

The ethnic Chinese constitute a powerhouse in the economy of each country in the region. Perhaps it is the economic prominence of the Chinese, more than any other factor, which contributes to widespread dislike – even hatred – of them among the more disadvantaged in countries such as Indonesia where there is a great discrepancy between rich and poor. In the 1965 coup in Indonesia, thousands of Chinese people were massacred, allegedly because they were communists, but more likely because they were different and hence unpopular. To this day, even though their families may have lived in Indonesia for generations, ethnic Chinese people cannot serve in the army or in the government. Although they are often very wealthy, Chinese Indonesians have very little political power and are in effect second-class citizens.

Another reason for their unpopularity is the fear that China with its huge population and military strength, may overrun its neighbours in South-east Asia. For example, in Vietnam, China is the age-old enemy always poised (the Vietnamese believe) to subjugate their country.

China ruled Vietnam for a thousand years after invading and conquering it in 111 BC, and for many Vietnamese the Chinese threat is still very real. The leap from seeing China as a potential invading enemy to punishing ethnic Chinese living in Vietnam has been a small and easy one for many Vietnamese to make. The Vietnamese have persecuted ethnic-Chinese in the same way that ethnic-Vietnamese have been persecuted and killed by Cambodians, and for the same reason – in Cambodian terms the ancient threat, always on the brink of invasion, is Vietnam.

The three countries of Indochina and their larger neighbour China are not known for their harmonious co-existence, and Indonesia and Malaysia are both barely keeping the lid on potentially massive social unrest if labour is ever allowed to organize against mainly Chinese and government factory owners.

The influence of Chinese culture is wide, and the following are some notes about aspects of South-east Asian culture that are, broadly, influenced by Chinese beliefs, customs and religion.

Buddhism

Buddhism is the main religion of the Chinese in South-east Asia. See above for more details about Buddhism.

Philosophies: Taoism and Confucianism

Taoism (pronounced *daw-ism*) is a poetic and spiritual philosophy based on the works of two Chinese philosophers, Lao Tzu (c. 6th–5th century BC) and Chuang Tzu (4th century BC). The gist of this complicated worldview is that reality is composed of two opposing forces, *yin* (female) and *yang* (male). The two forces must be kept in balance, whether in the world at large, or in the individual, where illness is a sign of too much yin or yang. Taoist beliefs affect Chinese medicine, eating habits (some foods are 'hot'/yang or 'cold'/yin) and politics. In practice, Taoism is conservative. Although traditional, familiar ways of life might not lead to exact balance, better the imbalance you know than the possible cosmic upheaval new approaches could bring! Popular Taoism also accounts for a lot of the genies, spirits, and monsters haunting the psyches of South-east Asia. (They certainly don't come from Buddhism, which downplays spirits and ghosts as 'gaseous extensions of the natural world.')

Confucianism is another stolid force for conservatism in the Chinese-influenced world. Originally it was wheeled in to bless the hegemony of the emperor: heaven gave him to us, so one must not resist him. It stresses family, marriage, and the veneration of ancestors. It is based on the ethical teachings of Confucius (551–479 BC), Chinese sage and philosopher, and to this day Confucianism is hugely influential in China and Vietnam, as well as among the Chinese diaspora. The 'Three Bonds' enshrined in Confucianism are the loyalty of ministers to the emperor, obedience of children to their parents, and submission of wives to their husbands. There is a democratic side to Confucianism: virtue can be acquired through learning, not just heredity, so upward mobility is possible, and education prized.

Ancestor veneration

Ancestor veneration is of enormous importance to the Chinese. To ensure a safe passage to the afterlife, a person must be provided with food, clothing, shelter and happiness while alive, and must be worshipped after they die. After a Chinese funeral, the family will burn paper houses, cars, clothes and money, and even representations of servants, TVs and mobile phones, to ensure that the person who died has everything she or he could want in the afterlife. The deceased will receive all these things when their essence is carried up to the spirit world in smoke as the paper objects are burned.

Good luck and bad luck

Good and bad luck are constant considerations for the Chinese. Chinese people might use a combination of any or all of: astrology, *I Ching,* numerology, all kinds of fortune telling including palm reading, and *Feng Shui* (the art of arranging objects in homes and offices to repel *chi,* or negative energy). There are also days, colours, and foods which are considered particularly lucky or unlucky. For example, red is considered a lucky colour. At Chinese New Year, black or dark colours are unlucky, and at funerals white, not black, is the appropriate colour.

Family

Of the 'Three Bonds' enshrined in Confucianism (see above), two relate directly to the family. Obedience of children to their parents, and submission of wives to their husbands are two reasons why family ties are still very strong for the Chinese. Traditionally the Chinese family is continued through the male line. A woman leaves her family to join the man's house and becomes part of his family, and so the birth of a son is cause for a much greater celebration than the birth of a daughter. A son not only ensures that the family name will be continued, but also guarantees that the older members of a family will have someone from their line to venerate them when they die.

For ethnic Chinese in South-east Asia in the countries where they are a minority, with little political power, and not yet fully integrated within the country, there is another reason for the emphasis on family unity. With little hope of government help to educate their children in Chinese ways or language, or of government jobs or positions in the police force or army, the extended ethnic Chinese family in South-east Asia is dependent on itself for job security, health-care and social welfare.

HEALTH

The health precautions you take before you leave and how you protect yourself after you arrive in South-east Asia will depend on which country you are planning to go to. Before you leave you should check with the relevant embassy and your doctor about which immunizations are currently required.

Take out a health insurance policy before you leave home. Many schools in South-east Asia provide their teachers with health-care cover. However, if your school has no such policy, or the policy is in some way inadequate, or if you become sick before you find your first job, you will at least be able to afford the treatment you want, in one of the best hospitals available, if you have your own health insurance.

Two insurance companies which are popular with EFL teachers are:

Bone and Company (International) Ltd, 69a Castle Street, Farnham, Surrey, GU9 7LP, UK. Tel: (01252) 724 140. Fax: (01252) 734 072.

Endsleigh Insurance Services Ltd, 97-107 Southampton Row, London WC1B 4AG, UK. Tel: (0171) 436 4451. Fax: (0171) 637 3132.

It is also worth remembering that as a teacher you are more likely to be working and living in a larger city or town, and the incidence of tropical illnesses is usually much lower in urban than in rural areas.

Without doubt the longer you live in South-east Asia, the stronger your resistance to local food-borne bacteria will get; you won't suffer from so many minor stomach problems as when you first arrived. Those who are new to South-east Asia are strongly advised to err on the side of caution where food and drink is concerned. You should peel fruit and vegetables, boil tap water before drinking it, and avoid uncooked meat or fish.

Singapore and Brunei are probably the safest countries, health-wise, in South-east Asia. Tropical diseases have been almost completely eradicated there and the medical help available in these countries is very good. Further down the economic scale, the Philippines, Thailand, Indonesia and Malaysia have fewer diseases and better hospitals and doctors than Laos, Cambodia and Vietnam. Indeed most foreigners who become ill in Laos, Cambodia or Vietnam usually opt for medical treatment in nearby Thailand or Singapore.

In the poorer counties of South-east Asia it is advisable to be protected against cholera, polio, tetanus, Hepatitis A, Hepatitis B, smallpox, rubella, TB and Japanese encephalitis. It is likely that some of your childhood illnesses and school vaccinations provide immunity from some of these diseases, and you may only need booster shots for them. If you require more than two live injections, it is worth making a couple of appointments with your doctor (up to three weeks apart, if possible), as the injections themselves and the after-effects can make you feel quite queasy.

If you are short of time before you leave your home country, and you are not as fully vaccinated as you would like to be, you can obtain further medical information and/or vaccinations in Bangkok from:

Travellers' Medical and Vaccination Centre, 8th floor, Alma Link Building, 25 Soi Childlom, Bangkok 10300. Tel: 655 1024, 655 1025.

You should carry a note of your blood type with you to Asia. If possible, you should also take a sterile medical equipment pack with you, as both AIDS and Hepatitis B can be spread through contaminated blood or non-sterile equipment. You can buy an equipment pack from:

Medical Advisory Services for Travellers Abroad Ltd (MASTA), London School of Hygiene and Tropical Medicine, Keppel Street, London, WC1E 7HT. Tel: (0171) 631 4408. Fax: (0171) 323 4547.

MASTA suggest the following five guidelines for dealing with injections and blood transfusions while abroad:

(1) Insist that injections are only given by qualified medical personnel using sterile needles and syringes. This includes local anaesthetic injections given by dentists.
(2) Wounds should be cleaned with an antiseptic and covered with a clean dressing. If the wound is deep, pull the edges together using sterile skin closure strips. If stitches are essential, insist that the suture material is sterile.
(3) Insist that any intravenous drip of blood or any other fluid is only given through a sterile needle.
(4) Should you need a blood transfusion abroad, try to get a colleague or embassy official to find out if the blood to be given is screened for AIDS and Hepatitis B.
(5) If you have to dispose of needles or syringes yourself do so with great care – it is best to bury them deeply.

The following is as list of *potential* health problems you may face in South-east Asia, how you can prevent them, and medical treatment you should seek should you become infected. Please do not be alarmed! In seven years of living and teaching in South-east Asia I have not caught any of the diseases below. Being sensible (without being obsessive) about what you eat and drink and protecting yourself from mosquitoes are probably the two most important precautions you can take.

AIDS (all countries in the region). AIDS is now pandemic, and the countries of South-east Asia with thriving sex-industries are epicentres. Thailand is perhaps the country with the most notorious sex industry, but developing countries in the region, such as Vietnam, Laos and Cambodia will soon not be far behind. The human immuno-deficiency virus – (HIV) – which can lead to AIDS and ARC (AIDS-related complex) can be contracted through having unprotected sex, sharing needles, and through transfusions of infected blood. The main precautions you can take against HIV are: using a reliable latex condom (not 100% effective); being wary of having a tattoo done, or getting your ears or body pierced in a shop that looks less than scrupulously clean; only going to a reliable hospital if you need a blood transfusion; and being extremely careful around blood. At the moment there is no cure for AIDS.

Cholera (all countries in the region except Brunei). This illness in caused by contaminated food and water. Often cholera epidemics spread after floods and there are usually press reports to alert you about which areas are dangerous and which are safe. The symptoms of cholera include acute diarrhoea, vomiting, weakness and cramps. If you have these symptoms, consult a doctor as soon as possible. Re-hydration is very important. There is a cholera vaccination, but it is considered to be only about 40% effective.

Dengue Fever (all countries in the region). The dengue-carrying *Aedes* mosquito is common in urban areas and is active during the day. The symptoms of this virus include severe headaches, bone-aches, a rash and a high fever. If you have these symptoms, consult a doctor as soon as possible. The symptoms come on suddenly, and if you can't see a doctor immediately, you should rest in bed, drink lots of liquids, and use cold sponges to ease the fever, but DO NOT take aspirin as it reduces the platelets in the blood and this can lead to dangerous haemorrhaging, instead use acetaminophin (Tylenol, Panadol).

Dysentery (all countries in the region). There are two kinds of dysentery – amoebic dysentery and bacillary dysentery. Both are caused by ingesting contaminated food or water. Amoebic dysentery is the more serious and is characterized by acute diarrhoea and blood or mucus in the stool. The symptoms of bacillary dysentery include a high fever, vomiting, headaches, stomachaches, and cramps. If you have these symptoms you should seek medical help. *Metronidazole* is the treatment used for amoebic dysentery and *tetracycline* is the treatment for bacillary dysentery. There is no vaccination available against dysentery.

Giardiasis (Vietnam). Giardiasis, sometimes known as giardia, is caught by ingesting contaminated water. The symptoms include nausea, stomach cramps, a bloated stomach, watery diarrhoea and frequent gas. If you have these symptoms, seek medical help. *Metronidazole (Flagyl)* is the recommended drug. There is no available vaccination against giardiasis.

Hepatitis A (all countries in the region). Hepatitis A is food- and water-borne. The symptoms of Hepatitis A include fever and chills, tiredness, headaches and body aches. These are followed by nausea and vomiting, loss of appetite, stomach pains, dark urine and light-coloured faeces. The whites of the eyes turn yellow and the skin becomes jaundiced. If you have these symptoms you should seek medical help immediately. Bed rest, re-hydration, eating lightly and avoiding greasy food is the best help you can give yourself before you get to a doctor. Hepatitis A attacks the liver, so doctors recommend that you not drink alcohol for 6 months, to help your liver recover. A preventative vaccine of *immune serum globulin* is available, and although it is not 100% effective, it is probably worth having before you leave for South-east Asia. This vaccine will help protect you for one year. The most effective injection for Hepatitis A is called Harvix.

Hepatitis B (all countries in the region). Hepatitis B is spread through contact with infected bodily fluids, and like HIV, can be prevented by using a condom, not sharing needles, being sure that any body piercing done is safe and that any blood transfusion is uncontaminated. The symptoms of Hepatitis B are similar to those of Hepatitis A but more severe; Hepatitis B can lead to liver cancer. A vaccination against Hepatitis B is available and you should consult your doctor in your home country about the possibility of having this injection before you leave for South-east Asia. As long as you protect yourself, teachers (as opposed to health workers) are less likely to need this vaccination. However, because up to 70% of people in Asia are carriers of Hepatitis B, you should discuss it with a healthcare professional before deciding if you need this injection or not. The injection is called Energix B.

Japanese encephalitis (all countries in the region except Brunei and Singapore). Japanese encephalitis is contracted from the *Culex* mosquito which is active during the night. As with many other diseases in South-east Asia, you are more at risk in rural areas, especially on farms where pigs are raised. The symptoms of Japanese encephalitis are sudden fevers, headaches, chills, and aching joints, followed by vomiting and delirium combined with an aversion to bright lights and sunshine. This disease can be fatal. If you are likely to be spending a lot of time in the countryside, especially during the rainy season, you should be vaccinated against this disease. There has been a recent outbreak of Japanese encephalitis in Vietnam and Laos, and consequently an increased risk in northern Thailand too. If this vaccine is not readily available in your home country, you can obtain it quite easily and cheaply in Singapore or Bangkok.

Malaria (all countries in the region except Singapore). Malaria is caught by being bitten by the female *Anopheles* mosquito which is active around dawn and dusk. The symptoms of malaria include: headaches, chills, a high fever which lasts a few hours, and perhaps diarrhoea. Any clinic or hospital can carry out a simple blood test to check if you have malaria. Treatment, if given early enough, is usually effective in completely ridding you of malaria. If you are treated too late, the malaria will return in cycles as the parasites move from your liver to the bloodstream, and back again.

Protection against malaria is a very controversial matter. *No* drugs currently available are 100% effective against the strains of malaria found in South-east Asia. Furthermore, the side effects from anti-malaria drugs can range from itching and rashes to retinal damage, fatal skin conditions and bone-marrow failure. Larium is a particularly controversial anti-malarial drug. For women there are further complications. During pregnancy women's resistance to malaria falls, and one of the side-effects of some anti-malarial drugs is an increased incidence of miscarriages and still-births. Most doctors advise that, if possible, women should delay conception while in a malarial area.

Rabies (all countries in the region except Brunei, Malaysia and Singapore). You can get rabies by being bitten, scratched, or licked by an infected warm-blooded animal. Dogs and bats are the two main carriers. If you are bitten you should treat the bite with soap, water and a strong alcohol-based solution and you should get medical help as soon as possible. Rabies, if contracted, is always fatal. Post-exposure to rabies treatment, a series of injections, is usually successful if it is started soon enough. A rabies vaccination is available and you should consult your doctor in your home country about having one before you leave for South-east Asia. Some Asian countries have a very limited supply of the serum you need if you actually get bitten, and the course of post-exposure treatment is often more expensive and painful than a preventative rabies injection.

Tetanus (all countries in the region). Tetanus occurs when a cut, wound or scratch becomes infected by a germ that lives in animal and human faeces. The symptoms of tetanus include difficulty or pain when swallowing, stiffening of the jaw and neck, followed by jaw and body convulsions. Tetanus can be fatal, but it is preventable – in fact, you may already be vaccinated against it. Before you leave your home country, however, you should check with your doctor to find out if you need a booster shot. Most doctors recommend a booster shot every five to ten years. Even if you are vaccinated against tetanus, you should still take good care of any cut or scratch you get in South-east Asia. A small wound can easily become infected in the heat of the tropics, and washing with soap and water and cleaning any wound with alcohol prevents infection setting in.

Tuberculosis (all countries in the region). TB is caused by *tubercle* bacilli and usually affects the lungs. It is mostly spread through airborne contact – eg a person with TB coughs and you breath in the tiny infected particles suspended in the air. The symptoms include a chronic cough with sputum (mucus you cough up) which may be bloody, and a fever. If you have a bad cough for more than three weeks, you should seek medical help and have a chest X-ray, as well as a sputum analysis. You were probably vaccinated against TB in childhood (in the UK, this would have been your BCG vaccination). Before you leave your home country, however, you should check with your doctor to find out if you need a booster shot.

Typhoid (all countries in the region). Typhoid is carried by food and water and, like cholera epidemics, typhoid is usually prominent after floods. Typhoid can be fatal. The symptoms of typhoid include: headaches, a sore throat, vomiting and diarrhoea or constipation. Typhoid is characterized by a slowly increasing temperature, which can eventually reach 40° C or more. (Normal body temperature is 37°C or 98.6° F.) The pulse often gets slower as the fever rises, unlike in usual fevers where the pulse tends to increase. In the second week of this illness, some pink spots might appear on the body. Further symptoms include trembling, delirium, weakness, weight loss and red spots on the chest and back. If you have these symptoms you should seek medical help immediately. Make-shift help can be given in the form of rehydration, keeping cool with sponge baths and eating only soft, non-acidic food. Doctors recommend *chloramphenciol* or *ampicillin* to treat typhoid. A vaccination against Typhoid is not 100% effective but you should consult your doctor about getting this vaccination before you leave for South-east Asia.

General protection

The best protection you can give yourself against most of the health risks listed above is to be careful about what you eat and drink, and try to avoid getting bitten by mosquitoes.

In the developing and under-developed counties in South-east Asia (Cambodia, Indonesia, Laos, Thailand and Vietnam) the tap water is *not* safe to drink, so you should buy bottled water or boil tap water for at least five minutes to kill off organisms. Even bottled water and locally-made ice cream in Laos and Cambodia show a certain level of bacteria present, however, this should prove harmless unless you are immuno-compromised. Avoid ice in restaurant drinks.

Stagnant water is the perfect breeding ground for mosquitoes, so be sure to change standing water regularly (for example, in saucers under plant-pots, refrigerator drip-trays, window boxes) and if you have any blocked drains, get them fixed as soon as possible.

To avoid being bitten by mosquitoes, you can use mosquito repellents, mosquito coils, electric mosquito mats and/or a mosquito net. Wearing long-sleeved shirts and covering up as much as possible when mosquitoes are around is also a sensible precaution.

WHAT TO TAKE

Most products you can buy at home are available in South-east Asia. This is, of course, not the case if you are going to one of the more remote parts of the region or are planning to work in a small, outlying village. However, since most of the TEFL work on offer is in the main cities, you will probably be living near supermarkets and department stores which are well-stocked with imported goods or excellent Asian-made versions of all your favorite biscuits, beers and make-up. It is sometimes difficult to find larger than Asian-size shoes and clothes (for women over UK size 12, US size 10 in clothes, and over UK size 5, US size 7 in shoes, and for men over UK size 37-38, US size 38 in clothes and UK size 10, US size 11 in shoes). However, you can usually have clothes and shoes copied from your originals quite cheaply when you arrive.

It is often difficult (although not impossible) to get a work permit without your original or a certified copy of your university degree certificate. Your home-country driving licence or an international one might be handy, if you want to hire or buy a motorbike or car.

An international plug adaptor is another useful item, if you are bringing electrical goods from home with you to South-east Asia. In most countries in the region locally made crash helmets are not up to international safety standards. If you think you might buy a motorbike or be riding one quite a lot it would be useful to bring a helmet from your home country with you.

If you have room in your suitcase you might want to pack: contact lens solution, tampons, condoms, bras, cotton underwear, and reading material if you are interested in books other than those written by Jackie Collins or Harold Robbins. All of these are available, especially in the major cities, in South-east Asia, but because they are imported goods they are much more expensive than they are at home.

How much money to take

The largest single expense faced by most teachers who go to South-east Asia without a pre-arranged job is setting up an apartment or home. The many cheap hostels for travellers are very useful initially, but eventually you will want somewhere of your own. Unfortunately in most countries in the region you will almost certainly have to pay two or three months' rent in advance (and in Indonesia you have to pay a year's rent up front). Some schools offer temporary accommodation and/or housing loans of two or three months' salary in advance, but this is not the norm. Most teachers take between four and six weeks to find a suitable house, and in the interim have to pay for short-term accommodation.

Another large financial outlay you may face is a return trip to a neighbouring country to obtain a work permit once you have found a job. If you find full-time work, the school will usually finance this trip, but if you find only part-time work you may be liable for between 50 and 100% of the costs.

All in all, it is advisable to take as much money as you can with you to South-east Asia if you have no job to go to. Of course it is possible to live very cheaply until you find work, and after that, to rent a house for very little money, but a reasonable minimum to live on and to avoid hardships is probably around £500-750/$750-1200.

Suggested reading

Buruma, Ian, *God's Dust: A Modern Asian Journey*, Vintage, New York, 1991.

Dingwall, Alastair, Ed, *Traveller's Literary Companion To South-east Asia*, In Print, Brighton, UK, 1994.

Floyd, Keith, *Far Flung Floyd: Keith Floyd's Guide to South-east Asian Food,* Penguin, London, 1994.

Dawood, Richard, *Travellers' Health,* Oxford University Press, Oxford, UK, 1992.

Jackson, Peter, *Dear Uncle Go: Male Homosexuality in Thailand,* Bua Lang Books, 1995.

Osborne, Milton, *South-east Asia, An Illustrated Introductory History*, Allen & Unwin, St Leonards, Australia, 1987.

Pilger, John, *Distant Voices*, Vintage, New York, 1994.

Ryan, Rob, *Stay Healthy Abroad*, Health Education Authority, London, 1995.

2

Finding a job in South-east Asia

TRAINING

In some countries in South-east Asia it is almost impossible to get EFL work without a recognized qualification. You will need either the Royal Society of Arts/University of Cambridge Local Examination Syndicate Certificate in English Language Teaching to Adults (RSA/UCLES CELTA),[1] or Trinity College, London Certificate in TESOL (Teaching English to Speakers of Other Languages). This is because is some countries (eg Singapore) you must be a qualified teacher to obtain a work visa. In major cities in other countries it is a buyers' market in private language school recruitment at the moment, and a recognized EFL qualification is the least most schools can, and do, demand.

The most popular course for first-time teachers is the one-month RSA/UCLES CELTA course which is run at many centres in the UK, the USA, Canada, Australia and New Zealand. Over the last two years there has been a substantial growth in the number enrolled on such courses, and in 1996 over 6 000 people gained this qualification. This is a practical introductory course in TEFL, usually containing 110 hours of theoretical input and teaching practice. There is no exam at the end of the course, but the grades are given on assessment of teaching over the length of the course, which may be full-time

[1] In October 1996 CELTA replaced the old Certificate in Teaching English as a Foreign Language to Adults (CTEFLA). This name change has meant very few actual course content changes; the main difference is a decrease in the number of written assignments that trainees have to do during the course. Also in October 1996 two new introductory courses for teachers became available from RSA/UCLES: CELTYL – Certificate in English Language Teaching to Young Learners in Language Schools; and CTLEA – Certificate in Teaching Languages other than English to Adults.

intensive over a month, or part-time spread over three months to a year. Although fairly expensive (£895/US$1 360 at International House, London, in 1996), the RSA/UCLES CELTA course is a highly-recommended first step if you are at all serious about teaching English as a foreign language. Apart from the pedagogical reasons given below, it is a qualification which will go a long way in helping you find work not only in South-east Asia, but almost anywhere in the world.

As well as helping you find work, training can give you the confidence and credibility to stand in front of a group of students, as well as giving you ideas on what and how to teach. It is not enough just to be a native speaker of English to cope with the challenges that come with teaching English. Without training, native speakers are usually unable to articulate the rules of English grammar and generally have few ideas about teaching these rules. Certainly your native speaker ear can help you enormously in recognizing when something your students say is wrong. But in these competitive days, with so many schools to choose from, students want more of an explanation from their teachers than 'Well, it's just wrong, that's all.' Enthusiasm, imagination, common sense and hard work are all qualities you will need in the classroom, but these alone do not make you a good teacher.

Training in the UK

It is possible to do a one-week introductory to EFL course. Although these courses contain no teaching practice component and are unlikely to be recognized by recruiting organizations or schools, they can give you a good idea about what teaching involves and might also help you decide if you want to spend the time and money that an RSA/UCLES CELTA course requires. The *EL Gazette* (see below) lists centres running this course.

There are schools in some South-east Asian countries which employ unqualified teachers. If you are thinking of going to South-east Asia and picking up odd teaching jobs along the way, this one-week course will at least give you some ideas about what to teach and give you some confidence when your are faced with your first classes. You should bear in mind, however, that schools offering work to unqualified teachers will probably be less reputable, and offer lower wages.

RSA/UCLES CELTA courses are run in many centres throughout the UK including at large organizations such as International House, Bell and Pilgrims. Because so many places now offer courses in EFL, it is worth researching them in detail before committing yourself to a particular course. Cambridge University and the Royal Society of Arts oversee the standard of tuition on these courses, so you do not have to worry about whether any particular course is of a higher standard of tuition than another. However, there are other considerations you may want to think about; whether the course is full-time or part-time, cost (often the part-time courses are cheaper than full-time ones), recent pass rates, and location.

In the UK, check the *Guardian* on Tuesdays, the monthly *EL Gazette* and the most current *EFL Guide* or your local library for a list of places which run EFL courses.

University of Cambridge Local Examination Syndicate (UCLES), Syndicate Building, 1 Hills Road, Cambridge, CB1 2EU, UK. Tel: (01223) 553 311. Fax: (01223) 460 278.

EL Gazette, Dilke House, Malet Street, London WC1E 7AJ. Tel: (0171) 255 1969.

The *EFL Guide* is an annual publication which gives a run down of centres offering various courses, from CELTA courses to MAs and Diplomas in TEFLA, in the UK and worldwide.

EFL Limited, Lightwood, Grove Mount, Ramsey, Isle of Man, UK. Subscriptions Tel: (0171) 255 1969.

Trinity College, London, offers TESOL (Teaching English to Speakers of Other Languages) courses at both the introductory and Diploma level. These courses are not as well-known internationally as the Cambridge courses, but are generally accepted as an equivalent qualification. Courses are usually 100 hours and are offered at about 20 centres throughout the UK.

Trinity College, London, Teacher Training Course Co-ordinator (language section), Trinity College, 16 Park Crescent, London, W1N 4AP. Tel: (0171) 323 2328, ext 2103. Fax: (0171) 323 5201.

Training in Ireland

At the moment there are only two centres in Ireland where you can do the RSA/UCLES CELTA course. University College, Cork, offers the CELTA course full-time, while The Language Centre of Ireland offers full-time and part-time certificate courses, as well as a RSA/UCLES Diploma in TEFLA.

University College, Cork, Language Center, Department of English, Cork, Ireland. Tel: (3021) 276 871.

Language Centre of Ireland, 45 Kildare Street, Dublin, 2 Ireland. Tel: (021) 716 266.

Training in the USA

At the moment there is no US equivalent to the RSA/UCLES Certificate, with its mix of theory and practice. However, increasingly the RSA/UCLES courses are becoming available in the USA. Most Americans interested in a career in EFL do a BA or MA in ESOL or Applied Linguistics. Although there is no teaching practice component in most MA courses, most employers in South-east Asia will accept an MA as readily as a RSA/UCLES CELTA.

In the USA the *Directory of Professional Preparation Programs in TESOL* is a guide to the courses on offer. The same organization publishes a bi-monthly *Placement Bulletin* with information of job vacancies.

TESOL, 1600 Cameron Street, Suite 300, Alexandria, Virginia, 22314 – 2751, USA. Tel: (703) 518 2522. Fax: (703) 518 2525.

Addresses of RSA/UCLES course centres in the USA include:

California

English International, 655 Sutter Street, Suite 500, San Francisco, CA 94102. Tel (415) 749 5633. Fax (415) 749 6729.

St Giles Language Teaching Center, 1 Hallidie Plaza, Suite 350, San Francisco, CA 94102. Tel: (415) 788 3552.

Coast Language Academy, 501 Santa Monica Boulevard, Suite 403, Santa Monica, CA 90401. Tel: (310) 394 8618.

New York

Center of English Studies, International House, 330 7th Avenue, at 29th Street, New York, 10001. Tel: (212) 629 7300. Fax: (212) 594 7415.

Oregon

Coast Language Academy, 200 SW Market Street, Suite 111, Portland, Oregon 97201. Tel: (503) 224 1960.

Washington, DC

Georgetown University, 3607 ‘O’ Street NW, Washington DC 20057. Tel: (202) 687 6045.

Training in Canada

Addresses of RSA/UCLES course centres include:

British Columbia

Columbia College, 6037 Marlborough Avenue, Burnaby, BC V5H 3L6. Tel: (604) 430 6422.

Nova Scotia

1496 Lower Walter Street, Halifax, Nova Scotia, B3J 1R9. Tel: (902) 429 3636.

Quebec

1455 de Maisonneuve Boulevard, Montreal, Quebec H3G 1M8. Tel: (514) 848 2452.

Training in Australia

Addresses of RSA/UCLES course centres include:

New South Wales

Australian TESOL Training Centre, Australian College of English, PO Box 82, Bondi Junction, Sydney, NSW 2022. Tel: (02) 389 0249.

Australian Center for Languages, 420 Liverpool Road, South Stratfield, Sydney NSW 2136. Tel: (02) 742 5277.

Insearch Language Center, Level 2, 10 Quay Street, Haymarket, Sydney NSW 2000. Tel: (02) 281 4544.

Western Australia

Milner International College of English, 379 Hat Street, Perth 6000. Tel: (09) 325 5444.

St Mark's International College, 375 Stirling Street, PO Box 8480, Perth 6000. Tel: (09) 227 9888.

Queensland

International House Queensland, 130 McLeod Street, PO Box 7368, Cairns, Queensland 4870. Tel: (070) 313 466. Fax: (070) 313 464.

South Australia

Centre for Applied Linguistics, 82-98 Wakefield Street, Adelaide, South Australia 5001. Tel: (08) 302 1555.

The South Australian College of English, 254 North Terrace, Adelaide, South Australia 5000. Tel: (08) 232 0335

Victoria

Holmesglen College of TAFE, PO Box 42, Chadstone, Victoria 3148. Tel: (03) 564 1819.

ITTC International College of English, 185 Spring Street, Melbourne, Victoria 3000. Tel: (03) 662 2055.

La Trobe University, Bundoora, Victoria 3083. Tel: (613) 479 2417.

Royal Melbourne Institute of Technology, PO Box 12058, A Beckett Street, Melbourne, Victoria 3001. Tel: (613) 639 0300

Training in New Zealand

Addresses of RSA/UCLES course centres include:

Auckland

Auckland Language Centre, PO Box 1652, Auckland City, Auckland. Tel: (09) 303 1962.

Dominion English School, PO Box 4217, Auckland. Tel: (09) 377 3280.

Languages International Limited, PO Box 5293, Wellesley Street, Auckland. Tel: (09) 309 0615.

Christchurch

ILA South Pacific Ltd, PO Box 25170, Christchurch 1. Tel (03) 795 452.

Hamilton

University of Waikato, Private Bag 3105, Hamilton. Tel: (647) 838 4193.

Wellington

Capital Language Academy, PO Box 1100, Wellington 6000. Tel (04) 472 7557.

Training in South-east Asia

At the moment the RSA/UCLES CELTA courses are offered in Thailand, Indonesia, and Malaysia. One of the advantages of doing the course in South-east Asia is that it is cheaper because the cost of living is lower than in the West. Furthermore, should you want to teach in South-east Asia the course will offer you a preview of typical Asian students and an opportunity to set up a job in the region more easily.

Indonesia

The British Institute, Setiabudi Building 2, Jalan H R Rasuna Said, Jakarta, 12920. Tel: (021) 525 6750

Malaysia

The British Council Language Centre, 3rd and 4th Floor, Wisma Hangsam, Box 20, 1 Jalan Hang Lekir, 50000, Kuala Lumpur. Tel: (03) 230 6304, 230 6305.

Thailand

ECC (Thailand), 430/17-20 Chula Soi 64, Siam Square, Bangkok, 10330. Tel: (02) 252 6488, 252 6489. Fax: (02) 254 2243.

Further qualifications

The Cambridge/RSA DTEFLA is primarily for teachers who have completed the Cambridge/RSA CELTA course and have a minimum of two years' recent classroom experience. This course is at a much higher level than the Certificate and goes into the theoretical aspects of language teaching in much more detail, although teaching practice plays an equally important role. It can be taken intensively over eight to weeks, or part-time over eight to ten months. Apart from the many centres in the UK that run such courses it is also currently offered at the British Council in Malaysia (address above) and it is also possible to do a distance Diploma course through International House, London wherever you are in the world.

A PGCE (Postgraduate Certificate in Education) is a UK qualification and an option for those wishing to move into state education, either in the UK or abroad. It is also a useful qualification if you are interested in working in private International Schools abroad. In all the countries of South-east Asia, there are International Schools where a PGCE is the recognized qualification.

Teachers interested in looking into a particular field in more depth may consider doing a Masters Degree for example, in Linguistics, Teacher Training, or ELT Management. In South-east Asia an MA is often preferred to a Diploma if you are competing for a high level job such as a position in a university or a consultancy in one of the aid agencies. This is perhaps because those organizations are often unaware of what the Cambridge/RSA DTEFLA involves, and presume that an MA is a better qualification. However, in most EFL schools in South-east Asia the Cambridge/RSA DTEFLA and an MA are equally well-regarded and rewarded.

CAREER POSSIBILITIES IN TEFL

A lot of people initially use TEFL as a means to work abroad and see some of the world for a few years. However, there are more and more opportunities now to pursue a career in TEFL, and the profession is becoming increasingly diverse. Enormous advances have been made in the field over the last 10 years, and these are likely to develop in the future, as English language teaching becomes more professional and the demand for EFL grows.

It is important to realize that, even after doing a one-month or part-time course, teachers should still consider themselves 'apprentices' until they have had about two years' classroom experience. When considering TEFL as a career you should also bear in mind that while experience is crucial, promotion very much depends on an individual's resourcefulness, energy and adaptability.

Some of the possibilities available after three or four years' experience teaching at all levels, and after gaining further qualifications include: Director/Assistant Director of Studies in a private school or institute, apprenticeship as a teacher-trainer; an administrative job in a school; teaching ESL (English as a Second Language) to immigrants; specializing in commercial or technical EFL; English for Academic Purposes (EAP); publishing; writing textbooks; starting your own school; broadcasting; specializing in teaching English to children; and developing information technology for EFL.

It is important that you take advantages of as many opportunities as possible at all stages of your career. When you are in South-east Asia, for example, learn the language of the country you are teaching in. Learn all you can about the educational systems and the background of your students. Join local and international teachers' associations, attend any conferences that are organized, give talks at them: anything directly related to your experience will almost certainly be interesting. Read as much as you can about EFL and the country you are in and assess any textbooks you come across in terms of the specific linguistic needs and cultural interests of Asian students. Observe other teachers and be observed as often as you can as this can give you valuable insight into how other teachers deal with challenges similar to those you face. Remember that you cannot always rely on your school or Director of Studies to help you develop as a teacher, and you should take responsibility for your own growth as a teacher.

FINDING A JOB

There are definite advantages in arranging a job before you go to South-east Asia. Travelling a long distance to a region with such different cultures, you will undoubtedly feel more secure if you have guaranteed employment beforehand. This will enable you to start earning a salary from the time you arrive. Your visa will be arranged for you, perhaps saving you an expensive trip outside the country to exchange a tourist visa for a work visa. Your flight will probably be paid for you and you will receive valuable help in finding accommodation, if accommodation is not provided by your employer.

Newspapers in the UK

In the UK you can look for schools which recruit from abroad in the *Guardian* every Tuesday, the *Times Educational Supplement* on a Friday and the monthly EFL newspaper, the *EL Gazette*. *The International Educator* (TIE) also advertises posts abroad, mostly in international schools. You can contact them at:

TIE (UK), 102a Popes Lane, London W5 4NS, UK. Tel/fax: (0181) 840 2587.

If you are living in London it is worth regularly checking the bulletin board at International House for jobs in South-east Asia.

Newspapers in the USA

In the USA, TESOL offers a placement service and publishes a list of jobs openings (address above).

For staff recruitment ads covering 500 worldwide international schools, consult *The International Educator*, a quarterly newspaper. Individual teachers can take out a subscription at $35 per year, or you can find *TIE* in public libraries.

TIE, PO Box 513, Cummaquid, MA 02637, USA. Tel: (508) 362 1414. Fax: (508) 362 1411.

Recruiting organizations

Recruiting organizations in the UK

The following organizations all recruit teachers in the UK for South-east Asia. The specific countries they recruit for are indicated in brackets after the name of the organization.

International House (Singapore). IH is a non-profit educational charity which was founded in 1953. It is now the largest UK-based organization for teaching English with nearly 100 schools worldwide. It is also a major teacher-training institute. International House employs qualified native speaker teachers from a number of countries. For detailed information contact:

International House, Teacher Selection Department, 106 Piccadilly, London W1 9FL. Tel: (0171) 491 2598. Fax: (0171) 495 0284.

Other recruitment organizations. These include: Bell Educational Trust (Indonesia and Thailand), inlingua, (Singapore and Thailand), TEFLNET (Thailand), The Anglo-Pacific Consultancy (Thailand and Malaysia and, in the near future, Vietnam and Indonesia), and the British Council (Brunei, Indonesia, Malaysia, Singapore, Thailand, Vietnam). In some countries, eg Indonesia, the British Council has no language school but does offer the occasional consultancy post for highly qualified and experienced teachers. When applying to the British Council at the addresses listed in relevant country chapters, you should direct your query to the DTOM (Direct Teaching Operation Manager). The inlingua Teacher Training and Recruitment service in the UK recruits not only for its own schools in the region but also for other private language schools in Indonesia, Malaysia and Thailand. Although Berlitz Schools (Thailand) no longer recruit for their overseas schools in the UK or the USA, if you contact them they will give a list of their schools abroad enabling you to contact the Director of Studies directly.

Anglo-Pacific (Asia) Consultancy, Suit 32 Nevilles Court, Dollis Hill Lane, London, NW2 6HG. Tel: (0181) 452 7836. E-mail: anglo-pacific@cygnet.co.uk

Bell Educational Trust, Overseas Department, Hillscross Redcross Lane, Cambridge, CB2 2QX. Tel: (01223) 246 644. Fax: (01223) 414 080.

Berlitz School of Languages, 9 -13 Grosvenor Street, London, W1A 3BZ. Tel: (0171) 915 0909. Fax: (0171) 915 0222.

British Council, Central Management of Direct Teaching, 10 Spring Gardens, London SW1A 2BN. Tel: (0171) 389 4931. Fax (0171) 389 4140.

inlingua, Teacher Training and Recruitment, Rodney Lodge, Rodney Road, Cheltenham, GL 50 1JF. Tel: (01242) 253 171. Fax: (01242) 253 181.

TEFLNET, The Language Works, 41 Low Petergate, York, YO1 2HT. Tel: (01904) 613 869. Fax: (01904) 613 8869.

Recruiting organizations in the USA

The United States Information Agency (USIA) has many teaching posts in South-east Asia. If you contact USIA directly they will give you a list of schools where they have teaching programmes in the region and you can then apply directly to the centers. You can contact USIA at:

Berlitz International Inc, 239 Wall Street, Princeton, NJ, 08540 1555. Tel: (609) 497 9731.

United States Information Agency (USIA) English Language Teaching Division, 301 4th Street, Washington DC 20547.

Volunteer recruitment organizations

For many people who want to teach or work in the poorer countries in South-east Asia, the main way to do it is through volunteer work. Getting the necessary work visa is very difficult if you are not sponsored by an organization and, as yet, some countries in the region (eg Cambodia) have not allowed many private language schools to open. Although as the free market economy expands in Laos, Vietnam and Cambodia, the possibility of working in those countries as a paid EFL teacher increases, for the moment, much of the teaching done there is through aid organizations .

Most voluntary organizations will pay your return air-fare, a small living allowance, find and pay for your accommodation, set you up with a job, and offer you a support system of other volunteers, as well as a field officer in the nearest city. Other organizations expect you to finance your trip and pay your own expenses. Most organizations are looking for a commitment of one to two years. Some organizations only recruit volunteers with particular religious beliefs, notably Christian organizations, while others, although Christian, accept volunteers of any or no denomination. I have indicated which organizations will accept only practising Christians.

Most volunteer organizations have a rigorous interview system to help you decide if you are suitable for volunteer work. If you are accepted as a volunteer, you might be working in a remote area, with few home comforts, and little chance to talk with English-speaking people. Volunteer organizations will want to check if you can work as part of a team and if you have the capacity to accept other cultures and different ways of doing things. Patience, understanding, and an ability to consider your world-view as not the only feasible one, are all characteristics that volunteers should have.

UK

Voluntary Services Overseas (VSO), 317 Putney Bridge Road, London SW15 2PN. Tel: (0181) 780 2266.

Methodist Church Overseas Division (Committed Christians), 25 Marylebone Road, London, NW1 5JR. Tel: (0171) 486 5502. Fax: (0171) 935 1507.

Concern Worldwide, 248-250 Lavender Hill, Clapham Junction, London, SW1W 1LJ. Tel: (0171) 738 1033.

Christians Abroad, 1 Stockwell Green, London, SW9 9HP. Tel: (0171) 737 7811. Fax: (0171) 737 3237

Youth with a Mission, (YWAM) (Committed Christians), 13 Highfield Oval, Ambrose Lane, Harpenden, Herts, AL5 4BX. Tel: (01582) 765 481. Fax: (01582) 768 048.

London Mennonite Centre (Committed Christians), 14 Shepherds Hill, Highgate, London, N6. 5AQ. Tel: (0181) 340 8775. Fax: (0181) 341 6807.

Ireland

Agency for Personal Services Overseas (APSO), 29-30 Fitzwilliam Square, Dublin 2. Tel: (01) 661 4411. Fax: (01) 661 4202.

USA

The Peace Corps, 1990 K Street (PO Box 941), NW, Washington, DC 20526. Tel: 800 424 8580 Ext 2293 (toll free).

World Teach Inc, Harvard Institute for International Development, 1 Eliot Street, Cambridge, MA 02138. Tel: (617) 495 5527. Fax: (617) 495 1239.

Global Routes, 5554 Broadway, Oakland, CA 94618. Tel: (510) 655 0321. Fax: (510) 655 0371.

Global Volunteers, 375E Little Canada Road, St Paul, Minnesota, MN 55117. Tel: (612) 482 1074. Fax: (612) 482 0915.

Mennonite Central Committee (MCC), (Committed Christians), Head Office, 21 South 12th Street, PO Box 500, Akron, Pennsylvania 17501–0500. Tel: (717) 859 3889. Fax: (717) 859 2622.

Presbyterian Church (USA) (Committed Christians), 100 Witherspoon Street, Louisville, Kentucky, KY 40202 - 1396. Tel: 1 800 524 2612 (toll free).

Canada

Voluntary Services Overseas (VSO), 35 Centennial Boulevard, Ottawa, Ontario, KIS OM6. Tel: (613) 235 4199.

Mennonite Central Committee (MCC) (Committed Christians), 134 Plaza Drive, Winnipeg, Manitoba R3T 5K9. Tel: (204) 261 6381. Fax: (204) 269 9875.

Australia

Overseas Service Bureau (OSB), 71–75 Argyle Street, (PO Box 350), Fitzroy, Victoria, 3065. Tel: (03) 279 1788. Fax: (03) 419 4280.

Interviews

Whether you are able to set up a job interview in your home country or in the country you actually want to work in, here is a checklist of 10 questions you should probably know the answer to when you come out of the interview. You should prioritize these questions according to your own specific wants and needs before an interview.

(1) *How many hours a week will I work?* The maximum should be 25 contact hours with another 15 for administration or preparation. In some schools, a teaching 'hour' includes a break, and so might actually only mean 45 or 50 minutes actual teaching.

(2) *How will these hours be arranged?* You probably want to avoid split shifts (eg working early in the morning, having a break of a few hours and then teaching again in the late afternoon or evening), and to make sure that there is a sufficient length of time between finishing teaching one evening and starting the next morning. But frankly, split shifts are not always the end of the world, and you might have to accept a few in order to prove your eagerness to a new employer. The relative pain of split shifts depends on what kind of city or town you live in. For example, in Singapore it is quite feasible to teach an early morning class, go for an excellent lunch and then laze beside an outdoor pool or work out in the gym, and then teach again in the evening. So think about transport and 'hanging around' facilities where you live when considering your stand on split shifts.

(3) *Will I work on weekends?* Some schools have Saturday and Sunday morning business and children's classes. You might be put on a Tuesday to Saturday schedule, or be asked to do an extra class on what would be your usual weekend day off. If you do have to work at the weekend, you might want a guarantee from the school that you will have two consecutive days off later in the week.

(4) *Where will I be teaching?* You may be asked to do classes 'off-campus', for example on site at a company. If this turns out to be the case, find out how long it is going to take you to get there, and whether you will receive compensation for time spent travelling. Most likely, only your actual travelling expenses will be paid, and travel time will be subsumed under the 15 hours of non-teaching time you are expected to do anyway.

(5) *What will I be paid?* If you will be working without a contract, you need to know the hourly rate, and also if you get paid at a higher rate for exam classes, English For Special Purposes, and other special classes. You also need to find out the procedure for cancelled classes. Will you be paid if there is no notice given? How much will you get paid – your normal teaching rate, or a non-

teaching rate? If you are working hourly, it is unlikely that you will have access to advances or settling-in loans, but if you need them, you might as well ask. If you have to pay for your own work permit costs, find out now. It is also worth asking if your employer is prepared to split your work permit costs 50/50 with you, if you are on a part-time contract.

If you sign a part-time contract, that should mean that you are guaranteed a minimum number of hours, and you are a salaried employee. You will want to know about the over-time rate and if taxes are deducted from your salary. If you are offered a full-time contract, you should ask about whatever is applicable from the above, and also about salary increments for service, further qualifications, etc. Don't forget to find out what *day* you actually receive your pay on, especially for your first month's salary – after working for four weeks without income the difference between being paid on the last working day of the month and the first day of the next one can seem quite enormous.

(6) *Do I receive any holidays?* If you are on a full contract, about four weeks paid holiday a year is normal. There may be some restrictions on when you can take time off, as many of the school holidays may be already fixed.

(7) *Who will I be teaching?* Teenagers, business people, children, or all of these? You will also want to know about class size, and if the school's placement system allows a range of levels in the same class. (An interviewer is unlikely to admit this but you can get a sense of whether this is the case by asking about the method of placing students – what reading, writing, listening and speaking tests do they use, is there an placement interview?)

(8) *What is the academic set-up?* This is probably the most important question after pay and hours worked. You won't be able to find out in the interview about all school facilities, but if the words *Headway, Cambridge* or other well-known coursebooks, and indeed 'tape recorder', 'photocopier', and 'whiteboard' do not trip off your prospective employer's tongue, you will know where you stand. Ask about the syllabus, what coursebooks are used, whether students have their own copies, and how long each level or term lasts. If you are actually at the school when you are interviewed, you can learn the most by asking to see the staffroom and classrooms – look for available teaching resources and supplementary material, classroom facilities and what the teachers already working there are like.

(9) *What kind of staff development is offered?* Will you have the opportunity of being observed with feedback, and of peer-

observation? Are there staff development workshops? How often are staff meetings? Will you be able to attend professional conferences that come up? Is there a Senior Teacher system?

(10) *Does the school provide health insurance?* In some countries, such as Cambodia, medical evacuation insurance is also important.

Arriving without a job

Probably most of the teachers teaching in South-east Asia now originally arrived here on spec and set up a job. Although this way of finding work can be stressful, it is feasible, even for a woman alone, and carries some advantages with it. The main one is that you can see the school and find out its local reputation before signing a contract. All schools have their own personalities which you can quickly divine; bad schools have their horror stories which will be repeated with relish by the local teaching community. Being on the scene means you can be pretty sure you are not being exploited. Occasionally the recruiters or agents for Asian schools that you meet in your home country are acting in complete good faith, but have themselves been bamboozled by the school they are representing. Glossy photos of computerized student resource centres and fern-filled staff-rooms may not be worth the paper they are printed on. Actually, unless you are completely certain that the school is legitimate, the implications of signing a contract before you arrive in the country are probably scarier than just seeing for yourself. There certainly are cowboy schools in Asia; some use intimidation and tactics such as locking up your passport and refusing to give it back to you lest you abscond. Just be careful. The questions you ask in an interview (see above) will help you weed out the bad schools.

Because there is a pool of teachers already present in most desirable teaching areas, sending out CVs from home is unlikely to meet with positive results. But arriving on the doorstep with CV in hand should lead to a demonstration lesson, being asked to cover a few classes, and then to bigger and better things.

A disadvantage of going to a country on spec is that you need enough money to tide you over for a while. You can use the country guides in this book (Chapters 4 – 12) to estimate how much money you would need to take to your target country. Even if you go on a contract, you need enough to get through the month before your first paycheque. It would be rare for airport immigration to ask a Westerner to produce an onward ticket or show sufficient funds on arrival, but for your own peace of mind it would be a good idea to take an onward ticket with you. Most teachers enter a country on a tourist visa, and even legitimate schools will employ you (illegally) on a tourist visa for a few lessons, if they think you might be suitable for them. Then they will arrange for you to pick up a work permit in a neighbouring country and return as a legitimate worker or 'consultant'. It is true that the process of obtaining a work permit takes a long time in all the countries in this book, but you probably will be paid the whole time anyway, and will have to do little more than sign your name to some forms, appear for a photo shoot at Immigration, and be amply fingerprinted. Leaving the country to pick up a visa can be a nice holiday.

When you get to the country you want to find work in and you've found some short-term accommodation, the next thing you need to do is buy a local phone-card. Then, find a phone-card phone, and start calling schools to make appointments with the Director of Studies (DOS) or the Assistant Director of Studies (ADOS). Use the local Yellow Pages to check if numbers or addresses have changed since this book was published. If you are staying in budget accommodation or a guest house known to be frequented by foreigners, then there is a good chance that some people who want to learn English will find you. True, they probably will want to do it for free, but in practising their English on you, they might actually prove helpful in getting you oriented or finding private lessons to get you started. Of course you should be a bit wary, especially if you are a woman, of locals (almost always male) who 'collect' foreigners. But these people are not likely to be dangerous, simply annoying in their attentiveness. Having said that, Bangkok has more of a reputation for taking foreigners for a ride than other major cities covered in this book – so be especially careful in Khao San Road and budget areas of the city. A tip-off is if the person you've met wants to practise English by talking about the gems he'd like to show you in a shop 'just around the corner'... you know the sting is not far off!

3

Teaching in South-east Asia

Once you have found a job, your work visa has been arranged, and you have found somewhere to live, your first lesson in South-east Asia and perhaps even your first ever lesson, will soon begin. What will the students be like? What will they expect of you?

There are a number of considerations to bear in mind when teaching in South-east Asia. Not least of these is the fact that most EFL coursebooks are written with European students in mind. The following section gives ideas on how you can adapt both coursebooks and your teaching methods to help address the special needs of students in the region.

SOUTH-EAST ASIAN STUDENTS' PROBLEMS

In this section I will look at the particular problems that South-east Asian students have in a typical EFL classroom. Some of these problems arise because their first-language background is so different from English. Some problems arise from their expectations of how they should learn and how they should be taught. Other problems arise from their cultural assumptions about what topics are appropriate and inappropriate to talk about in the classroom.

First language interference

One of the main features of English and European grammar is that verbs are inflected to show tense change, that is, the verb itself changes in some way (eg She *is working* now, She *worked* yesterday). None of the South-east Asian languages, however, inflect their verbs to show tense changes.

Other features of English grammar that are similar to European languages, but different from Asian languages include: an article system (*the, a, an,*), the use of auxiliary verbs in negatives and questions, and making nouns singular or plural. An Asian student's first language is therefore, more likely to hinder rather than help, when s/he tries to make sense of English grammar rules.

As a result of this first language interference, common Asian mistakes include:

I buy a CD yesterday. **(X)**
She go to the cinema tomorrow. **(X)**

Where is pen? **(X)**
I went to the bed at 8 o'clock **(X)**

You see her yesterday? **(X)**
I not Thai. **(X)**

I'd like two pen, please. **(X)**
He has five sister. **(X)**

Lack of cognates

For Europeans studying English, there are likely to be a large number of words which are similar between the two languages, for example, Latin-based words such as *situation* and *important* for students from southern Europe, and shorter words such as *house,* and *good* for students from central and northern Europe. For Asian students there are no such lexical roots common to their first language and English. (On the positive side, Asian languages are much more likely than European ones to have a large number of borrowed modern words, for example *computer*.)

To help Asian students overcome their fear of unknown words it is useful to build on the knowledge they already have, and help them make connections between words they know and words they don't know in the same family (eg if they already know *economy,* words such as *economist* and *economically* need not be frightening, unknown words). Encouraging students to make guesses about what words might mean from the clues they can gather from other parts of the text (ie from context) also helps Asian students feel less overwhelmed by unknown vocabulary.

Culturally inappropriate materials

For a European studying English, the topics covered in most coursebooks are likely to be ones which the student has previously been aware of, has a sound background knowledge of, may well be interested in, and is used to discussing and hearing discussed (in the media and among friends). For Asian students, however, many of the topics covered in coursebooks, are likely to make them feel very uncomfortable. The prospect of being asked to discuss, offer opinions and disagree with others on subjects such as the environment, nuclear energy, war, or poverty is likely to fill most South-east Asian students with dread. To help your students you can adapt your coursebook so that topics which they find irrelevant or embarrassing are left out, or you can use reading texts from the local English language newspapers about these difficult topics to introduce an Asian viewpoint which your students are more likely to respond to than a European, Australian or US one.

Most EFL coursebooks start from the assumption that some kind of British/Australian/American cultural understanding is necessary for students learning English. This is because many students study English because they are planning to live and work in an English-speaking country. For many of your students in South-east Asia, however, this is not the case. For them English is seen as a common language which can be used *within* the region so that a business meeting in Malaysia with Singaporeans, Thais and Vietnamese can be conducted successfully in one language. Learning about the culture of an English-speaking country is irrelevant to such students, so you might want to adapt your coursebook and leave out or change such lessons as the *Headway Intermediate* listening on a British woman forever failing her driving test or the *Cambridge English Course I* reading text on a naval battle between America and Britain more than 200 hundred years ago.

Different learning expectations

In most South-east Asian classrooms students will show little, if any, initiative. They expect the teacher to provide a lock-step lesson and they will follow this pattern if it is laid down. When you stop, they stop. There is generally little question of students taking over the lesson and moving it onto different areas. Rather, much more usual is for the teacher to have to pull students along, to get them to take that extra step beyond mere grammatical manipulation. Teachers are looked on with a respect which can seem almost god-like. They are given total responsibility for the running of the class and where a European student might think 'Why shouldn't I volunteer some opinion or irrelevance?' an Asian student is likely to think 'Why should I? It's my teacher's responsibility to tell me what to do'.

Most qualified EFL teachers apply the 'communicative approach', ie the belief that students should be involved in communication that is as real as possible, rather than translating endless sentences, or chanting unexplained words or phrases after the teacher. For South-east Asian students who are new to the EFL classroom, these communicative ideas might seem very radical. To introduce new ways of learning and teaching successfully, you should do so gradually, and if necessary, explain why you are doing particular activities. This is especially true with adults who are more likely to be set in their learning ways and who might find the 'communicative approach' unacceptable, particularly if no rationale is given.

A reluctance to speak

Perhaps the greatest overall problem is that students find it hard to verbalize their ideas. This is related to a number of factors:

- The non-communicative way in which English has traditionally been taught in Asian high-schools. Many Asians are not taught to think of English as a means of communication, merely a subject to be studied and an exam to be passed.
- You may be the first Westerner your students have ever spoken to – especially if you are teaching away from the major cities. Although the number of travellers in Asia is increasing every year, Western faces are still by no means an everyday sight for many Asians. This means that your students may be intimidated simply by your physical presence in the classroom.
- Silence, or at least a fair degree of reticence, is often more admired and desirable in Asia than volubility.
- Asians are, on the whole, rather more reserved with strangers than their Western counterparts. They are in general less used to speaking to people outside their normal circle of acquaintances which is made up of mainly their family and work/school friends. As a result, even when speaking in their own language they can be, in Western eyes, less than forthcoming with strangers. In fact, even when Asians are with people they know well, they may be content to sit in silence, rather than keep up with what to their minds would be an artificial stream of conversation.
- Asians are reluctant to disagree openly with others, especially if within the group there is an older person, or a person of higher social status whose views it would impolite to challenge. This means it is hard to maintain a discussion, and a confrontational exchange of ideas, such as a debate, is very difficult to arrange in the Asian classroom. Asians prefer to try to find a general compromise solution to which the whole group can agree, rather than voice an individual opinion which they would consider to be unnecessarily divisive.

To help students overcome their reluctance to speak you can use the *twenty tips to relax your students* (see pp 53-55). These tips will help you to create a more stress-free environment in your classroom, which in turn will encourage your students to relax and feel less threatened about speaking in English in front of other students and you.

A TYPICAL SOUTH-EAST ASIAN CLASSROOM

A typical South-east Asian primary or secondary classroom often looks like this: 50 to 60 students sitting in neat rows, learning by repeated drilling, and a teacher in the front speaking through a microphone, if he or she can afford one. Corporal punishment is common, and punishment is usually aimed at humiliating the student in front of his or her peer group. The image of learning in the South-east Asian classroom is that the teacher possesses a sort of quantifiable substance, knowledge, and the students must have it implanted in them somehow. This implantation can be more or less painful for teacher and students alike, depending on how much the students squirm or try to resist it.

Classroom testing reflects this view, and in a test, a South-east Asian teacher is asking the question, how much of what I said can they reproduce? This means there is a premium on memorization, not analysis or extrapolation from what has been taught. Perhaps naturally, since tests are often multiple choice and very concrete, cheating methods have entered the realm of high art, and are ubiquitous. Cheating is not harshly condemned, because there is not the same emphasis on individuals standing or falling on their own achievement as there is in the West. Formal written tests are part of most learning situations for students in South-east Asia and a group of students trying to outwit the teacher any way they can during a test is part of the group ethos. This may sound a bit harsh, but I have the impression that students cheat in the same spirit that they bargain: thinking, the cards are stacked against me, but I'll do the best I can to make small gains. It can be a sort of game; or, in any case, you can choose to view it that way when it comes up in your classroom. It would be culturally inappropriate to come down with an iron fist on students for cheating, particularly since working together is stressed constantly in the EFL classroom!

A typical EFL classroom might be a shock to your students. They may spend some time looking around for the microphone, or wondering where the rest of the class is. An EFL view of learning includes teacher–student cooperation and the use of analytical skills is encouraged. If you compare the underlying view of learning in an EFL classroom with the rote methods used in mainstream South-east Asian schools, you can imagine students' initial disorientation. Obviously there will never be a question of your using physical punishment in your classroom, but if you are not sensitive to South-east Asian students' anxieties about your unfamiliar teaching approach, you could unwittingly 'punish' them through body language, voice, and different cultural assumptions. You don't have to walk on eggshells in a South-east Asian classroom, but here are 20 tips – that will soon come naturally to you – to help you relax your students.

TWENTY TIPS TO HELP YOUR STUDENTS TO RELAX

(1) Sit down for all or part of the lesson. Except for certain stages of the lesson, such as writing on the board, it is quite feasible to run all but the very largest of classes from a seated position.

(2) Do not talk too loudly. Of course you must be heard, but do not be domineering or threatening either in the volume of your voice or the tone of your voice (eg avoid sarcasm) .

(3) Put students into pairs or small groups which can be rearranged from time to time to improve class harmony and mixing. Actually, students are almost as embarrassed at performing and afraid of making mistakes in front a large number of their peers as they are nervous of you. So reduce the size of their audience to a manageable number as often as possible. As well as being more relaxed about speaking in small groups, students will be more confident about repeating or reporting back to the whole class later.

(4) Have brief pauses between stages of the lesson to allow students' minds to settle. These may only be a matter of 20 seconds or so. You can use the excuse of cleaning the board, or setting up the tape-recording, or sorting our your papers.

(5) Correct as gently as possible – try to avoid the word 'No'. Try expressions such as: 'Well....', 'Maybe', or 'Anybody else?'. Use student-self correction and peer correction techniques (see pp 56-57).

(6) Explain that making mistakes is part of the learning process, everyone does it, and there is no penalty for it. Students should know that when they aim for fluency or try out new ways of expressing themselves, they will be praised. If you are learning the local language you can point out that you understand their difficulties, that you have made some howlers yourself and have learned from them. If you use either the *Headway* or *Hotline* series of coursebooks, you can do the translation exercises with your students. When you make mistakes translating the English phrase into *their* language this has two positive effects. First, students see you more as an equal, as a fellow language learner, not an all-knowing guru. And second, in explaining your mistake to you (in English) they are getting further practice in articulating the language point that the lesson has covered.

(7) Be positive and congratulate your students as often as possible. Show that you are pleased in your voice and face. But be sure to vary the actual words you use to praise students, or you could end up sounding like Polly the Parrot: 'Well done, well done, well done'.

(8) Encourage students to take responsibility for their own language learning. As students become less dependent on you (for praise or

correction) they will become more confident and, therefore, will be more relaxed in class.

(9) Give students a chance to take control of the class. For example let students run a game of hangman, take the register, or record a class brain-storming activity on the whiteboard. As a class, they can take control by choosing from a list of possible activities, for example, which grammar points they need more practice on in a revision class. Be careful, however, when you do let students set the agenda. Make it clear that what you are doing is part of the lesson and has a purpose, otherwise students will become uncomfortable that a figure of authority is abdicating the total control that teachers in South-east Asia traditionally have. Quite often if you give students a chance to choose they will say 'It's up to you'. Expect this, but persuade them to decide: this is all part of encouraging student autonomy (see point 8 above, but also see point 18; introduce a new idea slowly and carefully).

(10) Never ridicule students or belittle their efforts at English, or abuse your power in any way. This is very rude and destructive and can have grave repercussions on future lessons with that class and your teaching reputation at your school.

(11) Set clearly achievable tasks. You should steer a middle course between setting tasks which are too hard or too easy; both can demotivate students.

(12) Do not always win, or insist on having the last word. Remember your special advantages in this unbalanced situation – you are the native speaker, you have set the agenda for the class and you are the well-respected teacher. And, you are not always right either.

(13) Be wary of joining in class laughter if it is at the expense of a student. If you join in you can unwittingly give a seal of approval to the scapegoating of one student.

(14) Be sensitive and restrained about bringing up any negative aspects of the culture you are in, such as the 1965 coup in Indonesia, racism against ethnic Chinese in Malaysia or Thailand's 'neutrality' in the Second World War.

(15) Strengthen class dynamics by socializing as a group; in class order a pizza at the end of term or occasionally go out together after class.

(16) Be careful how and when you touch students. Both students and teachers in Asia are much less demonstrative than, say, Italians or South Americans. This is particularly true for a male teacher and a female student, where touching may cause acute embarrassment. In all of South-east Asia, never touch students' heads, and in Muslim countries in the region, do not touch students with your left hand.

(17) Don't worry if your students are not as fluent as you might like them to be, and there seem to be long periods of silence in your

classroom. Generally your students need longer to think about their answers, often because they do not want to make mistakes by rushing into an utterance. These periods of silence are unlikely to embarrass your students, and there is no need to let them embarrass you. Do not press students to respond quickly and do not show signs of impatience; this will only increase the stress level in the classroom.

(18) Introduce new kinds of activities gradually. Because the South-east Asian educational system is extremely conservative, students are often reluctant to embrace new or radical ideas. You should introduce such ideas slowly and be ready to give the rationale behind them.

(19) Give your students room to move, mentally as well as physically. Do not stand close to them; give them time to gather their thoughts; do not jump on every mistake. Do not intimidate your students by towering over them; perhaps crouch or kneel to have level eye contact.

(20) Finally, never show students that you are angry with them, either individually or as a group, unless it is a matter of disciplining children or teenagers.

See 'Suggested reading' below for useful books dealing with confidence building and group dynamics.

CORRECTION

Ways of correcting oral mistakes

Making mistakes is unavoidable when learning a language, but making students feel bad about them can be avoided.

How to correct

It is best to correct as gently as possible. Asian learners can feel vulnerable and exposed when they make a mistake when speaking in class because it means a loss of face in front of the group. You can correct effectively without saying the word 'No'. Try saying 'Not exactly, well…, hmm…', or looking quizzical. Asians are used to subtlety and it won't be difficult for them to figure out that they have made a mistake.

When and what to correct

Don't correct every mistake. Although a lot of students will tell you that this is precisely what they want you to do, in reality it is disheartening for students to be reminded of every slip that they make.

A rule of thumb is to correct most of the mistakes connected with that day's lesson, some mistakes relating to points covered in previous lessons, and hardly any that relate to points yet to be taught. For example, if a student, who has not yet learned the present perfect, says 'She has ever been to Bali', I would probably rephrase it as, 'She has been to Bali', but I would not expect the student to produce that, nor would I drill the student on the correct sentence.

The amount of correction should normally vary as the lesson progresses. If you are teaching a lesson using the Presentation, Practice, Production (PPP) model, you will probably correct almost every error connected with the point you are teaching at the presentation and drilling (practice) stages. While if the students are doing some fluency work (production) you will probably note some of the mistakes made, but leave actually correcting them until the end of the activity. This is because it has been suggested that if students are overly concerned with producing accurate language, they will never become fluent.

Error feedback

Who should correct

The student who made the mistake should be given a chance to self-correct. Often the student will do this without any prompting from you, so do not be too eager to jump in. If the student cannot self-correct, other students (either individually or as a class) should be asked for the correct answer. Finally, if none of the students can, you should give the right answer.

How to correct

When seeking self or peer correction, isolate the mistake if necessary. You can repeat the mistake with questioning intonation (although this method is sometimes frowned on as it is believed that students will pick up incorrect English if they hear their teacher saying it); say the sentence up to, but not including the mistake; or refer to or define the mistake by saying 'tense' or 'preposition'.

Another way to isolate a mistake is to hold up or point to one finger for every word in the sentence. This is useful if the mistake is one of omission. It is worth practising this technique privately before you do it in class. Imagine you are facing the students, hold up your right hand with the palm facing you, fingers spread out. With the fore-finger of your left hand point to your right thumb and say the first word of the sentence. Point to your right fore-finger for the second word, and so on. If the sentence has more than five words, put your left hand up beside your right hand in a fist, and lift your left little finger for the sixth word and, so on. This is not the only way to do finger work, but if you use a slightly different method, remember to raise your fingers from your right to your left so that the students see the sentence being formed from their left to right.

LISTENING AND SPEAKING

The two skills which often terrify South-east Asian students are listening and speaking. Years of rote learning, and of filling-in a million grammar substitution tables have made them excellent at identifying, for example, the past perfect continuous, but completely lost when faced with naturally spoken English – either in understanding it or being able to contribute to a conversation.

Listening

Listening can be very difficult for South-east Asian students because they often have little real-life experience of listening to natural English. Students are sometimes overwhelmed by both the speed and the content of the message when they have to listen to a tape recorder or a native speaker in person. While it is important for your students not to feel intimidated, you should also remember that making your lessons too easy can have a negative effect as well.

Particularly in elementary level coursebooks, tasks are often childishly easy and this can demotivate students. Where possible you should simplify the task not the text or your language. For example, a beginners class can listen to a very difficult, short radio interview where their task is only to write down the caller's name, age and address.

Here are some suggestions for making listening easier for South-east Asian Students:

- Ask simple, 'locating' questions to begin with (for example: What is the people's relationship with each other? Where are the people?) so that, although students are only ostensibly listening for a small, simple piece of information, they are also being exposed to the rest of the tape content, and will, therefore, not find it so difficult the next time they hear it.
- Break up listening texts into manageable chunks. This can help students not to panic if they lose the thread of the text or do not understand one part of it.
- Play the first part of the tape and get students to predict what they will hear next. This helps students to notice the patterns of, for example, the conversation possibilities of a customer and a shop assistant. This will also make listening to the tape easier, because

they have guessed what is coming next. And it makes their next shop conversation, in the English-speaking world, easier to predict and to participate in successfully.

- Teach students to listen for gist. Many Asian students in their high-school experience of learning English have been exposed to carefully graded language. In any given listening text they were sure to understand every word as it was only included in the text if it had previously been introduced to them. When students come into an EFL classroom, with its emphasis on 'authentic' natural, native-speaker English, they are often overwhelmed, not so much by the speed, but the content, and they want to understand every word of it. It is important to try to wean your students off this desire to comprehend every word when listening, as it slows them down, and it is not necessary. Asking questions about the gist of a listening text, rather than specific questions about particular parts of the text, is one way to encourage students to move away from trying to understand every word when they are listening.
- Teach communication strategies. Using the methods above will help prepare students very well for successful eavesdropping (ie listening to recorded conversations) but, of course, they will need to be able to hold up their end of a face-to-face conversation too. In their first language students will have many skills they use when listening to conversations, such as ways of interrupting, clarifying meaning, and stalling for time and you can encourage them to use those skills when they are listening in English. For example, you can use a short activity where pairs or small groups of students are given a topic and they have to try to keep the conversation going for as long as possible.

Speaking

Speaking English can be a frightening prospect for South-east Asian students. Their high-school experience of learning English probably involved little, if any, actual speaking. Such students can easily recognize complicated written English structures, but will often have great difficulty producing even a very simple utterance. Building confidence is an essential element of getting your students to talk. The 20 tips to relax your students (see pp 53-55), as well as ways of correcting oral mistakes (see pp 56-57) are both relevant here.

Here are some suggestions for making speaking easier for South-east Asian Students:

- Give students prompts to help them remember what to say. You can use pictures, mimes or single words.
- Use pair and small group work as often as possible, so that students don't feel intimidated by having to speak in front of the whole class.

- Give, and stick to, reasonable time-limits for speaking activities. Your students will feel much more ready to speak if they know that they have a definite time-frame, rather than thinking they have to talk to their partner forever about what they did at the weekend.
- Prepare students gently for speaking activities. Introduce the topic and vocabulary first and give students time to prepare what they want to say – you can let them write short notes to remind themselves of their main points.
- Give students plenty of time to practise. For example, if students are involved in a role-play which they will perform for the class, let them know that they are not expected to do so impromptu, but that there will be enough time for them to practice.

Pronunciation problems

Word stress. Speakers of tonal languages (Thai, Lao, Khmer and Vietnamese) have much greater difficulty with English pronunciation than speakers of non-tonal languages (Indonesian, Malay and Tagalog). Tonal speakers give equal weight and timing to each syllable which can make them sound very mechanical. For example they say Yes/ter/day/ I/ went/ to/ the/ cin/e/ma/.

Intonation. Changing from a pattern where each syllable has its own tone, to the English pattern where pitch is located on *groups* of syllables, is very difficult for tonal speakers. Tonal speakers also find it difficult to hear and reproduce the rise and fall we use when asking yes/no questions, or showing surprise, for example. In their own languages tones constitute the meaning of a word, and remain constant in every context (in Thai, the word *'haa'* said with falling intonation *always* means five – no matter if the speaker is bored, happy, or angry). So speakers of tonal languages need a lot of exposure to English intonation where the context is made clear. With analysis, they will be able to understand how the meaning of an utterance can change depending on the pitch and volume of your voice. The listening and speaking exercises in the *Headway Pronunciation* series are ideal for this.

Consonant clusters. Consonant clusters (two or more consonants together with no vowels in between, for example *scr*ape, pa*rch*) are much less common in the languages in the region than they are in English. And again, the tonal languages have fewer consonant clusters than the non-tonal languages. There are two favourite ways that students have for getting round difficult consonant clusters. Either they insert an extra vowel so that *steak* becomes *s**a**teak,* or they reduce the cluster to a manageable consonant, so that becomes *detect* becomes *detec.* When they do both, *swift* becomes *s**a**wif.*

COMMON SOUTH-EAST ASIAN MISTAKES

Most South-east Asian students at private language schools have already studied at least six years of English at Junior and Senior High School. They have usually been taught by non-native speakers who favour reading and writing over listening and speaking (which is understandable considering that there are often up to 50 students in a class). School students have usually been taught, both inside and outside schools, from books which are full of mistakes in spelling, punctuation, grammar and register. The following examples come from *Kursus Lengkap Bahsaa Inggeris* (A complete English Course) by H Abullah Maurur M.H. (an Indonesian book) and *English Khmer Conversation* (a Cambodian book), but could easily be from similar books published in almost any South-east Asian country.

Most of the recurring mistakes revealed in the extracts above can be categorized into five main groups. Each of these groups presents South-east Asian students with enormous problems, and although you might be aware of these problems, there is no magic remedy to help your students overcome them instantly. An awareness of their first language is a huge help, as is an understanding of the differences in

Happy Birthday.
Happy New Year.
Happy **The Same to you.**
I have **ever** been to Singapore twice.
He's a much talked about **write.**

I need a porter to carry it.
I need a broom to clean it.
I need a guide to **escourd** me.
I want to buy a couple of **raincoat**
I want to **drow flower.**

No **talk, pleas!**
She always does all the **talk.**
Oh Charles, do turn **of** the **wire less.** If you can't find anything better than that for us to listen to.
I think this music's so nice, father.
Go and learn **you** lesson.
Thanks to your advice.
How about **come** to my house for dinner tonight?
I'll have some **the** cheese.
I think the best watches **import from Swiss**
How do you do Dr Lin? **It's an honor to know you Dr Lin.**
Next week he **go** to Jakarta.
OK, waiter, bring us two **beer.**
I'm came from Phnom Penh.
Oh Kira, if you're going out I want to **buy some thing for me.**
Please stop here **about** five minutes.

grammatical concepts between English and your students' first language. It is also important for you to encourage your students to become aware of the ways vocabulary, grammar, register, stress, and intonation in their own language differ from English patterns. When they become more self-aware, they can monitor themselves so that they will make fewer of these 'classic' South-east Asian mistakes.

Use of articles

The article system of English (*a, an,* and *the*) is usually very confusing for Asian students, as most of the South-east Asian languages do not have articles. Students tend either not to use any articles at all (eg I want to **drow flower**), or hyper-correct when they realize that English uses articles (eg I'll have some **the** cheese).

Singular and plural nouns

In most languages in South-east Asia the context of a sentence makes it clear if we are talking about something that is singular or plural. In the sentence **OK, waiter bring us two beer**, an Asian student might think it excessive to put an 's' on the end of a noun, when we have previously, clearly indicated by the **two** that the number is plural.

Tenses

In South-east Asian languages context or marker words (eg yesterday) usually indicate tense, so it is difficult for your students always to remember to change the form of verbs. This leads to mistakes like **Next week he go to Jakarta.**

Register and style

The way we talk differs depending on who our listeners are. Our register changes if we are in a formal rather than an informal situation. If we are talking to children rather than adults, or we are using jargon among our colleagues rather than talking to people who are not familiar with our work, we adjust our register. For most South-east Asian students the main problem is one of being too formal. Because Asians are usually quite formal in their own language they often translate directly (see below) both phrases and concepts of formality. In English this can make them sound as if they are stuck 50 or 60 years ago, saying things like: **It's an honor to know you Dr Lin.**

Direct translations

Most students at some stage in their learning career, but particularly in the early stages, use direct translation. Although the language may be incorrect, they still manage to get their meaning across, and this 'success' encourages them to repeat their mistakes. As teachers we have to try to undo these learned (or fossilized) mistakes. Because students have so often repeated a pattern such as, **I have ever been to Singapore twice** or **I'm came from Phnom Penh** it can be an uphill struggle for them to relearn and remember to use the correct version. Being aware of your students' first language will help you recognize direct translation mistakes and enable you to point these out to your students when they make them.

Suggested reading

Cunningham, Sarah, and Bill Bowler, *Headway Intermediate Pronunciation*, Oxford University Press, Oxford, 1991.

Davies, Paul and Mario Rinvolucri, *The Confidence Book*, Longman, Harlow, UK, 1991.

Deller, S, *Lessons from the Learner*, Longman, Harlow, UK, 1990.

Hadfield, Jill, *Classroom Dynamics,* Oxford University Press, Oxford, 1992.

Moskowitz, G, *Caring and Sharing in the Foreign Language Classroom*, Newbury House, Massachusetts, 1978.

Swan, Michael, and Bernard Smith, *Learner English,* Cambridge University Press, Cambridge, 1994.

Thomson, A. J., and A. V. Martiner, *A Practical English Grammar,* Oxford University Press, Oxford, 1989.

4

Thailand

FACTFILE

History

4000 BC	Rice is cultivated in the north-east of Thailand in the Ban Chiang region.
6th century AD	Thailand's earliest recorded inhabitants are Buddhist Mons who form the Dvaravati kingdom. This loosely-based community survives until the 11th century.
8th century	For the next 300 years Hindu Khmers from Kampuchea (Cambodia) absorb the Mons into their empire, as the Khmers expand westwards.
11th century	The Tai (Thai) people arrive from southern China and settle among the Khmers and Mons already living in the central plains of Thailand.

Sukothai Period (1220–1378). Under the leadership of King Ramkamheng, Sukothai is the centre of a great Thai kingdom which combines Khmer and Mon traditions, arts and cultures. The first Thai alphabet is introduced. The kingdom's military and economic power allows it to rule a huge part of South-east Asia from Malaysia to Laos.

Ayuthaya Period (1378–1767). Within a hundred years of being founded, Ayuthaya is proclaimed to be the grandest city in South-east Asia. It has a larger population than London. A Greek adventurer, Phaulkon, who is employed in the court of King Narai tries to convert him to Christianity. Phaulkon is executed and all Westerners are expelled. During the next 150 years Ayuthaya and its people live in self-imposed isolation. In 1763 the Burmese attack, and after two years, the city is destroyed and most of its population dead.

Bangkok Period (1767–present). Within ten years of the Burmese invasion a new capital has been established in Thonburi, across the river from Bangkok, and the Burmese have been ousted. A new King, Rama I, is crowned. Fearful of further Burmese attacks, Rama moves the capital to the other side of the river, to Bangkok. During the reign of Rama III (1824–1851) the British defeat the Burmese and this allows Thailand to expand again into Malaysia, Laos and Vietnam.

King Rama IV (1851–1868). King Mongkut (Rama IV) is a monk for 25 years before coming to the throne in 1851. He successfully keeps Thailand free of colonizers who establish rule in Burma and Malaysia (the British) and Laos, Cambodia and Vietnam (the French).

King Chulalongkorn (1868–1910). Chulalongkorn outlaws slavery, and continues his father's policies aimed at transforming Thailand into a modern nation. Railways are built, and a civil service introduced.

King Vajiravudh (1910–1925). During King Vajiravudh's short reign he introduces compulsory education.

King Prajadhipok (1925–1935)

1932 A bloodless coup supported by the military topples the king. The coup is organized by a group of Thai students educated in France who oppose the idea of an absolute monarch. A constitutional monarchy is introduced.

1935 King Prajadhipok resigns and retires to Britain. The cabinet names his nephew, 10-year-old Ananda Mahidol as King Rama VIII.

King Rama VIII (1935–1946)

1941 The Thai government stays silent when the Japanese invade Burma and Malaysia. Thailand declares war on the USA and the UK, but the Thai ambassador in Washington refuses to deliver the declaration. After the war Thailand maintains that Thailand was therefore actually neutral during the Second World War.

1946 The King is shot dead under mysterious circumstances. His brother King Bhumibol Adulyadej (Rama IX) succeeds him.

King Rama IX (1946 –)

1949 Thailand becomes strongly anti-Communist, refuses to recognize the People's Republic of China and becomes a loyal supporter of French and US foreign policy in the region.

1958	A successful coup is led by General Sarit. He abolishes the constitution and bans all political parties.
1964–73	Thailand is ruled by the military who allow US army bases in Thailand to help the US war effort in Vietnam.
June 1973	Students demonstrate and demand a new constitution. A constitutional government is elected and rules until 1976.
1977–present	A series of short-lived governments rule, mainly replaced when ousted by a coup. Most of these governments have been made up of career politicians who have had more or less backing from the military.

Geography

Thailand has an area of about 517 000 square kilometres, making it slightly smaller than united Germany, or Texas. Thailand is bordered by Burma to the north-west, Laos to the north-east, Cambodia to the east, the Gulf of Thailand to the south and the Andaman Sea to the west. It is a long country from north to south and spans almost 16 latitudinal degrees, giving it a much more diverse climate than most countries in the region. Thailand has mountains in the north, beaches and rainforest in the south and the highly populated city of Bangkok in the central region of the country.

Climate

Because Thailand is so long from north to south, its climate is not uniform. For example, while it rains for six months of the year north of Chiang Mai, the rains last only for about two months south of Surat. There are three seasons in northern and central Thailand and two in the south. The northern climate includes a south-west monsoon which brings the rains around May or June and lasts until November. The cool, dry season follows from November to February. The temperature steadily increases until May when temperatures between 37°C and 39°C are common during the day.

The southern climate has a north-east monsoon from November to January as well as the south-west monsoon from May to November. The dry season is much longer than in the north and is from February to the end of April.

Time

Thailand is 7 hours ahead of Greenwich Mean Time, 12 hours ahead of New York, 15 hours ahead of San Francisco, 3 hours behind Sydney and 5 hours behind Wellington.

The people

Thailand has a population of about 58 million. The majority of people (about 75%) are ethnic Thais. Historically people have migrated to Thailand from nearby countries, notably Laos, Cambodia, Vietnam, Burma, Malaysia, India and China. Most recently, political refugees from Cambodia, Laos, Vietnam and Myanmar have come to live here.

The Thai people originated in south-eastern China. In 655 AD they founded the independent kingdom of Nanchao which survived for 600 years. Unwilling to join mainstream Chinese society, the people of Nanchao migrated southward into what is now Thailand.

The largest ethnic minority groups are the Chinese (often second or third generation) who make up about 10% of the population, and the Malays who make up about 4%. The remaining 10% is made up of Vietnamese, Khmer, and some non-Thai-speaking hill tribes in the north.

Politics

Thailand has a constitutional monarchy and a Senate, with a lower and upper house. Since 1932 Thailand has had more than 12 coups and as many constitutions. The most recent military coup was in February 1991 when the National Peace-Keeping Council (NPKC), led by the General Suchinda Kraprayoon, overthrew the democratically elected civilian government. When Suchinda replaced the next elected Prime Minister, thousands called for his resignation. In May 1992 dozens of people were killed while peacefully demonstrating against him at the Democracy Monument.

The new constitution that was introduced in 1991 stated that the Prime Minister and the 360 senators for the Lower House should be elected by a national vote, while the Upper House should be chosen by the National Peace-Keeping Council (NPKC) – the military group behind the 1991 coup. The present constitution allows the NPKC to enforce martial law at any time. There are no provisions for the dissolution of the NPKC in the near future.

Language

The Thai language or *Phasa Thai* consists of monosyllablic words whose meanings are complete by themselves. Thai vocabulary incorporates Pali, Sanskrit, Khmer, Malay, English and Chinese. Its alphabet was created by King Ramkhamhaeng the Great in 1283 by modelling it on the ancient Indian alphabets of Sanskrit and Pali but utilizing the old Khmer characters. After a history of over 700 years, the Thai alphabet today comprises of 44 letters (including 2 obsolete ones) representing 20 consonants, phonemes and 15 vowel signs which denote 22 vowels, diphthongs and triphthongs. Thai is a tonal language with five tones. The tones are: rising, falling, high, mid (or level), and low. The tone you use alters a word's meaning so, for example, the word *mai* can mean new, burn, wood, not?, or not, depending on which tone you use. For more information on tones see Appendix 2: Useful Thai words and phrases. You can study Thai in Bangkok at:

> **AUA Language Centre**, 179 Rajadamri Road. Tel: (02) 252 8170. Fax: (02) 255 0745.

Religions

More than 90% of Thais are Theravadin Buddhists, about 5% of Thais and Thai-Malays who live in the south are Muslims and about 1% of the people are Confucianists, Taoists, Mahayana Buddhists, Christians and Hindus.

Cultural considerations

Buddhism

As Thailand is mainly a Buddhist country it is important not to offend Buddhist sensibilities by behaving inappropriately when you visit a temple, or when you talk to a monk. (See Chapter 1 (Buddhism: Cambodia, Laos, Thailand and Vietnam) for further information on cultural considerations while in a Buddhist country.)

Respect for royalty

The Royal family is held in very high regard in Thailand and *lèse majesté* is still a prisonable offense. The national anthem is played twice a day, at 8am and 6pm. If you are in a public place and within earshot of a loud-speaker when the anthem is being played, you should stand to attention. The anthem is also played before performances in theatres and cinemas and you are expected to stand.

The present monarch is Bhumipol Adulyadej who was born in 1927 in Cambridge, Massachusetts. He became king in 1946 and is now the longest reigning king in Thai history.

Wai (Greetings)

Thais greet each other with a *wai.* To *wai* you should place your hands together as if you were a Christian praying, put your hands in front of your face, and then bow your head. It sounds more complicated than it really is, and once you have seen this being done a few times, it will be easy to do. There are quite strict rules of etiquette about who *wais* first, in what order they should *wai,* and how low a bow it should be. However, as a foreigner, you will be forgiven if you do not get it exactly right every time. As a general rule, a social superior does not initiate a *wai,* a younger person should *wai* first, and the lower the bow when *wai*ing the greater the respect shown is.

Terms of address

Thais use the title *khun* before a first name as a mark of respect. They also use *nang* before a woman's first name and *nai* before a man's. *Ajarn* or *ajhan* (which means teacher) will often be put before your name as a sign of respect.

TEACHING POSSIBILITIES

The busiest time of year for private language schools in Thailand is their summer which starts at the beginning of March and lasts to the beginning of May. This period covers the Songkran Festival (in April) when primary and secondary schools are closed and young people are looking for summer courses. Another good time is the beginning of term at private schools (early May and November). December is said to be a poor month to be job-hunting.

Language schools are listed in the English Language edition of the Bangkok, Chiang Mai and Hat Yai telephone directories (under 'Language Schools'). Other sources of addresses are the classified sections of the *Bangkok Post* or *The Nation* newspapers. The British Council does not to have a list of approved schools as it does in other countries in the region, however it does have a list of Thai universities which employ English teachers. The *EL Gazette*, a monthly newspaper for EFL teachers, which has job advertisements in it, is also available in the British Council library.

The British Council, 1 and 2 CU Building, 254 Chulalongkorn, Soi 64, Siam Square, Bangkok, 10330. Tel: (02) 252 6136. Fax: (02) 253 5312. E-mail: bc.bangkok@british.council.sprint.com

The British Council, English Language Teaching Centre, 198 Bumrungraj Road, Chiang Mai 50000. Tel: 053 242103. Fax: 053 244 781.

Bangkok has a reputation as a man's city and in the English teaching community you will probably meet a higher proportion of men to women than in other countries in the region (6:1 in two major schools in Bangkok). An Australian woman, teaching in a small school in Bangkok, who would like to remain anonymous, tells a common tale.

> There were three women teaching in the school I was working in but they left because they didn't like the attitude of the rest of the staff (20 men) or the kind of social lives they had and the bars they went to.

Going to a prearranged job

A few organizations advertise in the UK, Australia or the USA: for example ECC, inlingua, The British Council, Bell Language Schools and Voluntary Services Overseas (VSO). The last three of these will interview a prospective teacher before he or she goes to Thailand. They will probably offer a return flight, medical insurance and a work permit. Some organizations employing native-speaker English teachers will promise you work 'if they've got it' if you write to them before you arrive in Thailand. This is not quite as dicey as it sounds; however, how much work they will offer you and at what rate of pay is another matter. It is unlikely that you will arrive with the promise of a job and find no work at all since most schools and organizations only recruit locally. Few people go to Thailand with a prearranged job. (For more information on organizations which recruit from outside Thailand, see Chapter 2: pp 41-43).

Private language schools

The vast majority of teachers in Thailand find their jobs after arriving in the country by visiting different schools. Of course finding work this way gives you the opportunity to see round the school and perhaps meet potential colleagues and management. (See Chapter 2: Arriving without a job.) However, it also means you will probably enter on a tourist visa, necessitating a trip outside the country (usually to Penang, Malaysia) when your visa runs out. (See below: Visas and work permits.) You will also need enough money to last until your first pay cheque and a central place to stay from which you can visit schools.

Most EFL teachers who work in Bangkok work in private language schools. The schools range from establishments with 20 classrooms to those that do all their work 'in company', ie the teacher goes to the students' place of work or residence and the school has perhaps only an office. Qualifications required vary enormously too; from non-native, non-experienced, unqualified teachers to the RSA Diploma in TEFLA and MAs in TEFL. With the latter, you will probably find yourself a bit overqualified for the vast majority of jobs available although this is slowly changing.

Schools tend to operate from 7am to 9pm with a lot of work being in the evening. You might find yourself teaching one student or 20, teaching business people, elementary school students, teenagers or nine-year-olds. A class is likely to meet twice weekly for two to three hours each time. You will be working anything from 20 to 35 actual teaching hours per week. Where classes are paid hourly, how many classes you take on depends on how much money you want to make. If you have a full-time contract a certain minimum will be required. Lesson preparation, marking and other administrative duties are normally expected on top of these hours.

Below are some well-known language schools in Bangkok:

Assumption Bell Language Centre, Assumption College, Thonburi. Tel: (02) 421 0016. Fax: (02) 421 9666.

AUA Language Centre, 179 Rajadamri Road, Bangkok. Tel: (02) 252 8170/3. Fax: (02) 255 0745.

Berlitz School of Languages, Silom Complex, 22nd Floor, Silom Road. Tel: (02) 231 3652.

British American Language Centre, 50/299 Ladprao 58-60, Bangkok. Tel: (02) 514 0584.

The British Council, 1 and 2 CU Building, 254 Chulalongkorn, Soi 64, Siam Square, Bangkok, 10330. Tel: (02) 252 6136. Fax: (02) 253 5312. E-mail: bc.bangkok@british.council.sprint.com

ECC (Thailand), 430/17-24 Chula 64, Siam Square, Bangkok, 10300. Tel: (02) 252 6611/252 6319/254 2242. Fax: (02) 254 2243. E-mail: eccthai@ksc.net.th

ELS Language Centre, 419/3 Rajavithi. Tel: (02) 245 8953.

Inlingua School of Languages, 7th Floor, Central Chidlom Tower, Ploenchit, Bangkok 10330. Tel: (02) 252-7028/30.

King's School of English, 5A, 1093/19–21 Office Building City Bangna, Bangna-trad Road, Prakanong, Bangkok, 10260. Tel: (02) 745 6001-5. Fax: (02) 745 6000.

St John's Bell Language Centre, St John's College, Ladprao, Bangkok 10900, Tel: (02) 513 8587.

Siam Computer, Siam Square, Bangkok.

Private primary and secondary schools

Several of the large private schools in Bangkok employ teachers at anything from 8 000 baht outside Bangkok to 15 000 baht per month in Bangkok. Often you will get a job if they like the look of you. It has been said that this is more important even than having the right (or any!) qualifications. However, like a lot of language schools, private primary and secondary schools are beginning to realize that just having a native English-speaker in the classroom is not enough. Some of these schools will provide a work permit. Classes are large and there isn't much in the way of resources and, of course, most of the work is during the day; this leaves you free to do evening classes elsewhere. Some private schools include:

St Dominic's, 1526 Petchburi Road, Bangkok 10310. Tel: (02) 252 6220.

St Gabriel College, 565 Samsen Road, Bangkok. Tel: (02) 243 0065, 243 2156, 243 7001.

St John's College, Bell Primary Programme, Ladprao Road, Bangkok, 10900. Tel: (02) 938 7009. Fax: (02) 513 8588.

St John's College, College of Commerce, Ladprao Soi 2, Ladprao, Bangkok, 10900. Tel: (02) 511 4759.

St John's College, International Matriculation Programme, Ladprao Road, Bangkok, 10900. Tel: (02) 513 0166. Fax: (02) 513 8588.

St Joseph's Convent School, 7 Convent Road. Tel: (02) 235 1895, 266 5996, 234 0561.

State primary and secondary schools

Not surprisingly, state schools can hardly afford to pay extra staff much, if anything. Outside Bangkok a Thai teacher of English earns about 4 000 baht a month. Occasionally a school will take on a guest teacher and you might be paid 7 000 baht.

Don't count on more than about 100 baht per hour for private lessons outside the capital. Having said that, this is not such a small salary given the low cost of living (especially accommodation) outside Bangkok. In Bangkok, few teachers will look for work in state schools because there are so many private schools which offer better pay.

International schools

Most of these schools are for the children of expatriates. Sometimes they require the services of an ESL specialist or a classroom assistant. Classroom assistants are not usually qualified teachers, but as an ESL specialist you would be expected to be well qualified.

Bangkok Patana School, 2/38 Sukhumvit 195. Tel: (02) 398 0200. Fax: (02) 399 3179.

Rasmai International School, 48/2 Soi Rajvita 2 (Attavimol), Rajprop Road, Bangkok. Tel: (02) 246 3089. Fax: (02) 246 6363.

St John's International School, Ladprao Road, Bangkok, 10900. Tel: (02) 513 0579, 513 8590. Fax: (02) 513 5273.

Private universities

Some private universities employ native speaker English teachers. Thammasat and Chulalongkorn Universities in Bangkok, two of the most famous, pay English teachers about 23 000 baht a month.

Private companies

There are a few teachers working full-time for companies. The kind of companies that might require an English language teacher are large multinationals where expatriates have to work alongside Thais or where the business involves daily contact overseas (eg import-export or shipping companies). These posts are usually obtained by word-of-mouth, although there is nothing to stop you knocking on doors and asking to see the training manager. Of course it is entirely at the discretion of the company whether or not they provide you with a work permit. You will have to negotiate terms and conditions on your own. Ask around to find out about current salaries and conditions.

Freelance teaching

Getting business for yourself without the aid of a school depends very much on having the right contacts, and advertising in newspapers is very expensive. Freelance teaching is therefore mostly for people who have been in Thailand for a while, and is generally as a supplement to be earned outside your school schedule. The main disadvantage is that you are on your own as far as visas are concerned. It makes life easier if you have some kind of sponsor. You can charge pretty much what you like – be prepared for some haggling and requests for discounts from your students – but a common rate in Bangkok is currently about 300 baht per hour for a one-to-one class and more if you're dealing with a company.

BEFORE YOU GO

Insurance

Take out travel and health insurance. Government hospitals in Thailand and particularly in Bangkok are good and fairly cheap although perhaps not quite up to the standard you are used to. The staff have limited English. For any serious ailments you will probably be happier to know that with a health insurance policy you can afford the best treatment that is available. See Health below.

Vaccinations

See Chapter 1: Living in South-east Asia: Health for information on diseases which are prevalent in Thailand and for advice about what vaccinations you should consider having before leaving your home country and what precautions you should take once you arrive here.

Shipping/air freighting personal effects

If you are sending a shipment of belongings out to Thailand in advance you may be liable for duty on any electrical goods. You will have to pay this duty before any of your belongings are released from customs.

Check *thoroughly* with your shipping company before you pack about who will be liable for the duty payment. Unfortunately, several English teachers have found out too late that the duty they had to pay (anything from 30% to 400%) on larger items, plus the price of sending the items, ended up being more expensive than just buying the electrical goods new in Thailand. Negotiating personal electrical goods out of customs is a bureaucratic headache you might want to avoid.

What to bring

In Bangkok there is almost no product you can't get, if not the brand you are used to then probably a good alternative. There are two main supermarkets which stock Western goods; Villa (with a branch on Sukumvit and one on Ladprao Road) and Foodland (on Patpong Road)

Outside Bangkok you might want to stock up on tampons, contact lens solutions and reading material. Traveller's cheques and bank drafts are safe ways to carry money. Money changers and banks are on virtually every street corner and opening a bank account and getting an ATM card is quite straightforward.

ARRIVAL AND VISAS

Visas, work permits and tax clearance certificates

It is a time-consuming, bureaucratic and costly process obtaining a work permit in Thailand. Usually, teachers who go independently to Thailand work illegally on tourist visas, leaving the country every three months to renew them. Visa runs to Penang, Malaysia are still the most common means of keeping yourself on a valid visa but are best avoided if possible because these trips are time-consuming, expensive, and although you may have an up-to-date visa you will probably still be working illegally if you do not have a work permit. So far the authorities seem to have turned a blind eye to English teachers without work permits.

All visas issued from abroad must be used within 90 days. When you enter the country on a tourist visa (even if you do not stay for its full duration) you cannot leave Thailand and enter the country again on the same visa. There is no such thing as a multiple-entry visa but if you want to go out and come back again you can get a double visa which will cost the price of two visas but this will mean you don't have to bother reapplying before you return to Thailand.

Transit visa (15 days). This can be obtained at the point of arrival in Thailand but can only be extended if you hold a passport from a country that does not have a Thai embassy. It doesn't cost anything.

The visa run to Penang
Penang is the first place over the Malaysian border where you can get a new visa. *By train:* It's a 20 hour journey. The number 11 special express departs Hualamphong Railway Station at 3.15pm daily and arrives in Butterworth at 12.10pm the following day. It costs about 650 baht each way for a second class sleeper. From Butterworth you can cross to Penang Island by ferry. *By bus:* Guesthouses on Khao San Road can organize transport, usually a minibus, for you. Otherwise, private bus companies operate services to Penang. *By plane:* A return flight from Bangkok costs about 5 200 baht.

Getting the visa: Many of the hotels and guesthouses in Penang offer a visa processing service which will cost you an extra dollar or two but will relieve you of some of the hassle. 60-day tourist visas are M$45. Allow at least three days for the whole trip or longer if there is a public holiday (the office takes the numerous Malaysian holidays as well as the Thai ones). Make sure you get your application in before 3pm if you want to pick up the visa the next day. *Accommodation:* A favourite, basic but cheap, is the New Asia Hotel.

Transit Visas (30 days). These are available from Thai embassies abroad. They cannot normally be extended.

Tourist Visas (60 days). Available from Thai embassies abroad, they may be extended by one month in Bangkok at the discretion of immigration officials.

Non-immigrant B visa (90 days). This visa is often obtained by people going to Thailand on business, to do research or to work. Some kind of proof is usually required by the issuing office, for example a letter from your employer or institute 'guaranteeing your repatriation'. A letter from a school saying that you are studying Thai or from a temple saying you are studying meditation would do. Once you have this visa you can apply for an extension for 12 months. If you have a job you can apply for a work permit, although your employer usually submits the application. Once you have a 12-month visa and you want to leave Thailand and return again it is important to apply for a re-entry permit before you go. Otherwise you'll have to start the whole process again when you get back.

Work permits. These are obtained from the Labour Department at the Labour-Control-for-Aliens Section. You have to have a non-immigrant visa before you can apply for a work permit and to get a non-immigrant visa you need a letter from your employer (see above). However, once you get as far as having an employer who is willing to provide you with a work permit, you won't have to deal with all the bureaucracy by yourself. Your school will deal with most of the paper work on your behalf.

A work permit without an employer is not possible, so that makes freelance teaching (see above) out of the question, if you want to do it legally.

Re-entry permits. These are required for all holders of extended visas and work permits who wish to leave the country temporarily. Failure to obtain one will result in you having to apply for a new visa and work permit on your return. Take a photograph, 500 baht and your passport to the Immigration Department. Fill in the appropriate form and the permit will be issued to you there and then.

Tax Clearance Certificates. These are not necessary for holders of non-immigrant or tourist visas.

Immigration

It is advisable to arrive in Thailand looking reasonably presentable. The *key nok* or 'bird shit' foreigner is widely despised by a people who set great store by their dress and you will not be doing yourself any favours by turning up at immigration in old or dirty-looking clothes. Women should cover their shoulders and men should wear long trousers. For men, a conservative hair cut is also advisable when passing through immigration.

Transport from the airport

There are three airport buses (A1, A2 and A3) which leave from the front of the international and domestic terminals on Viphavadi Rangsit Highway. The bad news is that there is no bus stop, so in the baking noon-day heat or heavy rain of the monsoon season it is not a very comfortable wait. The good news is that buses leave about every 15 minutes, so you won't have to wait very long for a bus. The journey can take anything from 50 minutes to 2.5 hours, depending on the traffic, and the flat fare is 70 baht. Khao San Road (in Banglampoo) is where most of the cheap accommodation is located and the A2 bus goes there.

A metered taxi to Khao San Road is between 150 and 200 baht depending on the traffic. It is usually easier to persuade a taxi-driver to use his meter if you go upstairs to the departures hall in the airport. Most taxi drivers in Bangkok are polite and honest, the exception seems to be at the airport arrivals hall. Here there are two clearly marked queues for metered and non-metered taxis. Unfortunately, even after waiting in the arrivals hall for a metered taxi, once you get outside a lot of taxi drivers refuse to use their meters. If this happens to you, especially if you have just arrived in Thailand and don't know much Thai, 'Stop!' is still a well-enough-known word for the driver to understand. Don't feel embarrassed about getting out of the taxi and going back into the airport, with the taxi-driver, if possible, explaining at the taxi-desk in arrivals what has happened, and asking for another taxi. If you use a non-metered taxi there is a fixed charge of about double the fare in a metered taxi. If you have booked your first night in a hotel from your home country you can often get the hotel to pick you up at the airport. There is also a helicopter service from the airport to town if you're pressed for time – it costs a mere 3 000 baht.

ACCOMMODATION

Short-term accommodation

Before you find your own place the cheapest temporary accommodation is in small hotels for Western travellers (many forbid Thais to even enter them) known as 'Guesthouses'. Generally people rent a room in a guesthouse for a few weeks (although some people stay in them for months) and then find a room or small apartment to rent for the longer term.

The main budget accommodation areas are Banglamphu (Khao San Road area), Sukhumvit Road and Siam Square. Many of the private language schools are around Siam Square, so finding accommodation around Siam Square might cut down on some of your travelling time when you are doing the rounds of schools when you first arrive in Bangkok. Some popular budget hotels, approximately 100-400 baht a night, include:

Siam Square

A-One Inn, 25/12 -15 Soi Kasem. Tel: (02) 215 3029. Fax: (02) 216 4771.

Bed and Breakfast Inn, Soi Kasem, opposite the A-One Inn.

The Muangphol Building, 938/1 Rama 1 Road, (on the corner of Rama 1 Road and Soi Kasem San 1 Road).

The Pranee Building, next to the Muangphol Building.

Sukhumvit

The Atlanta Hotel, 78 Soi 2 Sukhumvit (Soi Phasak). Tel: (02) 252 1650, 252 6069.

Thai House Inn, between Sukhumvit Soi 5 and 7. Tel: (02) 255 4698. Fax: (02) 253 1780.

Khao San Road

C.H Guesthouse, 216 Khao San Road. Tel: (02) 282 2023.

Nith Charoen Hotel, 183 Khao San Road. Tel: (02) 281 9872.

A.A. Guesthouse, 84 Pra Sumeru Road. Tel: (02) 282 9631.

Long-term accommodation

Other teachers are usually the best source of information about where houses are available, and how much they are currently renting for. You can also check the property sections of the *Bangkok Post* or *The Nation* newspapers although a lot of properties will be out of your price range. Have a look anyway – you'll be amazed by some of the places on offer with rent prices comparable to London, New York and Sydney.

Rent is normally paid monthly and a two to three month deposit is required. It is unlikely that you will have to commit to a long lease. Contracts for housing are the exception rather than the rule. You could ask for one, but the chances are it will come down strongly on the side of the owner and you are probably better off without it. It is unwise to commit yourself to a particular place until you know what area of Bangkok you will be working in, because extended travelling time can ruin your life here. If you live alone, expect to live either in a two-room apartment or a single room. Property and land prices have rocketed during the economic boom of the last few years in the cities of Thailand, so space is at a premium. Remember that, like most things in Asia, the cost of your accommodation is probably negotiable. When discussing the price you could ask the owner to include repainting the apartment, adding furniture or providing a cleaning service. This is a good face-saving way to get a discount.

Considerations when looking for a place to live:

- If there is a telephone, is it a direct line or not? Many apartment blocks have only a few lines and to call in or out you have to go through a switchboard. This can result in two problems. Firstly, if the switchboard operator doesn't speak English well and your friends' Thai is not good (let's be realistic here) they will have difficulty getting through. They might be connected to another foreigner's room or just be told that you are out! This is especially aggravating if it's an expensive overseas call. Secondly, there might only be a few lines into the block for a hundred people in which case it's hardly worth having a private phone. As few phones allow IDD (International Direct Dialling), you will almost certainly have to go through the Thai operator to phone abroad.
- Do you want air-conditioning? If you aren't house-hunting in the hot season it is difficult to imagine just how badly you might want AC in your bedroom come next April. This is particularly true in Bangkok. Try to find out how much the bills are, as air-conditioning is greedy on electricity.
- Is there a construction site nearby? Buildings are going up in Bangkok like there's no tomorrow so the answer to that question is probably YES. Noise is something you have to learn to live with but

if you can find a place that doesn't have a crane nestling beside your window, you'll probably be that bit more contented.

- Is there an independent water supply or a good sized tank in your apartment block? Nearly every year the hot season water shortage gets more acute and an independent water source is becoming almost essential in Bangkok. It is a very serious problem not to be able to have a shower after a day in Bangkok's heat and grime. One tip is to buy yourself a large dustbin and fill it with water for emergency baths during the hot season.
- Is furniture included?
- Is a laundry service available? How much does it cost? How long does it take? And are you prepared to have your clothes thrown in an industrial machine with everyone else's?
- Is there a cleaning service? Does it cost extra?
- Is the apartment on the ground floor or on very low-lying land? If you think regular flooding is going to be a serious problem and you don't fancy the thought of wading home through sewage, well....

Finding addresses

This can be quite daunting, especially in Bangkok. It is difficult to pronounce street names unless you have heard them many times and virtually impossible if you have only seen them written down. Street signs are in Thai and English but beware of inconsistencies in spelling. There is no single system for transcribing Thai sounds into the Roman alphabet so Phetburi, Petchburi and Petchaburi Road are one and the same. There is, however, a useful system of *sois*. A *soi* is a street which branches off a main road. *Sois* are numbered with odd numbers on one side of the main road and even numbers on the other. A school might be located on Sukhumvit soi 103. This means that the street you are looking for is street number 103 off Sukhumvit Road.

A full address might look like this: 1899/16-8 Ramkhamheang 15. Once you've found soi 15 off Ramkhamheang Road the address of the building can still be very tricky. The list of numbers refers to the property lot number and the buildings constructed on that lot. They don't necessarily run consecutively so you can waste a lot of time walking up and down the road hoping to spot a particular set of numbers. The moral of this tale is, before you visit the school, find out on the telephone: (1) how to pronounce the name of the road, (2) the soi number, (3) any useful landmarks by which the school can be identified (hotels, shops, etc). If you can get to the right area, a local *tuk-tuk* or a motorcycle taxi-driver might know the place you're looking for.

Electricity, gas and water

Most teachers live in rented rooms or apartments in Bangkok, and your utility bill comes with your rent bill once a month. Your electricity meter is usually outside your flat, the flat-owner will read it once a month and your bill will usually show how many units you used that month (the rate is about 5 baht a unit). Most apartment blocks will deliver a new gas canister to you and bill you at the end of the month (each canister costs about 150 baht). Most people pay a flat fee for their running water (about 500 baht a month) and the apartment-owner can usually deliver your bottled water, or you can buy it at your local shops.

Household help

Most teachers have some household help. Other teachers usually know if their household help is looking for more work, or know someone else who's looking for work. Most teachers have help with cleaning, washing and ironing clothes, two or three days a week. Salaries are negotiable, but generally household help costs about 1 500 baht per person, per month.

LIVING COSTS

How expensive is Thailand?

Thailand is as expensive or as cheap as your lifestyle makes it. Many expats try to recreate a Western lifestyle which costs them a lot more than it would at home, since they have to pay for imported goods. On the other hand there are some teachers in Bangkok who take home no more than 7 000 baht (£200) a month and who are by no means living in poverty. Utilities, food and entertainment can be much cheaper than in the West. Probably your most expensive outlay will be rent. Rent in Bangkok in rated among the highest in the world – higher even than New York or London.

Salaries

EFL teachers earn anything from 10 000 to 60 000 baht a month. Well-qualified teachers working for the better-paying schools in Bangkok have quite a high standard of living and on average earn about 30 000 baht a month. It is difficult to compare lifestyles to those in the West. No matter what you are earning as a teacher in Thailand, you'll be able to afford to eat out every night, but buying or cooking Western food might be a luxury (potatoes and cheese are for special occasions!). Your living space will probably be cramped, but then you are likely to have a swimming pool in your apartment block. You won't have a washing machine but you may well be paying someone to do your cleaning or washing. Holidays on palm-lined beaches with fresh seafood on the grill will almost certainly be affordable, and your cassette collection will grow speedily at minimal expense. A bottle of wine, on the other hand, might be a rare luxury. So, although as an English teacher you will not be in the league of having a chauffeur-driven car, or be able to go on weekend shopping trips to Singapore, you will probably have considerably more material advantages than most Thais and be able to enjoy a reasonable standard of living.

Taxes

Income tax. If you are in the minority position of having a work permit, you will have to pay tax. Your tax will be in the region of 5–8%. If you aren't working officially, then you won't be expected to pay tax. Before leaving the country work permit holders should obtain a tax clearance certificate.

Departure tax. The airport departure tax in Thailand is currently 200 baht per person for international flights and 30 baht for domestic flights.

How far does the money go?

Overall, 20 000–25 000 baht will keep you reasonably well for a month, if you are being careful, and will enable you to put down the deposit on a flat.

Once you have got a job and started earning, after paying rent and taxes, you will be left with between 12 000 and 20 000 baht. Although this might not seem much compared to what you can earn at home, apart from rent, the cost of living is much lower in Bangkok than it is at home.

Eating and drinking can be very cheap in Thailand, especially if you buy your food at the abundant roadside food stalls and markets. These seem to be open at all times of the day and night – Thais are constantly snacking. If you like rice, coconut milk, chillies, lemon grass, coriander and seafood you can have a gastronomic field-day every day. You can't drink copious amounts of alcohol without running up a large bill unless you can develop a taste for Mekong or Sangtip (many people do) which are Thai whiskies.

Supermarket costs

There are a number of supermarkets which carry Western goods in Bangkok. Two of the most popular ones with teachers are Villa and Foodland (locations above). Below is a list of some supermarket costs, but you should bear in mind that costs in the markets and in small local shops are often lower than in supermarkets. However, many of the goods listed below, because they are imported, are available only in supermarkets (prices in Thai baht).

Bread (small sliced loaf)	25	Tea (50 tea-bags)	68
Beef (100 g)	18	Coffee (200 g jar instant)	88
Milk (1 litre)	27	Beer (bottle)	46
Sugar (1 kg)	13	Vodka (750 mls)	270
Eggs (1 dozen)	22	Cigarettes (20 Marlboro)	40
Rice (2 kgs)	30		

Here are the prices of some dishes at an average food-stall in Bangkok:

Fried rice with seafood	20	Thai noodles	15
Fried rice with chicken	15	Papaya salad	15

EATING AND DRINKING

Food is inexpensive and you will probably find that it is much cheaper to eat out than to cook for yourself. Even a cheese sandwich is more expensive than a plate of rice. There are eating places everywhere, from the *Somtam* woman in the street with her baskets over her shoulders, to very expensive French haute cuisine or Chinese sharks-fin soup restaurants. In fact there are restaurants to suit almost every taste and budget.

Etiquette

A traditional Thai meal consists of boiled white rice for each person and several plates of food which are placed in the middle of the table and shared. (It is considered a bit strange to eat on your own in a restaurant.) Your plate will come only with boiled rice on it and it is polite to take a small spoonful of this before you start. Take small portions of one dish at a time. Thai food is eaten with a spoon in the right hand and a fork in the left. Nothing comes in large enough chunks to warrant a knife. With noodles or in a Chinese restaurant you'll probably be given chopsticks, but using a fork and spoon is quite acceptable too.

If you are taken out for a meal, your host might ask you to choose a dish. If you are not sure of what to order or you cannot understand the menu, either ask your Thai friends to order for you, or ask for a staple dish of seafood, beef or chicken.

If Thais invite you out for the meal, it would be considered very rude if you got your wallet out when the bill came – whether you tried to pay all the bill, or even your share of it. In Thailand whoever organized the evening will expect to pay for the meal. The vision of a group of people scanning the bill for what they ate and then discussing exactly what everyone owes is excruciatingly embarrassing to Thais. If you are out with good friends, offer someone money after you leave the restaurant and out of sight of the others, if you want to. But usually, it's better to repay your hosts by asking them out for another meal.

It is not necessary to leave a tip unless you are in an air-conditioned or more expensive place, and often in more expensive restaurants a service charge will already be included in your bill.

Traditional ingredients

Thai food is almost always cooked with fresh ingredients. Traditional Thai ingredients include mushrooms, small white egg plants, tiny green 'pea' eggplants, shallots (small red onions), garlic, pumpkin, cucumber, a variety of gourds (from the marrow or cucumber family), bamboo shoots, baby sweet-corn, small, sweet peas in the pod, and various leafy spinach-like greens. Common herbs, spices and flavourings are coriander root and leaves, lemon grass, kaffir lime leaves, fish sauce, shrimp paste, tamarind, soy sauce, ground peanuts, ginger, coconut milk. The most common fruits are coconut, banana, papaya, mango, rose-apple, water-melon, rambutan, durian, longan, pomelo, lime, lychee, mangosteen and mandarin orange.

Chillies

If it's green and it looks rather like part of a French bean or if it's red and it looks like a red pepper, be wary. The smaller they are, the hotter they are and the most lethal are the *phrik kii noo*. This translates as 'mouse-shit chillies' which is not a bad description of their shape.

Thai specialties

Popular Thai dishes include: *Tom yam kung* (shrimp soup with lemon grass and mushrooms); *Paw pia sot* (fresh spring rolls); *Paw pia tod* (fried spring rolls); *Poo pat prik* (crab with chilli); *Gai ho bai toey* (fried chicken in pandanus leaf); and *Gang keo wan pla* (green fish curry with coconut milk).

Restaurants

There are very cheap road-side stalls, where a plate of fried rice and seafood will cost you about 20 baht and cheap indoor Thai restaurants with air-conditioners where the same meal will cost about 50 baht. If you want to take your meal home or to work, street stalls, noodle shops and small restaurants can put your food and drinks in a bag. Ask them '*Sai thoong dai mai?*'

At the moment, street stalls are forbidden on Wednesdays in

Bangkok – one transport minister's attempt to alleviate the traffic jams in the capital once a week.

An interview isn't much fun (a traffic jam even less so) with diarrhoea, so be a bit discriminating about which stalls you patronize, especially when you first arrive in Bangkok.

Western food

There are plenty of fast food outlets in Bangkok – Pizza Hut, McDonald's, Sizzlers and Burger King. Prices in these restaurants are about the same as those you would pay at home.

Almost all foreign food is available in Bangkok, although most of these restaurants cater for the wealthy expat population, so you might find that you can't afford to eat there quite as often as you would like. There are Italian, French, Mexican, Vietnamese, Spanish, Lebanese, Swiss and Japanese restaurants, and Irish and British pubs, too, that offer pub meals.

Drinking

A night out for a group of young upwardly-mobile Thais is commonly spent in a restaurant. It is not considered a fun night out unless you are in a group. Likewise, having a meal on your own makes you the object of some suspicion. Restaurants often have live music so it's not a case of sit-eat-leave. A bottle of whisky is bought and drunk to the end with soda or coke. In slightly more up-market establishments you are not expected to pour your own whisky from the bottle – a waiter is hovering ready to fill the glass as customers finish (bad luck, slow drinkers).

The most well-known Thai-brewed beers are Singha and Singha Gold which are available in bottles, in cans and on draft in restaurants and pubs in Bangkok. Singha is a light, fizzy beer, with a 5% alcohol content.

Other beers are available, including draft Guinness at Delaney's (an Irish pub) and draft Tetley bitter at Bobby's Arms (a British pub). The Paulaner Brauhaus is a microbrewery in Bangkok which makes and sells fresh, wheaty German beer which you can watch being made while you drink. (For addresses of these and other pubs, see below: Bars and discos.)

TRANSPORT

Thais drive on the left-hand side of the road, in right-hand drive cars. There is an expressway around Bangkok and the toll-fare is 30 baht. The horror stories of Bangkok traffic jams are mostly all true! If it's rush hour and you want to get into the city centre, going by taxi can be very expensive. If you are going to be stuck in traffic for a couple of hours you might as well go by bus, and save yourself some cash. Often the best way to get around in a traffic jam is by *motocy* (motorbike taxi). Although the drivers seem to value speed above traffic laws, they do get you to your destination a lot quicker than any other form of transport. For short journeys *motocy* drivers will not always have a helmet for you, and even when they do have one for longer journeys into the city, it is rarely very sturdy. If you think you might buy a motorbike while you are in Thailand or are likely to being using *motocys* regularly it is worth considering bringing a helmet with you.

Bus

The cheapest way around Bangkok is by bus (regular 2.5 baht, red non-aircon 3.5 baht, blue aircon 6 baht, micro, air-con buses 30 baht).

The bus destinations are written in Thai on the front of the bus, but the numbers are written in English. At present there is no completely reliable bus map available, so it's probably best to ask other teachers or foreigners for bus information. There is a leaflet available at major bus-stops showing micro air-con bus routes.

All but the red, micro air-con have bus-conductors. For these micro-buses you need either the exact fare or a coupon which you put into the machine beside the driver, and collect your ticket from a little machine further down inside the bus. You can buy books of micro-bus coupons at major bus-stops or from inspectors who regularly come onto the buses to check your ticket. A book of 10 coupons costs 285 baht, saving you 15 baht and the headache of needing exact change.

Taxi

Taxis in Bangkok are metered and the flag-fare 35 Baht. Not many taxi drivers speak English, so it is useful if you have the address you are going to written out in Thai for the driver.

Train

Thailand has a very good rail service which runs as far north as Chiang Mai and as far south as Hat Yai and then on into Malaysia. The State Railway of Thailand (SRT) offers a combination of ordinary, rapid and express trains and first, second and third class tickets. The cheapest, slowest and most uncomfortable is a third-class seat on an ordinary train and the most expensive, fastest and most comfortable is a first-class seat on an express train. You can buy tickets for any Thai destination at Bangkok's Hualamphong station (Tel: (02) 223 3762, Fax: (02) 225 6068.)

Boat

There are river boats in Bangkok with designated stops at small piers on the Chao Phraya river. Travelling by boat is much faster than travelling on the roads during the rush hours and is often a much more pleasant way of getting to your destination. You have to be quick at getting on and off the boat because the driver doesn't wait long at any stop. You should wait by the back of the boat in good time before you want to get off because if there is no-one waiting for the boat, the driver won't stop at each pier and you could easily be two miles downriver before you know where you are.

Tuk-tuk

Tuk-tuks are three-wheeled cars which can carry two to three people, although you will often see a lot more than that in one. Minimum fares start at about 15 baht and you should bargain and agree a price before you start your journey. Apart from around tourist areas *tuk-tuks* are usually only used for very short journeys.

Motocy (motorcycle taxis)

Motocys are useful for short trips and also for trying to beat the traffic jams during the rush hours. For a very short journey the minimum fare is 5 baht and for longer journeys you should bargain and agree a price before starting the trip.

Groups of *motocy* drivers wait together at the junction of main roads. You can approach them when they are stationary, or you can flag them down on the road. You can recognize *motocy* drivers by the brightly coloured, numbered waistcoats they wear.

Plane

Thai Airways International is the national and international carrier. Domestic destinations from Bangkok include: Pattaya, Phuket, Ko Samui, Hua Hin, Chiang Mai and Chiang Rai.

SERVICES

Shopping

Shopping is a national pastime or, to be more accurate, it is the single most popular hobby in Bangkok. You can guarantee that if you ask your students what they did at the weekend almost all of them will tell you they went shopping. It is a social occasion, and a time for cruising other well-dressed young people. You will see couples flirting over the toothpaste and fawning over the cooking oil. Though you might think incessant Thai mall-crawling sounds boring, don't knock it till you've tried it!

Public phones and fax services

Some post-offices have an overseas telephone, and the larger hotels will allow you to use their fax machine at an inflated price. The guesthouses in Khao San Road offer these facilities too, but at a much cheaper rate.

Public phones generally take 1 and 5 baht coins. Some shops, restaurants and stalls have a freestanding pay-phone. You need 5 baht for these and when the receiver is picked up at the other end remember to press the button on top of the phone or you won't be connected. From these phones, you can't dial through to an extension once you're connected.

Phone-cards are available at some banks, and larger shops. There are separate phone-cards for international and domestic calls.

Libraries

There are two main libraries in Bangkok for English language books, the British Council and the Neilson Hays library. Both libraries have a joining fee.

The British Council Library, 1 and 2 CU Building, 254 Chulalongkorn, Soi 64, Siam Square, Bangkok, 10330. Tel. (02) 611 6830.

Neilson Hays Library, 195 Suriwong Road. Tel: (02) 233 1731.

Bookshops

Khao San Road is the best place for second-hand books. There are lots of bookshops in Bangkok with English-language books. Asia Books is the best-known chain of bookstores in Thailand, with branches all over Bangkok.

Asia Books, 221 Sukhumvit Road (between Soi 15 and 17). Tel: (02) 252 7277. Fax: (02) 251 6042.

Asia Books, World Trade Centre, 3rd Floor (Skydrome Area), Rajadamri Road. Tel: (02) 255 6209. Fax: (02) 255 6211.

Asia Books, Times Square, 2nd Floor Times Square (opposite Robinson Department Store). Tel: (02) 250 0162-5. Fax: (02) 250 0164.

In Chiang Mai the best bookshop is:

Suriwong Book Centre, 54/1-5 Sridonchai Road, Chiang Mai 50100. Tel: (053) 28 1052-5. Fax: (053) 27 1902.

Banks and financial matters

Major Thai banks include the Thai Farmers' Bank, the Bangkok Bank, and the Thai Danu Bank. At the larger branches there's more chance someone will be able to help you in English. Opening an account is easy enough and if you apply for your ATM card at the Bangkok Bank, you can now choose your own PIN number. From the time you open your account it can take anything from ten days to a month before you can pick up your ATM card. Your ATM card can usually be used in any bank machine (although there is a charge for using them outside Bangkok). Almost everyone in Thailand is paid on the same day at the end of the month and on pay day you can usually only get cash from your own bank's ATMs.

Health

There are some excellent hospitals, doctors and specialists in Bangkok.

Government hospitals

Chulalongkorn University Hospital, Rama VI Road (near Dusit Thani Hotel). Tel: (02) 252 8181-9

Ramathibodi University Hospital, Rama VI Road, Tel: (02) 246 0024, (02) 246 1073-99.

Siriaj University Hospital, Prannok Road, Thonburi. Tel: (02) 411 0241, 411 3192, 411-4230.

Private hospitals

The Bangkok Nursing Home, 9 Convent Road, North Sathorn (Nua) Road, Tel: (02) 233 2610/9

Bumrungrad Hospital, 33 Soi 3 Sukhumvit Road, Tel: (02) 253 0250/69.

Phyathai II Hospital, 943 Phahonyothin Road.

MEDIA

Television

There are five TV channels in Bangkok, which are owned by the government, the military or private companies. Channel 9 has an English language news programme every weekday morning at 7am. At 7.30pm. you can tune into the radio and receive English soundtracks for the news on Channel 3 (105.5 FM), Channel 7(103.5 FM), Channel 9 (107 FM) and Channel 11 at 8 PM (88 FM). Many of the newer apartment blocks have access to satellite TV – the most popular is Satellite Television Asian Region (STAR), which is beamed from Hong Kong and shows a mixture of sports, music, and BBC news and current affairs.

Radio

Bangkok has over 80 radio stations playing a mixture of classical, modern and traditional music. English news broadcasts are on Radio Thailand (97 FM) at 7am, 12.30pm and 7pm.

Newspapers

There are two main English language daily newspapers, *The Bangkok Post* and *The Nation*. Newspapers from abroad are available, in the international hotels and some supermarkets and bookshops.

RECREATION

Bars and discos

There is no shortage of night-life in Bangkok, although you might believe before you arrive that the city only has bars filled with strippers, dancers and prostitutes. The most notorious area for such pubs are the Patpong Sois which are off Silom Road. However, there are actually numerous other bars in Bangkok where beer, music, food, and no sex transactions are on offer. Some bars popular with teachers include:

Bobby's Arms, 2nd floor car park building, Silom Soi 2 (Patpong Soi 2). Tel: (02) 233 6828.
Delaney's, 1 Convent Road, Silom. Tel: (02) 266 7160.
Hard Rock Café, 424/3-6 Siam Square, Soi II, Rama 1 Road. Tel: (02) 251 0792.
Saxophone, 3/8 Victory Monument, Phyathai Road. Tel: (02) 246 5472.
The Bull's Head, 595/10-1 Sukhumvit Soi 33/1. Tel: (02) 259 4444.
The Old Dutch, 9/4 Sukhumvit Soi 23. Tel: (02) 258 9234.
The Paulaner Brauhaus, President Park (at the end of Sukhumvit Soi 24). Tel: (02) 661 1210.

Cinema

There are lots of cinemas in Bangkok, often on the top floor of large shopping centres. Most of the movies shown are Hollywood blockbusters, but occasionally French films and other less mainstream films are shown too. The cinema is quite a cheap night out, with tickets costing only about 75 baht.

The national anthem is played before the film begins and you should stand while it is being played.

Video rental stores are also available, although, again, the choice is often Hollywood blockbusters or Kung Fu films.

Theatre

If you are interested in amateur dramatics, the Bangkok Community Theatre puts on about six performances a year, and is always keen to enlist new members for acting, directing, producing or helping behind the scenes.

The Bangkok Community Theatre, PO Box 1279, Bangkok, 10112.

Sports

Football, tennis, badminton, volleyball and basketball are all popular sports in Thailand, so you shouldn't find it too difficult to find a game, team or club you can join. Public tennis courts are available for about 100 baht an hour at the Central Tennis Club, Sathorn Tai, Soi Attakarnprasit (Tel: (02) 286 7202.)

Most apartment blocks have swimming pools, and even if you don't have one, it is likely that another teacher will, so keeping fit by swimming every day is a cheap option for most teachers. The more modern apartments have a swimming pool and a weights-room and gym as well.

Thai kick-boxing

You can see traditional Thai kick-boxing in Bangkok at two venues. Tickets costs between 150–800 baht, the more expensive the ticket, the nearer the boxing you are. But actually the cheaper tickets often have a better view of the whole show. From the cheap seats, high above the boxing ring, you are surrounded by men frantically calling out the odds and others desperately trying to lay bets before each round finishes. The boxing itself consists of five three-minute rounds where the boxers can use their fists, elbows, feet and legs to try to beat their opponents.

Lumpini Boxing Stadium, Rama IV Road (near Lumpini Park). Tel: (02) 280 4550.

Ratchadamnoen Boxing Stadium, 1 Ratchadamnoen Road (near TAT). Tel: (02) 281 4205, 282 5953.

Help-lines

Police		191 or 123
Tourist police (English spoken)		221 6206 – 6210
Ambulance	Bangkok Nursing Home	233 2610 – 9
	Bumrungrad Hospital	251 0415 – 6
	Samitivej Hospital	392 0011
The Samaritans		249 9977
Alcoholics Anonymous		253 0305, 253 8422, 253 8578

APPENDICES

Appendix 1. Case histories

Emma Robinson

Emma Robinson from Edinburgh worked for a year as an unpaid volunteer in a refugee camp, called Shoklo, on the Thai side of the Thai/Burma border. She heard about the job when she met other teachers while travelling in the area. She said 'If anyone is interested in teaching, the best idea is simply to travel to Mae Sot where you can easily meet teachers who are staying at the Mae Sot Guest House'.

She had a tourist visa which she had to renew every three months by travelling to Malaysia. 'Sometimes there were rumours that the authorities were going to crack down on foreigners working in the camps but I never had any problems'.

She lived with a local family who cooked her meals. 'All the houses in the camp were made of bamboo, thatched with dried leaves and built on stilts. They were very small and privacy was non-existent.' There was usually no electricity so Emma was in bed most nights by 9 o'clock. 'We slept on the floor, but it was quite comfortable. In the cool season it was very cold at night and I often wished I had brought a sleeping bag with me.'

Apart from getting a little bit run down, Emma had few health problems. She made sure that she was up-to-date with the recommended vaccinations, tried to avoid being bitten by mosquitoes and took vitamin pills. 'However, malaria is a huge problem in this area, and although I never got it, several teachers at other camps did. Prophylactics don't help at all and also the drugs that are used to treat malaria have high failure rates. Luckily Shokla has a hospital staffed by Medicins Sans Frontières and I knew I could receive high-quality medical care if necessary'.

Teaching in the camp was 'a really incredible experience. The people were always so kind, friendly and welcoming. I was always being invited to weddings, religious festivals and Full Moon celebrations.' Asked about her most memorable day in the refugee camp Emma recalled 'Without doubt it would be "Honour the Teacher Day". This was when all the children gave thanks to the teachers. They decorated the school, sang and danced, made garlands for all the teachers, knelt at our feet reciting Buddhist mantras and washed our hands with holy water.'

Anthony Green

Anthony Green was born in Nottingham in England and graduated in English Literature from Queen Mary and Westfield College, University of London in 1992. After graduating, he worked for a credit reference agency for two years, as a manager in customer services. He enjoyed the training aspects of his job, but felt he needed more of a challenge. He started studying Japanese while he was working and in 1995 originally intended to travel to Japan, via the Middle East and South-east Asia.

In Cairo, he studied for his CTEFLA in International House, Cairo, and when he arrived in Thailand he decided to work here for a while because he liked the country so much. At first he worked in Ramkamhaeng (about 10 kilometres north east of Bangkok) for a private language school, ECC

(Thailand). Within six months he was offered a Head Teacher position in the school's main branch in Siam Square.

The main things Anthony likes about Bangkok are the students, the variety of work available, Thai food and the easy access to beautiful towns and beaches. 'Thais have enormous respect for teachers which means they are very receptive as students, and rarely present teachers with discipline problems. They also have a good sense of fun which means they don't take themselves too seriously in the classroom.' In his short time as an EFL teacher, he has already taught children, teenagers, exam classes, business English and one-to-one students. The rapidly expanding economy in Thailand has a number of effects for EFL teachers. 'There are literally hundreds of language schools in Bangkok, and thousands of students who see learning English as one of the major ways of furthering their careers. This means that there are plenty of openings for teachers, but since this city certainly has some real disadvantages, it also means that Bangkok has one of the highest rates of teacher-turnover in the world.'

The main disadvantages of life in Bangkok are the pollution, the traffic jams and the rainy season. 'Wading through rain-water, sewage, rubbish and who knows what else in the monsoon season certainly isn't my idea of fun exercise' he said. But without doubt, the advantages far outweigh the disadvantages for Anthony. 'I know a lot of people would hate Bangkok, but that great Thai catch-phrase works for me – *mai pen rai* – don't worry, it doesn't matter.'

For anyone who is thinking about coming to Thailand to teach, Anthony has this advice: 'Smile, smile, smile, dress smartly and take time to get to know your students and you're sure to love Thailand.'

Appendix 2. Useful Thai words and phrases

As mentioned above, Thai has a completely different script from English. It is also a tonal language, and has more vowel sounds than English. The following words and phrases have been written as close as possible to how you would pronounce them using English transliterations. The tone is always said on the vowel sound, and in this guide the tones are marked above the vowel. I have followed the tone-markings used in the *Lonely Planet Travel Survival* and *Language Survival* books. This will make it easier for you if you are moving between this book and one in the *Lonely Planet* series. Other guide-books and language books use other tone-markings, but since the *Lonely Planet* books are probably the most well-known and readily available books both in Thailand and abroad, I have decided to use their system of tone-markings.

Tones are relative to each person's voice range, so a high tone is said in the highest part of your voice range which might be considerably different from someone else's high tone. There are five Thai tones:

- A high tone is said at the top of your voice range and has a flat sound (it neither rises or falls). It is marked – á.
- A mid or level tone is said in the middle range of your voice and has a flat sound. There is no mark for it – e.
- A low tone is said at the bottom of your voice range and has a flat sound. It is marked – ì.

- A falling tone is said as if you were calling someone from far away. It begins at your high or mid tone level and ends lower. It is marked – ô.
- A rising tone is said as if you were asking a one-word question 'coffee?'. It begins low and ends at a higher pitch. It is marked – ũ.

Polite endings and pronouns

A polite ending to questions, requests, invitations, etc is *kaa* – used by women and *krap* or *kap* – used by men. For first person pronouns use *dee-chan* if you are a woman and *phom* if you are a man. A general polite form of 'you' is *khun.*

Numbers

1	*nèung*	9	*gâow*	17	*sìp jèt*	60	*hòk sìp*
2	*sõng*	10	*sìp*	18	*sìp pèt*	70	*jèt sìp*
3	*sãam*	11	*sìp èt*	19	*sìp gâow*	80	*pèt sìp*
4	*sèe*	12	*sìp sõng*	20	*yêe sìp*	90	*gâow sìp*
5	*hâa*	13	*sìp sãam*	21	*yêe sìp èt*	100	*ráwy*
6	*hòk*	14	*sìp sèe*	30	*sãam sìp*		
7	*jèt*	15	*sìp hâa*	40	*sèe sìp*		
8	*pèt*	16	*sìp hòk*	50	*hâa sìp*		

Days

Monday	*wan jan*	Friday	*wan sòok*
Tuesday	*wan ungkahn*	Saturday	*wan saõ*
Wednesday	*wan póot*	Sunday	*wan ahtít*
Thursday	*wan préuhàt*		

Months

January	*deuan mókaraa-khom*	July	*deuan krakdaa-khom*
February	*deuan kumphaa-phan*	August	*deuan sĩnghãa-kkhom*
March	*deuanmiinaa-khom*	September	*deuan kanyaa-yon*
April	*deuanmehesãa-yon*	October	*deuan tùlaa-khom*
May	*deuan phréutsàphaa-khom*	November	*deuan phréutsàjìkaa-yon*
June	*deuan míthùnaa-yon*	December	*deuan thanáwaa-khom*

Times and dates

Today	*Wan née*	Next week	*Aatít nâa*
Tonight	*Kheun née*	What time is it?	*Kèe mohng laéw?*
Yesterday	*Mêua waan née*	When?	*Mêua rai?*
Tomorrow	*Prûng née*		

Greetings and small talk

Hello (used by women)	*Sawàdee kâa*
Hello (used by men)	*Sawàdee kráp*
Good-bye	*Sawàdee kâa/kráp*
How are you?	*Sabai dee rẽu?*
I'm fine.	*Sabai*
Please	*Kaw roo nah*
Thank you	*Kòp kun kâa/kráp*
Excuse me	*Kãw tôot*
I am sorry	*(I) Kòr tòht kâa/kráp*

It doesn't matter	*Mâi pen rai*
Can you speak English?	*Koon pôot pah-sãh angkrìt dâi mãi?*
No	*Mâi*
I can't speak Thai	*(I) Pôot thai mâi dâi*
I don't understand.	*(I) Mai khâo jái*

Shopping

How much does it cost?	*Thâo rái?*
Do you have any...?	*Mii...mãi? or ...mii mãi?*
Where is the...?	*...yòo tee nai?*

Appendix 3. Public holidays

13 to 15 April is the Songkran Festival Celebration at the start of the new lunar year in Thailand when Buddha images are 'bathed' and monks receive the respect of younger Thais by the sprinkling of water over their hands. If you are in Thailand for this, the most important Thai Festival, you'll notice that it is mainly celebrated by throwing a lot of water about. Expect to get wet if you go out and you should carry a change of clothes or a towel, especially in Bangkok if you don't fancy the idea of being soaked in smelly canal water! This is the height of the hot season and seems to be a welcome opportunity for an, otherwise very restrained, people to let their hair down. You have been warned.

Fluctuating dates are marked with an asterisk *

1 January	New Year's Day
* February	*Magha Puja (Makkha Buchaa)*
6 April	Chakri Day
1 May	Labour Day
* May	*Visakha Puja (Wisakha Buchaa)*
5 May	Coronation Day
* Mid July	*Khao Phansaa*
12 August	The Queen's birthday
23 October	Chulalongkorn Day
5 December	The King's birthday
10 December	Constitution Day
31 December	New Year's Eve

Appendix 4. Embassies and consulates

Selected Thai embassies and consulates abroad

Australia: Royal Thai Embassy, 111 Empire Circuit, Yarralumla, Canberra ACT 2600. Tel: (06) 273 1149/273 2937.

Canada: Royal Thai Embassy, 180 Island Park Drive, Ottawa, Ontario K1Y 0A2. Tel: (613) 722 444.

Ireland: Royal Thai Consulate, Bland, Payne, Dineen, 19 Harcourt Street, Dublin. Tel: (01) 781 599, 781 599.

New Zealand: Royal Thai Embassy, PO Box 17266, 2 Cook Street, Wellington 1. Tel: (04) 768 618.

England

Birmingham: Royal Thai Consulate, Exchange Building, Smith Keen Cutler, Stephenson Place, Birmingham, B2 4NN. Tel: (0121) 643 9481.

Hull: Royal Thai Consulate, Exchange Building, 5 Spyvee Street, Hull, North Humberside, HU8 7AD. Tel: (01482) 29925.

Liverpool: Royal Thai Consulate, Boodles House, 35 Lord Street, L2 9SQ. Tel: (0151) 255 0504.

London: Royal Thai Embassy, Consular Section, 1–3 Yorkshire House, Grosvenor Crescent, London SW1X 7EP. Tel: 0171 584 2384.

Scotland

Glasgow: Royal Thai Consulate, Pacific House, 70 Wellington Street, Glasgow G2 6SB. Tel: (0141) 248 6677

Wales

Cardiff: Royal Thai Consulate, Ledger House, 38 Station Road, Llanishen, Cardiff CF4 5LT. Tel: (01222) 766 993

USA

California: Royal Thai Consulate, 801 N LaBrea Ave, Los Angeles CA 90038. Tel: (213) 937 1894.

Washington DC: Royal Thai Embassy, 1024 Wisconsin Ave NW, Washington DC 20007. Tel: (202) 483 7200.

Selected embassies and consulates in Bangkok

Australia: 37 South Sathorn Road. Tel: (02) 287 2680.

Canada: 11 – 12th floors Boonmitr Building, 138 Silom Road, PO Box 2090. Tel: (02) 237 4125.

Ireland: 205 United Flour Mill Building, Tatchawong Road. Tel: (02) 223 0876.

New *Zealand:* 93 Wireless Road, PO Box 2719. Tel: (02) 251 8165.

UK: 1031 Wireless Road. Tel: (02) 253 0191

USA: 95 Wireless Road. Tel: (02) 252 5040.

Appendix 5. Suggested reading

Australian-New Zealand women's group, *Bangkok Guide- A Comprehensive Guide to Living in Bangkok.*

Buckley, Michael, *Bangkok Handbook*, Moon Publications, California.

Cummings, Joe, *Bangkok Lonely Planet City Guide*, Lonely Planet Publications, 1995.

Cummings, Joe, *The Lonely Planet Travel Survival Kit, Thailand*, Lonely Planet Publications, 1996.

Cummings, Joe, *The Lonely Planet Language Survival Kit, Thai Phrasebook,* Lonely Planet Publications, 1992.

Moore, John and Saowalak Rodchue, *Colloquial Thai*, Routledge, London, 1994.

Teach Yourself Thai, Hodder-Headline, London.

Thailand, Footprint Handbooks, Bath, UK/NTC, Chicago, 1997.

Walker, D, and R. Ehrlich, *Hello My Big Big Honey! Love letter to Bangkok Bar Girls and Their Revealing Interviews*, Dragon Dance, Bangkok, 1992.

Appendix 6. Suggested videos

The King and I

Good Morning Vietnam (filmed in Thailand)

Killing Fields (filmed in Thailand)

The Man With the Golden Gun (filmed in Thailand)

5

Laos

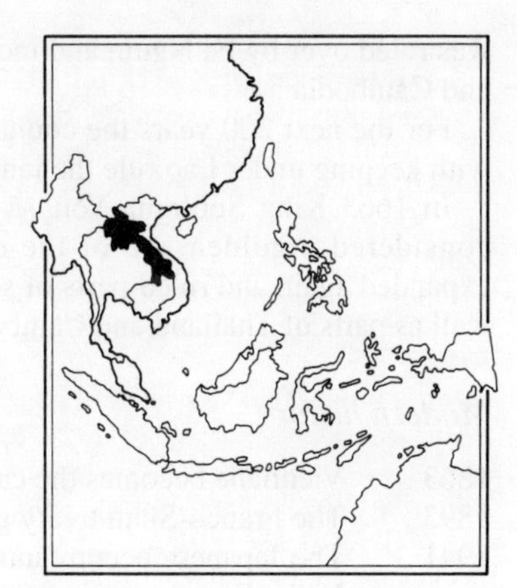

FACTFILE

Legend has it that Khoum Borom was a king who came out of the sky. He cut open a gourd in Vietnam and inside were his seven sons. His sons became the fathers of the Lao-Thai people and established the great Tai kingdoms of the region.

History

The history of Laos is filled with battles and bloodshed. Its strategic location bordered by China, Vietnam, Thailand and Burma has resulted in each of its neighbours, at one time or another, being intent on overrunning Laos. Laos has also been threatened from beyond the region. In the 19th century, Laos was a French colony and, during the Second World War, it was occupied by the Japanese. More recently, it was the war between the USA and Vietnam that devastated Laos, which has the distinction of being the most heavily-bombed nation on earth, per head of population. Of the 6 300 000 bombs dropped on Indochina by the US, one third of them fell on Laos.

Early history

There is evidence of settlements in Laos from Neolithic times. Recent excavations have found dinosaur remains, stone axes and copper tools.

Linguists and archaeologists believe that the Lao people arrived from south China in the 10th century. This migration continued in the 13th century when Kublai Khan invaded from Mongolia and many fled again to Laos from Southern China.

The first written historical records in the 14th century tell of the Kingdom of Lan Xang or land of a million elephants. This kingdom was ruled over by Fa Ngum and included parts of present-day Thailand and Cambodia.

For the next 200 years the country, under each king, was concerned with keeping under Lao rule the lands already conquered.

In 1663 King Souligna Vongsa began his 61 year reign, which is considered a golden age of the country. During this period Laos expanded again and ruled parts of south China, Burma and Vietnam, as well as parts of Thailand and Cambodia.

Modern history

1863	Vientiane becomes the capital city.
1893	The Franco-Siam treaty gives French control of Laos.
1941	The Japanese occupy much of South-east Asia and allow the Vichy French nominal control of Laos.
1945	French paratroopers land and declare Laos a French protectorate again.
1949	The French and the Lao royal families reach an agreement for a more independent Laos.
1950	Prince Souphanouvong forms a resistance government, which includes Nouhak Phounsavanh and Phoumi Vongvichit (both members of past and present-day Lao governments).
1953	The Franco-Laotian Treaty is signed, granting full sovereignty to Laos.
1954	The French are defeated at Dien Bien Phu. The Geneva Accord is signed in July guaranteeing Laos freedom and neutrality. But with Ho Chi Minh in control of all territory north of the 17th parallel in Vietnam, the USA is not prepared to allow Laos to be in the role of neutral neighbour. Laos becomes the first country in the US 'domino theory' and in an effort to keep communist Vietnam at bay, Washington pours millions of dollars in military aid into Laos.
1957	The First Coalition Government is formed under Prince Souvanna Phourma (brother of Prince Souphanouvong) in Vientiane.
1964	US bombing raids begin inside Laos. These raids soon expand along the Ho Chi Minh Trail and other parts of northern Laos.
1965–74	During the Vietnam War, US bombers stationed in Thailand conduct secret saturation bombings of Laos – more than 2 000 0000 bombs are dropped on Laos. As late as 1970 America is still maintaining that it is only involved in 'armed reconnaissance' flights over northern Laos. Souvanna Phouma refers to this period of Lao tragedy as 'the forgotten war'.

1975 Despite the continual bombing and the secret war financed by the CIA, when the USA withdraws from Vietnam, the Communist Pathet Lao (Lao Nation) takes control of the country. The monarchy is abolished, opposition leaders ousted and Kaysone Phomvihane is appointed premier.

1975–85 The People's Democratic Republic of Laos follows a Marxist-Leninist philosophy similar to those followed in Cambodia and Vietnam. During this period 300 000 people, or 10% of the Lao population flee the country and between 300 000 and 400 000 more are sent to 're-education' camps.

1986 The government launches an economic reform programme called the New Economic Mechanism (NEM) which is designed to introduce a market economy.

1991 The hammer and sickle are removed from the state emblem and the State motto is changed from 'Peace, Independence, Unity and Socialism' to 'Peace, Independence, Democracy, Unity and Prosperity'.

Geography

The Lao People's Democratic Republic, or Lao PDR, has a population of about 4.17 million (1991 figures), which is small compared to neighbouring countries. Although the country is about the size of the UK (or a third of the size of Texas), 85% of the surface is mountainous, dominated by the Annamite Chain. Only about 8% of the land is arable, and most of the population live in the valleys of the Mekong and its tributaries. The Mekong flows through Lao PDR for 1 850 kilometres of its length, but not every stretch of the river is navigable. Since the road system is still underdeveloped and Laos has no coast, Laos is very dependent on its neighbours, especially Thailand, for transporting of imports and exports. Only a tenth of the villages in Laos are anywhere near a road and three quarters of the population are subsistence farmers. Life expectancy is 47 years for men, 50 for women and annual per capita income is $300.

Climate

Laos has three seasons, all of which are hot. The wettest months are from June to November, while for the rest of the year Laos is drier. The rains are heaviest in the more mountainous regions of Laos, and as much as 400 centimetres of rain fall around the Bolovens Plateau every year. January and February are the coolest. Probably the most pleasant time of the year is in the dry season, from November to March. In the highlands you will need warm clothes, as night temperatures can be very cold.

The dry, hot season begins in February. March, April, and May are the hottest months with temperatures often in excess of 35°C. June to October is the rainy season, with temperatures over 30°C. During the rainy season, the average rainfall in the lowlands is 125 centimetres a year. The Mekong River rises and flooding in the surrounding areas is common. The cooler, dry season is from November to late January, with average temperatures of 18°C.

Time

Laos, like Thailand, is 7 hours ahead of Greenwich Mean Time, 12 hours ahead of New York, 15 hours ahead of San Francisco, 3 hours behind Sydney, and 5 hours behind New Zealand.

The people

Laos has a population of about 4.17 million, and over 250 000 people live in Vientiane, the capital.

There are three main ethnic groups in Laos, which in turn can be subdivided into more than 60 smaller groups. The main groups are the *Lao Loum* (who live in the lowlands), the *Lao Theung* (who are semi-nomadic and live mainly on the mountains), and the *Lao Sung* (who include most of the hill tribes with their very distinctive colourful, traditional clothes).

Politics

In December 1975, a bloodless coup by the Pathet Lao marked the beginning of the People's Democratic Republic of Laos and the end of King Samsenthai's reign. Compared to its neighbouring countries, the communist revolution in Laos was initially remarkably peaceful. The king was not executed or expelled, but was invited to be a 'special adviser' to the new politburo.

This peacefulness did not last, however. It has been estimated that over 300 000 people fled from Laos during the revolutionary period and a further 40 000 who did not manage to escape were sent to re-education camps.

The new government of 1975 was headed by Kaysone Phomvihane, the son of a Vietnamese civil servant. He led the country until his death in November 1991. During his years, the country followed a Marxist-Leninist philosophy. However, this changed in the 1980s, and in March 1986 the Lao People's Revolutionary Party voted to introduce a New Economic Mechanism (NEM). This was designed to encourage private ownership and foreign investment, and by 1994 over 500 such foreign licences had been granted, totalling US$3 billion. Laos is slowly emerging as a new semi-capitalist country, but the legacy of years of communist bureaucracy is still very much in evidence.

Language

The official language of Laos is Lao. Spoken Lao is very similar to spoken Thai, and like Thai it is tonal. However, while Thai has five tones, Lao has six. The tones are: low, mid, high, rising, high falling, and low falling. The tone you use alters a word's meaning so, for example, the word *sao* can mean girl, twenty, morning, or pillar depending on which tone you use. For more information on tones see Appendix 1: Useful Lao words and phrases.

Written Lao is slightly different to written Thai. However many educated Laos can understand written Thai because so many of the academic textbooks in Laos are written in Thai.

If you want to learn Lao, the following schools in Vientiane offer language courses:

Centre de Langue Francaise de Vientiane (CLF), Lane Xang Avenue. Tel: 215 764/5.

The Lao-American Language Centre, 152 Thanon Sisangvon, Ban Naxay. PO Box 327. Tel: 414 321. Fax: 413 760.

Mittaphab School, Km 3, Thanon Thadeua. Tel: 313 452.

Saysettha Language Centre, Thanon Nong Bone, Ban Phonexay. Tel: 414 480.

Vientiane University College, Thanon That Luang (opposite the Ministry of Foreign Affairs). P O Box 4144. Tel: 414 873. Fax: 414 346.

Religions

Over 90% of the people in Laos are Theravada Buddhists. This branch of Buddhism is the same as that practised in Thailand and Cambodia. The remaining 10% of the population are Christians (mostly Catholics) or Muslims. Some ethnic minorities practise animism (the belief that spirits inhabit natural objects, such as rocks and trees).

Cultural considerations

Buddhism. As Laos is mainly a Buddhist country, it is important not to offend Buddhists by behaving inappropriately when you visit a temple, or when you talk to a Monk. (See Chapter 1: Buddhism (Cambodia, Laos, Thailand and Vietnam) for further information on cultural considerations while in a Buddhist country.)

TEACHING POSSIBILITIES

At the moment, the main teaching possibilities are through volunteer organizations. There is little chance of turning up in Vientiane and finding decent-paying, full-time teaching work. However, as Laos continues to open up to the outside world, the 'New Economic Mechanism', as well as the loans negotiated with the IMF and World bank, will, no doubt, lead to liberalization of foreign investment, privatization, etc. Foreign language school owners will probably soon find Laos a congenial country to set up schools in. For information on Non-Governmental Organizations (NGOs) seeking to counter possible negative effects of the new market economy, working for sustainable growth, and offering teaching positions see Chapter 1: Volunteer Recruitment Organizations.

Private language schools

It would be useful to send off a CV to a school before you arrive in Laos. Starting off with a little bit of part-time work is often a usual way of getting your foot in the door. Once you have proved yourself, and full-time work becomes available, you are likely to be able to land yourself a full-time contract. Listed below are the main language schools in Vientiane.

The Lao-American Language Centre, 152 Thanon Sisangvon, Ban Naxay. PO Box 327. Tel: 414 321. Fax: 413 760.

Malaysian Management and Educational School, 311 Siamphone Road, Ban Watnak, Km 3, Thadeua Road, P O Box 4569. Tel: 314 150. Fax: 313 508.

Saysettha Language Centre, Thanon Nong Bone, Ban Phonexay. Tel: 414 480.

Vientiane University College, Thanon That Luang (opposite the Ministry of Foreign Affairs). PO Box 4144. Tel: 414 873. Fax: 414 346.

International schools

There are a number of international schools in Vientiane which cater mostly for foreign children living in Laos, although some Lao children also attend these schools.

The Vientiane International School, Thanon Sokpaluang (near the roundabout). Tel: 315 008.

Santisouk Montessori Pre-school, Thanon Phon Kheng (opposite the UNDP office). Tel: 413 723.

Mittaphab School, Km 3, Thanon Thadeua. Tel: 313 452.

BEFORE YOU GO

Insurance

If you are going to a pre-arranged job, or are working with a volunteer organization, you will have medical insurance provided for you. If you are not going to a pre-arranged job, then take out a health insurance policy, as health care in Laos is very basic, and if you become seriously ill, you will probably have to go to Thailand or Singapore for expensive medical treatment.

Vaccinations

There are no vaccination requirements for Laos, but most doctors in your home country would advise, at a minimum, that you have a tetanus, measles and polio booster, and that you are vaccinated against Japanese encephalitis. For further information about health precautions to be taken both before and after you arrive in Laos see Chapter 1: Health.

ARRIVAL AND VISAS

Visas

The visa situation is constantly changing, especially as Laos continues to open up more and more to the outside world. So it is essential that you check with your home country Lao embassy to get the most up-to-date information about visas. The prices mentioned below are in US dollars. At the time of writing there were five types of visas available for foreigners.

Transit Visa. This is a five-day, non-extendable visa, which is issued on arrival in Laos. It is mainly used by people who are stopping-over in Laos. To be issued with this visa you will need to have proof of confirmed tickets for the two countries you are travelling between and a valid visa for the country you are going on to. The Transit Visa costs between $10 and $12.

Visit Visa. Visit visas are valid for up to 30 days and extendible for a further 30 days once in Laos. An expat in Laos has to apply for this visa on your behalf. This visa costs $35.

Tourist Visa. Tourists visas can be issued through an authorized travel agent, when you book your ticket, or through a Lao Embassy in your home country or abroad. Tourist visas are valid for 15 days and can be extended for a further 15 days, once in Laos. This visa costs between $35 and $100, depending on which country you apply from, and if you do it through a travel agent or directly through a Lao embassy.

If you apply for a visa from Thailand, beware of travel agents who try to charge you up to 10 times the cost the embassy charges for the visa, which is 300 baht, or $12.

Non-immigrant Visa. As a teacher or a volunteer you are likely to have this visa, or a Business Visa (see below). To obtain this visa you have to have a sponsor in Laos who will confirm that you will be a volunteer or paid teacher. It is valid for 30 days and extendable for a further 30 days and costs $35.

Business Visa. A Business Visa is issued if you have a sponsoring agent in Laos, and once you have found work in Laos, this is likely to be the visa you will get. This visa is valid for up to 30 days and can then be extended each month for a further 30 days.

This visa costs $12 at the Lao Embassy in Bangkok. If you go through a broker to help you with the paperwork and the extensions, the fee, of course, will be higher (one company in Vientiane charges $60 to obtain this visa for you).

Most teachers in Laos arrive here on a tourist visa, and then after finding work, and completing the necessary paper-work, leave for a short trip to Bangkok and apply for either a Non-immigrant or Business Visa.

Where to get a visa. You can get your visa at the Lao embassy in your home country (see Appendix 3 below), or from the following embassies in the region:

LPDR Chancellory, 111, 214th St, Phnom Penh, Cambodia. Tel: 251 1821.

LPDR Consular Office, 2nd floor, 40 Quang Trung St, Hanoi, Vietnam. Tel: 52588.

Transport from the airport

Vientiane's international airport is at Vattay, about 4 kilometres from the city centre. The taxi fare costs about US$5, and you should agree on a price before you start your journey.

ACCOMMODATION

Short-term accommodation

There is a choice of guest houses and hotels in Vientiane ranging in price from US$5 to US$150 a night. Many of the smaller hotels give a discount for long-staying guests, so if you think you will be living and working in Vientiane for more than a month, it is worth trying to negotiate a price-cut. Some guesthouses in the US$5–20 price bracket include:

Lani 1 Guesthouse, 281 Thanon Setthathirat (Tel: 4175). This guesthouse is popular with volunteer workers and long-term visitors. It is often full, so reserve in advance. Write to Lani 1 Guesthouse, PO Box 58, Vientiane.

Lani 2 Guesthouse, 268 Thanon Saylom (Tel: 2615. Fax: 4174)

Syri Guesthouse, Quartier Chao Anou (Tel: 2394. Fax: 3117)

Long-term accommodation

Other teachers and foreigners are good sources for finding houses. There is also a noticeboard in The Scandinavian Bakery, 74/1 Pangkham Road, (near the fountain), which has ads for houses and rooms to rent.

Rent is from around $250–350 a month, with a hefty six- month deposit which the house-owner uses to make any improvements or changes you ask for before you move in.

Electricity, gas and water

Electricity. Electricity in Laos uses 220 volts, and most outlets have a two-prong flat or round socket. Adaptors and transformers are useful to bring from your home country if you are taking any electrical goods with you to Laos. You can also buy adaptors for European plugs in Vientiane.

Blackouts are still common in Laos, especially during the rainy season, so be sure to pack a torch, and have a supply of candles in your room at your hotel, or in your house.

Electricity costs $10–12 a month. Your bill will be delivered to your house in person by someone from the electricity company, and you can either pay your bill directly to that person, or pay it at the Electricity Company of Laos, PO Box 309, Thanon Samsenthai (behind Wat Sisaket), Tel: 212 800.

Gas. Gas comes in large canisters and is mainly used for cooking on a small two-ringed stove. Pransansak, Thanon Nong Douang (before the Belvedere) picks up and delivers gas. Tel: 214 702.

Water. Water is charged at different rates for Lao nationals, foreigners, businesses, factories, etc. Bills are delivered to your house, and like your electricity bill, you can either pay the bill directly to the deliverer or pay it at the Lao Water Supply Office Company, (Nam Pa Pa), Thanon Phon Kheng, Tel: 412 885.

The tap water in Laos in not safe for drinking. You should either boil it for five minutes or buy bottled water. Phommalinh, Thanon Loie Sam, Tel: 313 020, will deliver 20-litre bottles to your house.

Household help

Most teachers employ someone to help with house cleaning, clothes washing and cooking. Household help costs about $60 a month and other teachers or volunteers can usually help you find someone.

LIVING COSTS

How expensive is Laos?

Laos is a very cheap country to live in. Food can cost as little as $2 a meal in a restaurant, and only 70 – 80¢ for a bowl of noodles or rice from a side-walk stall. Travel in Laos, however, is very expensive since you still have to go through travel agents and hire guides to go anywhere outside Vientiane, Luang Prabang, or Pakse. The government's resolve to control tourism means that budget travellers are not yet common.

Salaries

Teachers' salaries start from around $1 200 a month and after paying rent and utility bills you will be left with about $850. If you are a volunteer you will probably be living on an allowance of about $300 a month, and if you are working part-time you might only be making about $10 an hour.

Taxes

Income tax is charged at the rate of 10% and it will be automatically deducted from your salary.

Supermarket costs

There are a number of supermarkets carrying Western products in Vientiane. A popular one with teachers is Phimphone Market, which has a branch at 110/1 Thanon Samsenthai, (Tel: 216 609) and another branch just across the road at 380 Thanon Samsenthai, (Tel: 216 963). Below is a list of some supermarket prices, but you should bear in mind that costs in the market and in small, local shops are often much lower than in supermarkets. However, many of the goods listed below, because they are imported, are only available in supermarkets (prices are in Lao kip).

Bread (small, white, sliced loaf)	1 000	Sugar (1 kg)	700
		Eggs (10)	900
Beef (100 kg)	6 500	Rice (1 kg)	700

Milk (1 litre)	800	Tea (25 tea-bags)	1 600
Instant coffee (100 g)	3 100	Cigarettes (20 Marlboro)	1 000
Lao coffee (500 g)	1 800	Vodka (75 ml)	7 000
Beer (big bottle)	1 200		

EATING AND DRINKING

The staple food of Laos is rice. Lao food is similar to Thai food in that it relies heavily on spices such as lemongrass, chillies, and soups which are often made with coconut milk. There is also still a strong French influence in Lao cooking, and a popular breakfast is *khao jii pa-teh*, a French baguette filled with luncheon meat and dressings; you can buy lovely fresh baguettes for breakfast from vendors on bicyles.

Lao specialties

One of the most popular dishes is *laap,* meat marinated in lemon and mixed with chillies, mint and bean-sprouts. This is the national dish of Laos and is also served at traditional ceremonies. *Laap sin* is meat based, *laap kai* is chicken based, and *laap pa* is fish based. *Phaneng kai* is chicken stuffed with peanuts and coconut, *tom yam paa* is fish and lemongrass soup *Kung pung* is sautéed prawns

Restaurants

Vientiane has lots of cheap Lao road-side stalls and small restaurants where you can eat for a couple of dollars. Lao and foreign restaurants which are popular with teachers include:

Belle Île Pub and Creperie, 21-1 Lane Xang Avenue. Tel: 214 942.
Just for Fun, 57/2 Thanon Pang Kham. Tel: 213 642.
Kua Lao Restaurant, 111 Thanon Samesnthai. Tel: 215 777.
L'Opera, Nam Phou Circle. Tel: 215 099.
The Taj, 75/4 Thanom Pang Kham. Tel: 212 890.

Drinking

Lao-brewed beer, *Beerlao,* is available in bottles and on draft in Vientiane. It is a light, fizzy beer, with 5% alcohol content. The traditional alcohol is rice wine, and there are two varieties – white and red. White rice wine called *lao-lao* (Lao alcohol) and is made from fermented sticky rice. Red rice wine, *fanthong,* is fermented with herbs. Traditionally rice wine is drunk out of a clay jug with long straws *(lao hai).*

TRANSPORT

Bus

Buses travel between the morning market and the bus terminal to the outskirts of the town. The bus destinations and prices are shown in English on a notice board in the bus terminal. There are no official bus-stops, so just flag down the bus on the road.

Taxi

Most taxis in Vientiane are old cars without meters, although increasingly, metered taxis are becoming available. You can book a taxi by phoning 213 918, 213 919 (they speak English) and pay the taxi driver what is shown on the meter. Alternatively you can agree an hourly or daily rate if you want to visit several places.

Bike

Particularly in Vientiane, one of the easiest ways to get around is by bike. You can rent bikes by the day, or longer, at most guesthouses, or buy one in Vientiane. Bikes cost about $2 a day to rent, or you can buy a new, standard bike for $80-90 or a new, Taiwanese, mountain bike for between $100-140. Most bikes available in Laos are heavy and not very shock-absorbent, but the rustic scenery around Vietiane makes riding worth it.

Motorbike

Motorbikes are popular with teachers. Vientiane is a small, city it is easy to get around and the traffic is not even vaguely comparable to Bangkok or Jakarta. If you are thinking about buying a motorbike, you should bring a helmet with you from your home country, as the helmets available in Laos are not of a very high standard. You can buy second-hand motorbikes from teachers who are leaving, or check the noticeboard at The Scandinavian Bakery, 74/1 Pangkham Road, (near the fountain). Honda and Suzuki are the two main brands of motorbike available in Laos, and there are numerous small garages around town where you can get your bike serviced or buy spare-parts. The main Honda showroom is at 193 Setthathirath Road, Ban Kaonhot (Tel: 214 621, Fax: 213 360.)

You can use an international driving licence when you first arrive in Laos, and then apply for a Lao licence at the Office of Vehicle and Driving Licence Control, Thanon Dong Pain. At the time of writing there were plans to change the office to the corner of Thanon Setthathirath and Thanon Sakharindh.

Samlor, Tuk-tuk and *Jumbo*

All these forms of transport are good for short distances around town. Prices are not fixed, and you should negotiate the fare before you start your journey.

Samlor. A *samlor* is a trishaw, with the driver who pedals at the front, and a small buggy at the back which can carry two or three people.

Tuk-tuk and Jumbo. A *tuk-tuk* is a small, three-wheeled vehicle, with the engine and driver at the front, and room for two or three people in the back. A *jumbo* is a bigger version of a *tuk-tuk.*

SERVICES

Public phones and fax services

You can make international calls and send faxes from the Enterprise Telecommunication Laos (ETL) bureaux service on Thanon Setthathirath (near Nam Phou Circle). The office is open every day from 8am – 10pm.

Libraries

There are a few libraries in Vientiane with a choice of French, Russian and English-language books.

Australian Embassy Library, Thanon Nehru (opposite the Australian clinic). Open Tuesday and Thursday 1pm – 4pm and on Saturday from 9am – 1pm.

Centre de Langue Francaise de Vientiane, Lang Xang Avenue. Tel: 215 764, 215 765. Open Monday to Friday 10am – 12.30pm and 2.30– 7pm, and on Saturday from 10am – 12 noon.

National Library, Corner of Thanon Setthathirath and Thanon Pang Kham. Open Monday to Friday 8.30 – 11.30am and 2.30 – 4.30 pm, and on Saturday 8.30 – 11.30am.

Russian Cultural Centre Library, Corner of Thanon Luang Prabang and Thanon Khoum Boulom.

Bookshops

There are only a few bookshops in Laos, with a fairly limited stock of English-language books. If possible, you should bring some books with you which you can exchange at the second-hand book-shop.

JJ Bookstore, 374 Thanon Samsenthai. Tel: 217 125.

Raintree Bookstore (new and second-hand books), Thanon Pang Kham (opposite Lao Aviation). Tel: 217 260.

Banks and financial matters

The official currency of Laos is the kip (K), although the Thai baht and the American dollar are also widely used, especially in the larger towns of Vientiane and Luang Prabang. There are very few coins, *aat,* in circulation. There are notes of 1, 5, 10, 20, 50, 100 and 500 kip. Banks are open from Monday to Friday from 8.30am to 4pm.

It is possible, as a foreign resident, to open a US dollar account at a number of banks in Vientiane including at:

Banque pour le Commerce Èxterieur Lao (BCEL), 1 Thanon Pang Kham, PO Box 2925. Tel: 213 200, 213 210. Fax: 213 202.

Health

Laos has a very poor health care service, and if you need medical help here it is advisable to go to nearby Thailand or Singapore for treatment. (For advice on health care before you leave for Laos and while you are living here see Chapter 1: Health.)

The main health care precautions you should take while in Laos are: take care with what you eat (wash and peel fruit, and in restaurants watch out for raw or unwashed vegetables, uncooked fish or meat, or food that has been re-heated); drink only bottled or boiled water (and only use treated ice in your drinks); and avoid being bitten by mosquitoes.

The main clinic that teachers use in Vientiane is:

The Australian Embassy Clinic, Australian Embassy compound. Tel: 413 603 (daytimes), 312 343 or 314 924 (weekends and evening). The clinic is open Monday, Tuesday, Thursday and Friday 8.30 – 12am, and 2 – 5pm and on Wednesday, from 8.30 – 12am.

MEDIA

Television

There are two TV channels, Channel 3 and Channel 9, which broadcast in Lao. It is possible to tune into Thai Channel 5 which gives English news at 7.30 pm.

Radio

BBC World Service, Radio Australia, Voice of America and Radio Manila can be received in Vientiane on short-wave, although the reception is often quite bad. If possible, you should bring your own short-wave radio from home along with a fine-tuning device.

Newspapers

Passason and *Vientiane Mai* are the two Lao-language daily newspapers. There is only one English-language 'newspaper', which is actually a government news-sheet, with very little news. For national and international news the two Thai English-language newspapers, *The Bangkok Post* and *The Nation,* are available daily in Vientiane.

RECREATION

Bars

Bars which are popular with teachers include:

Belle Île Pub and Creperie, 21-1 Lane Xang Avenue. Tel: 214 942.
Nam Phu Fountain Garden, Nam Phou Circle.

Cinema

There are no English-language cinemas in Laos, but you can see films at:

American Embassy Movies, American Embassy, Thanon Bartoloni. Wednesdays at 7.30pm.

Australian Embassy Recreation Club (AERC), Km 3 Thanon Thadeua. Movies are shown fortnightly – members only.

Centre de Langue Francaise de Vientiane, Lang Xang Avenue. Tel: 215 764, 215 765. Thursdays at 7.30 pm.

Sports

Cycling is very popular around Vientiane, and there are some lovely routes to explore as well as good picnic sites. Tennis is possible at the larger hotels. If you want to jog or do Tai Chi in the morning with the locals, try the parade ground at the National Stadium.

About three kilometres out of Vientiane on Thanon Thadeua is the Australian Club. This rather expat club has a lovely swimming pool, squash courts, billiards, table-tennis, darts and cheap drinks. Membership is US$100 a year plus a $100 joining fee, but it is also possible to join for a shorter time (Tel: 314 921).

Some of the larger hotels in Vientiane have sports facilities, and for a small fee (between 550 and 2 000 kip) you can use them even if you are not a hotel guest. Hotels with sports facilities include:

Lane Xang Hotel, Thanon Fa Ngum. Tel: 3672. Fax: 5448. This hotel has two badminton courts and a swimming pool.

Belvedere Hotel, Thanon Luang Phabang. Tel: 9991. Fax: 9470. About two kilometres out of town on the way to the airport. This hotel has tennis courts and a swimming pool.

Help-lines

Police	190
	191
	212 707
Fire	190
	212 708
International operator	170
Directory inquiries	178
Airport inquiries	512 028

APPENDICES

Appendix 1. Useful Lao words and phrases

As mentioned above, Lao has a completely different script from English. It is also a tonal language, and has more vowel sounds than English. The following words and phrases have been written as closely as possible to how you would pronounce them using English transliterations. The tone is always said on the vowel sound, and in this guide the tones are marked above or below the vowel. I have followed the tone-markings used in the *Lonely Planet Travel Survival* and *Language Survival* books. This will make it easier for you if you are moving between this book and one of the *Lonely Planet* series. Other guide-books and language books use other tone-markings, but since the *Lonely Planet Survival* books are probably the most well-known and readily available both in Laos and abroad, I have decided to use their system of tone-markings.

Tones are relative to each person's voice range, so a high tone is said at the highest part of your voice range which might be considerably different from someone else's high tone. There are five Lao tones:

- A high tone is said at the top of your voice range and is a flat or level sound (it neither rises or falls). It is marked – á.
- A high falling tone begins at or above your high tone and falls to about your mid-tone. It is marked – ê.
- A low tone is said at the bottom of your voice range and is a flat or level sound. It is marked – i̖.
- A low falling tone begins about the mid-range of your voice and falls to about your low tone. It is marked – ò.
- A rising tone is said as if you were asking a one-word question 'coffee?' It begins low and ends at a higher pitch. It is marked – ũ.
- A mid or level tone is said in the middle of your voice range. There is no mark for it – e.

Numbers

1	*neing*	9	*gâow*	17	*síp-jét*	60	*hók-síp*
2	*sãwng*	10	*síp*	18	*síp-pàet*	70	*jét-síp*
3	*sãam*	11	*síp -ét*	19	*síp-gâow*	80	*pàet-síp*
4	*see*	12	*síp-sãwng*	20	*sáo*	90	*gâow-síp*
5	*hàa*	13	*síp-sãam*	21	*sáo-ét*	100	*hâwy*
6	*hók*	14	síp-see	30	*sãam-sìp*		
7	*jét*	15	*síp-hàa*	40	*see-síp*		
8	*pàet*	16	*síp-hók*	50	*hàa-síp*		

Days

Monday	*wán jạn*	Friday	*wán sóok*
Tuesday	*wán ạng-káan*	Saturday	*wán são*
Wednesday	*wán poot*	Sunday	*wán ạa-tit*
Thursday	*wán pa-hát*		

Months

January	*dẹuan mángkạwn*	July	*dẹuan kạwlakót*
February	*dẹuan kụmpháa*	August	*dẹuan s͠ĩnghãa*
March	*dẹuan mináa*	September	*dẹuan kạnyáa*
April	*dẹuan méhsãa*	October	*dẹuan tuláa*
May	*dẹuan pheut-sápháa*	November	*dẹuan phajík*
June	*dẹuan mithúnáa*	December	*dẹuan thánwáa*

Times and dates

Today	*mêu nêe*	Tomorrow	*mêu eun*
Tonight	*khéun nêe*	Next week	*ạathit nàa*
Yesterday	*mêu wáan nêe*	What time is it?	*Ják mõng?*

Greetings and small talk

Hello	*sábạidẹe*
Good-bye	*láa gawn*
How are you?	*sábạidẹe baw?*
I'm fine	*sábạo-dẹe*
Please	*gá loo ná*
Thank you	*khàwp jạ̀i*
No	*baw*
I can't speak Lao.	*Khàwy páak pháa-saa láo baw dâi*
I don't understand.	*Báw khòa jạ̀i*
Can you speak English?	*Jâo páak pháasaa ạngkít dâi baw?*
No	*Baw*
What's your name?	*Jâo seu nyang?*
My name is...	*Khàwy seu...*
Where do you come from?	*Jâo máa tae sai?*
I come from...	*Khàwy máa tae...*

Shopping

I'm looking for...	*Khàwy sàwk hãa...*
How much does it cost?	*Tao dại?*
Do you have any...?	*Mịi...baw*
Where is the...?	*...yoo sãi?*

Appendix 2. Public holidays

Fluctuating dates are marked with an asterisk *

1 January	New Year's Day
8 March	Women's Day (a holiday for women only)
14 – 16 April	Lao New Year
1 May	Labour Day
* Mid/end of October	End of Buddhist Lent
2 December	Liberation Anniversary

Appendix 3. Embassies and consulates

Selected Lao embassies abroad

Australia: 1 Dalman Crescent, Canberra, ACT 2606. Tel (06) 286 4595.

USA: Embassy of the Lao People's Democratic Republic, 2222 South Street, NW, Washington DC, 20008. Tel: (202) 332 6146.

Selected embassies in Laos

Australia: Thanon Siphanthong, Nua Area. Tel: 314 952. Fax: 312 584.

USA: That Dam Area. Tel: 212 580, 312 609. Fax: 212 584.

Appendix 4. Suggested reading

Cummings, Joe, *Lonely Planet Travel Survival Kit: Laos*, Lonely Planet, South Yarra, Australia, 1994.

Cummings, Joe, *Lonely Planet Language Survival Kit: Lao Phrasebook*, Lonely Planet, South Yarra, Australia, 1995.

Evans, Grant and Kelvin Rowley, *Red Brotherhood at War, Vietnam, Cambodia and Laos since 1975*, Verso, 1990.

Laos, Footprint Handbooks, Bath, UK/NTC, Chicago, 1997.

Manich Jumsai, M L, *A New History of Laos,* Chalermnit Books, Bangkok, 1971.

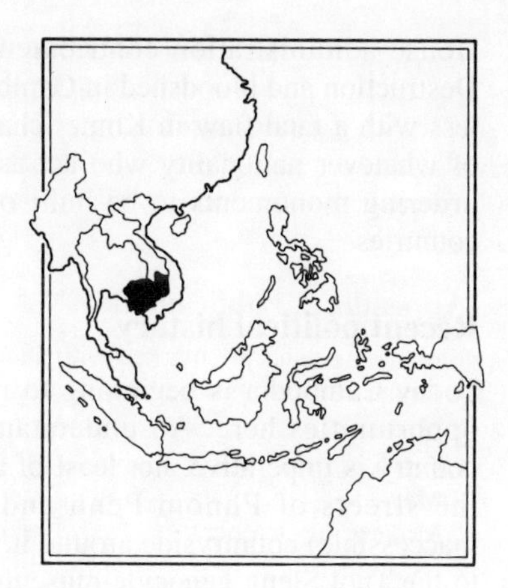

6

Cambodia

FACTFILE

In the last 20 years Cambodia has been called the Khmer Republic, Democratic Kampuchea, the People's Republic of Kampuchea and the State of Cambodia. Most Cambodians today refer to their country as Kampuchea.

History

Cambodia today is what is left of the widely influential Khmer Empire which ruled Thailand, Vietnam, and Laos during the Angkorian period (9th to 14th centuries). By the 18th century, the Khmers' power had declined to the point that its neighbours, Thailand and Vietnam, were vying for political control of the country. It was dominated by its neighbours until it became a French protectorate in 1864.

One way of interpreting Cambodia is to contrast the magnificence of the temples of Angkor – now regrettably marred by time and neglect, but still testimony to the cultural richness of the Khmers – with the self-immolation of the Killing Fields and the suffering called up by the word, 'Kampuchea'. A Khmer legend links the two images. Khmers say that so many workers died to build Angkor Wat that their blood has soaked through the soil of the country and curses it to this day. Since the Angkor complex was ordered to be built by Khmer god-kings of the time who meant to link their own personality cults with those of deities in Hindu cosmology (Shiva, then Vishnu), and later with the Mahayana Buddhist enlightened being, Avalokitesvara, Angkor may actually lend itself to concepts of hubris and tragedy. What many Cambodians might not realize is the role the USA played in fulfilling this 'curse'. Perhaps the 'Curse of Angkor' interpretation would break down if Cambodians knew how an amoral White

House administration contributed to the rise of the Khmer Rouge. Destruction and bloodshed in Cambodia might then appear to be linked less with a fatal flaw in Khmer character and society than with people of whatever nationality who act as if they were 'god-kings', whether ordering monuments to be built or bombs to be dropped on neutral countries.

Recent political history

Today Cambodia is beginning to revive and there are some teaching opportunities here. An understanding of the recent history of the country is imperative, not least of all because the past is so present in the streets of Phnom Penh and the land-mined (and currently inaccessible) countryside around it. *Cyclo* drivers will offer to take you to the Tuol Sleng genocide museum, where for a contribution you can walk around the high school that the Khmer Rouge turned into a torture and detention centre. Over 17 000 people – the nation's best and brightest, or simply the unlucky myopic who wore spectacles that made them look like intellectuals – were tortured here. The survivors were sent out to Choeung Ek, the Killing Fields, to receive the blow to the skull that killed them and saved a bullet for the Khmer Rouge. At Tuol Sleng there are no velvet ropes or glass cases between you and the torture instruments, between you and the photographs (pre- and post-torture) of the victims, or between you and the guides. (Lundi, one of the guides at the Tuol Sleng museum, believes his brothers were killed in the place where he works; he would have liked to have been a doctor rather than a guide, but corruption at the university made the cost too high for him.) At Choeung Ek, some of the mass graves have been exhumed, but you still see bones sticking up out of the ground. Cambodia is filled with killing fields, but that's not the whole story. Phnom Penh is a charming, if understandably highly-strung city.

In this timeline below I have followed William Shawcross's invaluable book *Sideshow: Kissinger, Nixon, and the Destruction of Cambodia*, in noting how American involvement in the region contributed to Cambodia's political woes. According to Shawcross, Cambodia was a quiet, neutral country before Kissinger and the Nixon administration began to treat it as an extension of the American war in Vietnam. The combination of massive bombing, actual invasion, and corruption-inducing economic and military 'aid' directly contributed to the destruction of Cambodia, and to the rise of the Khmer Rouge.

1864 France imposes a protectorate over the kingdom of Cambodia (*le Royaume du Cambodge*).

1941 The Japanese occupy much of South-east Asia and allow the Vichy French nominal control of Cambodia. Prince Norodom Sihanouk is crowned king of Cambodia.

1945 The Japanese take full control from the French and declare the colonialist period over. They order Sihanouk as well as the emperor of Vietnam and the King of Laos to declare independence for their countries. When the war ends, the French take control again.

1953 Sihanouk gains Cambodia's independence from France.

1954 Cambodian neutrality is recognized by the Geneva Conference on Indochina.

1955 Sihanouk abdicates the throne to his father in order to stand for election. He claims he want to get rid of the 'whole hierarchy of court mandarins amongst whom slide the intriguers, like bloodsucking leeches that fasten to the feet of elephants.' He wins a sweeping victory.

1963 Sihanouk renounces the US economic and military aid that he has been accepting since 1955, partly because he suspects that Hanoi will win the growing war in South Vietnam.

1965 On 28 February the USA announces 'continuous limited airstrikes' against North Vietnam. On 8 March US Marines land in Danang, South Vietnam. On 3 May Cambodia breaks diplomatic relations with the USA.

1966–67 Sihanouk tolerates Vietnamese communist use of Cambodian border areas. The USA begins carrying out a series of illegal, small raids across the border, code-named 'Daniel Boone'. Cambodia protests these incursions into a neutral country.

1967 Sihanouk's military savagely represses a peasant revolt in Battambang. Disgruntled left-wingers leave Phnom Penh, and Sihanouk names this small insurgent movement, '*les Khmers Rouges*'. They claim to number about 4 000, but the true figure is probably closer to a few hundred. They are capable only of isolated provincial assassinations and enjoy little support from country-people.

1968 Nixon is elected as president of the USA; Vietnamese Tet offensive.

1969 Nixon approves Operation Breakfast, a series of secret B-52 bombing attacks on Vietnamese communist 'sanctuaries' inside Cambodia. Sihanouk tolerates the bombings in hopes of avoiding a full-scale invasion.

March 1970 Sihanouk is overthrown in a coup by Prime Minister, General Lon Nol. The USA immediately recognizes the Lon Nol government. From Peking, Sihanouk announces that he has formed an alliance with his former enemies, the Khmer Rouge, called the National United Front of Kampuchea. China and North Vietnam recognize his government in exile. On 20 April Nixon announces the withdrawal of 150 000 US troops from Vietnam; ten days later he announces the invasion of Cambodia by US and South Vietnamese troops to attack communist bases in Cambodia. On 29 June US ground troops withdraw from Cambodia, having pushed the communists further west into the heart of Cambodia and destroyed and looted countless towns. The Khmer Rouge have now been armed by Hanoi and are enjoying some peasant support because of effective anti-American propaganda and their association with Sihanouk.

1971 A US Senate committee reports that more than 2 million of the 7 million Cambodians have been made homeless by the war and that 20% of property has been destroyed. US bombing continues. US economic aid, on which Lon Nol has become almost completely dependent, wrecks the economy and inflation soars in Phnom Penh.

1973 The Paris agreement on ending the war in Vietnam is signed in January; in February, massive F-111 and B-52 bombing resumes after a one-month respite. In August, eight days after an off-target bomb from a B-52 slams into Neak Luong, a government-held town, US bombing of Cambodia finally ends. The USA pulls out of a country to which it supplied arms and economic aid that was swallowed up by the corrupt military, but denied requested medical supplies and humanitarian aid – which might have benefitted the Viet Cong, it was argued.

1974 The Khmer Rouge, supplied with arms by Hanoi, begin shelling Phnom Penh, killing 139 and leaving 10 000 homeless.

1975 Year Zero. On 17 April Phnom Penh falls to the Khmer Rouge; Lon Nol leaves for Hawaii. The Khmer Rouge begin emptying Phnom Penh in order to restructure society along agrarian, Maoist lines. The entire population left living will have to labour in the countryside for three years and eight months. The wounded and dying in the hospitals are the first to be marched out of the city. In September: Sihanouk returns after a five-year absence.

1976 Prince Sihanouk resigns as head of state; two days later, a new government of Democratic Kampuchea is announced. Khieu Samphan is head of state, Pol Pot Prime Minister.

1977 The Khmer Rouge launch attacks on Vietnamese villages. On 25 December Vietnam attacks Cambodia; subsequently Cambodia severs relations with Vietnam.

1978 In December, the Vietnamese invade Democratic Kampuchea.

1979 Phnom Penh falls to the Vietnamese on 7 January. The conquerors are greeted as saviours by those who have been toiling in the countryside for almost four years. The Khmer

Rouge has already killed about 2 million people, and is actually becoming more barbaric and paranoid. Hundreds of thousands of Cambodians have fled to the Thai border to be housed in refugee camps, where they will still be living in the 1990s. In fighting, the 1979 rice crop is destroyed and famine threatens. Heng Samrin, the Vietnamese-installed Prime Minister, appeals for assistance, warning that 2.5 million Cambodians face death by starvation.

1980 The Vietnamese, with Soviet Bloc help, try to build up Cambodia's infrastructure and distribute food aid; China, supported by Thailand, continues to arm the Khmer Rouge.

1980–89 During this period of Vietnamese occupation, all young men are conscripted to fight against the Khmer Rouge and the US backed royalist factions. Many young men flee the cities (for a second time) to avoid conscription and spend their youth in border camps, separated from their families

1989 The Vietnamese withdraw from Cambodia. Hun Sen becomes Prime Minister.

1990 The Khmer Rouge begin making military advances again when Soviet aid (80% of Cambodia's income) is withdrawn.

1991 The Paris Peace agreement is signed on 23 October 1991. Prince Sihanouk has been instrumental in bringing opposing groups, including the Khmer Rouge, together for negotiations in Thailand and Indonesia.

1993 The UN Security council is mandated to ensure the success of the peace accord and to oversee elections in 1993 through UNTAC (UN Transitional Authority in Cambodia). The Khmer Rouge refuse to participate in the election, and also refuse to demobilize. In May elections are held and FUNCINPEC (National United Front for an Independent Neutral Peaceful and Cooperative Cambodia), the Royalist party, win with 42% of the vote. The previous government's Cambodia People's Party receives 38%. The two parties subsequently form a coalition government with two Prime Ministers – Hun Sen, and Prince Ranaridh (one of Sihanouk's sons). Sihanouk is the titular head of state, and the Royal Kingdom of Cambodia is a constitutional monarchy.

1994 The National assembly outlaws the Khmer Rouge.

Geography

Cambodia is a small country (about the size of England and Wales) of 181 035 square kilometres, or about 69 890 square miles. Along with Vietnam and Laos, it makes up what the French dubbed Indochina. Cambodia is bordered by Laos to the north; by the South China Sea to

The Khmer Rouge today

In his book *Distant Voices* (Vintage Books, 1994) John Pilger reports on the role of the Khmer Rouge in Cambodia today. Actually, the UN prefers not to call them the Khmer Rouge, since that name collocates with genocide. However, the UN seem to be alone in referring to the Khmer Rouge as NADK – the National Army of Democratic Kampuchea. The Khmer Rouge had a modern office building in Phnom Penh behind the Grand Palace until 1994 when it was closed down after they refused to go to 'roundtable' talks in Korea. At the time of writing it controlled about 50% of the countryside including areas that generate wealth through sales of timber, rice, and gems via safe supply lines to Thailand. According to the *New York Times*, the secret alliance of the Khmer Rouge and the Thai military has benefited both to the tune of US$500 million a year in timber and gems sales.

Craig Etcheson (*Phnom Penh Post*, 13-26 August 1993) writes: 'Pol Pot is better positioned today than at any time since 1979. The Vietnamese are gone. The 'puppet regime' [Heng Samrin's] is defeated, replaced by an unstable conglomeration. Pol Pot still has highly placed friends in China and Thailand. He is wealthy. He has hugely expanded his territory and population. He has deeply infiltrated the opposing parties, and once again he has both overt and covert operatives in Phnom Penh. And he has convinced most of the world that the Khmer Rouge threat is no more.'

If the Khmer Rouge actually are a major threat today, that is partly thanks to US funding, which began secretly in January, 1980. The US provided them with $85 million from 1980 to 1986 (Pilger, p 409) as part of a Cold War policy of appeasing China and trying to damage Vietnam. Through the Thai army, US and UN food aid and American weapons have been supplied to the Khmer Rouge. The British Special Air Services (SAS) actually trained Cambodian guerrillas allied to Pol Pot at secret bases in Thailand, Malaysia, and Singapore for more than four years. The guerrillas were trained in sabotage: how to attack bridges, railway lines, and power lines, how to lay mines and set booby traps.

On the other hand, in 1994 the Royal Cambodian Armed Forces implemented an amnesty to encourage Khmer Rouge defections. Although no figures are available, in Cambodia it is believed to have been, and continues to be, a very successful policy.

The most significant defection came in September 1996 when Ieng Sary, former Foreign Minister of the Khmer Rouge government and long-time associate of Pol Pot, defected to the government forces. Although Ieng Sary had been sentenced to death *in absentia* by a Cambodian court, Sihanouk has granted him a royal pardon. Ieng Sary claims he knew nothing of the killings, although Cambodia expert Stephen Heder argues that this is 'totally implausible' (*Far Eastern Economic Review*, 26 September 1996).

the south; by Thailand to the west; and by Vietnam to the east. The Mekong River, which rises in Tibet, flows into Cambodia from Laos, flowing through the eastern part of the country before entering Vietnam and the South China Sea. The annual flooding of the Mekong enriches the farmland around it.

In the middle of the country are plains and the Tonle Sap, or Great Lake. During the dry season water from the lake drains into the Tonle Sap River, which joins the Mekong at Phnom Penh. Strangely, when rainy season water and run-off from melting Himalayan snows make the level of the Mekong rise enough (mid-May to October) the Tonle Sap is forced to begin flowing backwards, up to the Great Lake again, often flooding the plains. Then, in the dry season, usually around the middle of October, the river reverses its current again and flows into the Mekong. (Colourful boat races are held in Phnom Penh to celebrate the reversal.)

There is a highland region in the southwest of the country formed by the Cardamom and the Elephant Mountains.

Climate

Cambodia has two monsoons. The one from November to March is a dry, north-eastern monsoon, and the other, from May to October, is a south-western monsoon . The May monsoon brings both strong winds and heavy rains. The wettest months are August and September. In the rainy season, rains usually come in the afternoons and in the form of showers, not a constant downpour. The hottest month is April, with highs around 35°C. January is the coolest month with lows in the 20s, making it quite chilly, for South-east Asia.

Time

Cambodia, like Laos, Vietnam and Thailand, is 7 hours ahead of GMT, 12 hours ahead of New York, 15 hours ahead of San Francisco, 3 hours behind Sydney and 5 hours behind Wellington.

The people

Before 1975, Cambodia had a population of more than 7 million. Over the next four years, this figure dropped to less than 6 million. This drop in population during Pol Pot's reign was the result of starvation, torture, execution and the many people who fled Cambodia. Ben Kiernan estimates the 1975–79 toll to be 'at least 1.5 million' (see Suggested Reading). Today the population is thought to be about 10 million. More than 90% of the population are ethnic Khmer, while the rest are Chinese, Vietnamese, Cham (Khmer Islam), and indigenous hilltribes (Khmer Loeu).

Politics

After the UN-supervised elections in May 1993, the Royal Cambodian Government was formed as a coalition between the National United Front for an Independent, Neutral, Peaceful and Cooperative Cambodia (FUNCINPEC), the Cambodian People's Party (CPP) and the Buddhist Liberal Democratic Party (BLDP). A new constitution for Cambodia was drawn up and was adopted in September 1993. The new constitution provides for a constitutional monarchy with separation of powers among the executive, legislative and judicial branches of government.

Language

The official language of Cambodia is Khmer, which belongs to the Mon-Khmer family of languages. Khmer includes Pali, Sanskrit, Thai and French influences. Unlike other languages in nearby Laos, Thailand and Vietnam, Khmer is not tonal. Khmer has no tenses, however it does have 23 vowel sounds and 33 consonant sounds. Khmer is written from left to right, with no separations between words. You can study Khmer in Phnom Penh at:

The Cambodian Development Resource Institute, Toul Kork 315/56. Tel: (023) 68053/66094.

In any foreign country, showing willingness to learn the local language will make your stay so much easier and endear you to the local people, and Cambodia is no exception to this rule. Useful self-study books include:

Colloquial Cambodian by Daniel Smyth, Routledge, 1995.

Religions

Buddhism

The majority religion in Cambodia is Theravada Buddhism. During the Pol Pot reign Buddhists were persecuted, and no young men were allowed to become monks. Before 1975 there were an estimated 64 000 monks living in 3 000 monasteries. Under Pol Pot as many as 62 000 monks were executed or died working in the rice fields. In 1979 Buddhism was revived when a visiting delegation of monks from Vietnam ordained Cambodian monks and re-consecrated temples which had been defiled during the Khmer Rouge regime. In 1989 Buddhism was re-introduced as the national religion and young men were, once again, allowed to become monks. (Between 1979 and 1989 only men over 45 were allowed to become monks; the younger men were needed for the army.)

Islam

There are about 100 000 Cham-Muslims who are descendants of the Malays who settled in Champa (Vietnam) in the 15th century. The Chams settled in Kampot in Cambodia in the 1640s, and were mostly cattle traders, silk weavers and butchers (Buddhists are forbidden to slaughter animals).

During the Pol Pot regime the Muslims in Cambodia suffered greatly; the Nur ul-Ihsan Mosque was used as a pig-sty and hundreds of Muslims were killed. So far only 20 of the 113 mosques that were defiled or bombed during the Khmer Rouge time have been rebuilt and reconsecrated.

Christianity

There are about 80 000 Christians in Cambodia. The largest group, 60 000, is made up of mostly Vietnamese Catholics. In addition, there are some 20 000 Protestants.

Taoism/Confucianism

The Chinese population of Cambodia – about 100 000 – are almost all Taoist/Confucian.

Cultural considerations

Cambodia's isolation

A major cultural consideration is that Cambodia was cut off from Asia and from most of the rest of the world for 15 years. The only outside contact Cambodians had was through Soviet TV and radio. Nearly all Cambodians you will meet lost someone in their families during the Pol Pot era, and although most EFL teachers and volunteers say that Cambodians will readily talk about their recent tragic national and personal history, you should be sensitive about discussing this subject too quickly, or too often.

Greetings and terms of address

Cambodians greet each other in a similar way to the Thais – they *wai* each other (see pp 67-68).

There are four main terms of address which you should use in Cambodia. With people your own age and friends, use first names. With people who are older than you, use *Bong Srey* for women and *Bong* for men. Elderly people should be addressed as *Yeay* for women and *Ta* for men. And finally, officials and bureaucrats should be addressed as *Lok Srey* for women and *Lok* for men.

Teaching considerations

Most of Cambodia's school teachers, professors, and intellectuals were systematically exterminated by the Khmer Rouge. That whole generation of expertise was lost, and today the typical school teacher is a 19-year-old with rudimentary training addressing a class of up to 60. An English class in English Street is similar, plus megaphone, with each student paying 500 riel to attend. Keep in mind when teaching English that Cambodians may lack basic skills in their own language, particularly critical thinking and questioning skills. This situation will certainly require from you patience, and perhaps deep thinking about course-content. On the other hand, if you are becoming demoralized, tell yourself that an EFL teacher cannot be expected to right the wrongs of decades. Do the best you can – don't be afraid to abandon inappropriate or demotivating material – but remember that showing your kindness and respect for the individual students in front of you may do more for them than teaching about prose style ever could. Chapter 2 contains 20 tips to relax your students (see pp 53-55) which are particularly relevant here, since getting Cambodians – especially female students – to speak aloud in class can be a real challenge, even for experienced teachers.

Punctuality

Punctuality is not a highly-valued trait in Cambodian society, so you can expect this to be reflected in your students. If you are teaching in a private language school, your students may be better off, but if you are working for an Non-Governmental Organization (NGO) or with poorer students, you can expect low or irregular attendance since many adults need to have more than one job to make ends meet.

Low motivation

If you are doing teacher-training, poor motivation on the part of your trainees can usually be taken for granted, at least initially, partly because they are so poorly paid. Although teachers in Khmer society are generally highly respected, the poor living standard of Khmer teachers is well-known, and they may not get much respect from better-off pupils. This lack of respect will almost certainly not affect you, as a foreign teacher, but it is probably a source of friction for your trainees or Khmer teaching colleagues.

In general, Cambodian governmental organizations are run inefficiently, and show reluctance to initiate change. If you come up against this, keep in mind, again, that a generation of expertise has been lost, and that 'corruption' is often subsumed for poorly-paid bureaucrats under 'survival'.

TEACHING POSSIBILITIES

There are three major teaching possibilities in Cambodia: working for a non-governmental organization (NGO), working for an EFL school, or working for an international school with an ESL or EFL programme. There is a street called English Street, but don't be misled by the name into thinking you could find work there on arrival. At the moment, the teaching is done by Khmer teachers, and the pay (maximum of $4/hour for early morning and evening classes) would not be enough to survive on considering the cost of accommodation in Phnom Penh.

Non-governmental organizations

Most of the volunteer aid organizations working in Cambodia recruit volunteers in their home countries after rigorous interviews and screenings. Some of the major aid organizations and language schools are listed below. Obviously, working as a volunteer entails a different lifestyle from paid EFL work. See an APSO (Irish aid recruiting organization) volunteer's case study on p 133 to get an idea of what working for an NGO is like.

The two major volunteer TEFL organizations working in Cambodia at present are VSO (UK and Canada) and APSO (Ireland). For further information about these two organizations, see Chapter 2: Volunteer recruitment organizations.

Private language schools

Some private language schools in Phnom Penh:

Australian Centre for Education (ACE), #4-6, 75 Street. Tel: 018 810 443, 018 810 474. Fax: (023) 426 608

The Banana Centre, #7, 9 Street, Kapkor Market. Tel: (023) 60 394, 60 517.

Cambodian-British Centre, PO Box 922. Tel: (023) 27 541. Fax: (023) 27 541.

International schools

International schools in Phnom Penh are:

The American School, #24, 184 Street. Tel: (023) 60 148. Fax: (023) 60 148.

The International School of Phnom Penh, 158 Norodom Blvd. Tel: (023) 60 041. Fax: (023) 60 041/26 209.

British International School, #213, 51 Street (Vithei Pasteur). Tel: (023) 62 781.

Children's Garden Pre-School, #11A, 29 Street.

London Montessori Center (Cambodia), #219, 51 Street (Vithei Pasteur). Tel: (023) 64 243.

BEFORE YOU GO

Insurance

If you are going to a pre-arranged job or are working with a volunteer organization, medical insurance will be provided for you. If you are not, take out a health insurance policy, as health care in Cambodia is very basic, and if you become seriously ill you will probably have to go to Thailand or Singapore for expensive medical treatment.

Vaccinations

The only official health requirement for Cambodia is to be vaccinated against cholera if you are coming from an infected area. However, most doctors in your home country would advise, at a minimum, that you have tetanus, measles and polio boosters, and are vaccinated against Japanese encephalitis. For further information about health precautions both before and after you arrive here see Chapter 1: Health.

ARRIVAL AND VISAS

Visas

You should check in your home country to find out if there is a Cambodian embassy there yet. At the moment no Western country has Cambodian representation, so if you want a visa in advance, you will have to apply through the Cambodian embassy in Bangkok, Ho Chi Minh City or Hanoi.

Tourist visas

At present there are no visa requirements for a stay of up to one month in Cambodia. You can get a visa at Phnom Penh's Pochentong airport on arrival. You need to fill in the application form in the arrivals hall, have one passport photo (but take more just in case), and pay US$20 for a visa which is valid for one month.

Visa extensions

You can extend your visa while you are in Cambodia at the Immigration Office on Thonsamat Road (near the Japanese embassy).

It usually takes one day to process and costs: US$10 for a one week extension, US$40 for a one month extension and US$100 for a six month extension.

Work permit

It is possible to obtain a work permit, but it is a slow process. If you are employed by a legitimate school, or a volunteer organization, they will process your work permit for you.

Transport from the airport

Phnom Penh's Pochentong international airport is about seven kilometres from the centre of Phnom Penh. There are unmetered taxis (ie ordinary cars) at the airport, and the trip into Phnom Penh costs US$5 or less – you should negotiate the price before you begin your journey.

ACCOMMODATION

Short-term accommodation

Phnom Penh has a limited amount of short-term accommodation, compared to most other cities in South-east Asia. Since the UNTAC forces left, however, there have generally been more rooms available and at slightly lower prices. Some popular budget hotels in Phnom Penh (US$5–10) include:

Bert's Books and Guesthouse, 79 Sisowath Quay. Tel: (023) 015 916 411.
Capitol, Streets 182 and 107.
Happy Guesthouse (near the Capitol).
Seng Sokhom's Guesthouse, Street 111.

Long-term accommodation

Most teachers pay between US$300 and US$400 a month for rent. You can find accommodation by looking for ads posted in many of the bars listed below, checking the English-language newspapers which carry ads for accommodation, or by signing on with an accommodation agency. Other teachers or foreigners are also a good source for telling you about houses for rent, or popular areas for teachers to live in. You can also see signs posted outside houses for rent, which are often written in English if the owner is interested in renting to foreigners.

Most teachers live in a house which is attached to the owner's house, usually with a separate entrance, but with a shared garden. Most owners expect a three-month deposit and will give you a contract for six months or a year.

Electricity, gas and water

Electricity. Electricity in Cambodia is 220 volts. Black-outs are frequent, so you should have a ready supply of candles or a torch, and find out if your house has a private generator. City electricity costs about $30 a month and a generator will cost you a further $20–25 a month if you use it three or four nights a week.

Gas. Gas, used for cooking, comes in a large canister. A canister usually lasts about three months, and costs $10 to replace.

Water. Tap water is not safe to drink. You can either boil tap water for 5–10 minutes or buy large, refillable bottles of water.

Household help

Most teachers and volunteers have some kind of household help. Usually you can arrange for a Khmer woman to come to your house to do washing and ironing and household cleaning. How much you pay for household help depends on the number of days she comes to your house, the size of your house, the amount of work you want her to do, how much you earn, and your bargaining powers. Most teachers pay between $30 and $40 a month, while expats usually pay between $60 and $100 a month.

LIVING COSTS

How expensive is Cambodia?

At the moment Cambodia is one of the cheapest countries in South-east Asia if you are a good bargainer and are paying in riel. Because UN troops and personnel were here recently, almost any imported good you can think of is still available, but imported goods are priced in US dollars and are considerably more expensive than in the USA. The cost of living can be fairly high, and the minimum for monthly rent is about $350, although if you are a volunteer, this will be paid for you.

Salaries

Teachers' salaries vary enormously, depending on whether you are living on a volunteer allowance, working for a private language school or working for an international school. A British VSO volunteer is given a living allowance of about US$280 per month, an Irish APSO volunteer is given about US$400 a month and a United Nations volunteer is given US$1 500 a month. If you are working for a private EFL school you can earn US$8–16 per hour, while The International School of Phnom Penh pays a minimum of $1 300 a month. All these living allowances or salaries will go a lot further in Cambodia than they would in the USA or the UK, although as pointed out before, rent and imported goods tend to be more expensive.

Taxes

Income tax. Income tax has been threatened, but at the time of writing has not been instituted, although if you are teaching as a volunteer you will not have to pay tax, even if it is introduced.

Departure tax. Departure tax is US$15 for international flights and US$5 for internal flights.

Supermarket costs

There are a number of supermarkets carrying Western products in Phnom Penh. Two of the popular ones with teachers are:

Seven Seven Supermarket, #13, Street 90. Tel: 60077
Lucky Supermarket, #160 Sihanouk Boulevard.

Below is a list of some supermarket costs, but you should bear in mind that costs in the market and in small, local shops are much lower than in supermarkets. However, many of the goods listed below, because they are imported, are available only in supermarkets.

Bread (small, white loaf)	0.80	Rice (1 kg)	0.70
Beef (1 kg)	8.60	Tea (50 tea-bags)	2.30
Milk (1 litre)	2.50	Instant coffee (200 g)	5.00
Sugar (1 kg)	0.80	Beer (can, 330 ml)	0.80
Eggs (10)	1.10	Cigarettes (20 Marlboro)	0.90

Tipping

Tipping is not necessary in Cambodia, but considering that local salaries can be as low as US$10 a month, you might want to leave a tip to share some of your wealth around.

EATING

Khmer food is very similar to Thai and Lao food, and there is also a strong influence from Vietnam and China. Rice is the mainstay of any

Khmer meal. Most Cambodian meals consist of soup, rice, meat or fish, and vegetables. All dishes are served together, rather than as separate courses.

Traditional ingredients

Traditional Khmer ingredients include: garlic, cucumber, bamboo shoots, baby sweet-corn, small, sweet peas in the pod and various leafy spinach-like greens. Common herbs and spices and flavourings are coriander root and leaves, lemon grass, kaffir lime leaves, fish sauce, fish sauce, shrimp paste, tamarind, soy sauce, ground peanuts, ginger, coconut milk.

Khmer specialties

Some of the most popular dishes include: *Samlo machou bangkang* (a prawn soup with ginger, lemon grass, and chillies which is similar to Thai *tom yam kung*); *Samla machou banle* (fish soup, with a sour, hot taste, similar to Thai soup); *Trey Aing* (grilled fish, usually wrapped in spinach or lettuce leaves and dipped in a fish sauce and ground peanuts); and *Khao phoun*e (noodles in coconut milk).

Restaurants

There are lots of road-side stalls, and small Khmer restaurants in Phnom Penh where you can eat really cheaply. There are also increasing numbers of foreign restaurants moderately to expensively priced. Some Phnom Penh restaurants which are popular with teachers and volunteers are:

Apsara Khmer Restaurant, 363 Sisowath Quay (next to The Foreign Correspondents' Club). Tel: (023) 427 757. Fax: (023) 427 758.

The Foreign Correspondents' Club (FCC), 3rd Floor, 363 Sisowath Quay

Happy Herb Bistro, 345 Sisowath Quay. Tel: (023) 62349.

Cactus, 94 Norodom Sihanouk Blvd.

TRANSPORT

Transport and travel in Cambodia

At the time of writing, travel in Cambodia, apart from in Phnom Penh and the carefully protected tourist area of Siem Reap and Angkor Wat, was not advisable. Even overland or boat travel to Angkor is not always possible; you may have to fly. (You can, however, make the overland journey to Vietnam safely on Highway One.) Certain south-western beaches are accessible if you travel in a convoy, but you should seek local advice before going outside Phnom Penh. If you are advised locally that a trip is feasible, be sure to let someone know when and where you are going; stick to the main roads, though these are not necessarily safe; travel between 0700 and 1500 hours; and bring a supply of cigarettes and 100 Riel notes to smooth your way with drunk/obstructive soldiers at checkpoints. It is not always clear if they are bandits or officials. Be polite and friendly. If it comes to giving money to someone with a machine gun, remember all you have to live for and hand your cash over with a smile.

Within Phnom Penh you should also take care, particularly if you are out and about after dark. Occasionally, foreigners are the targets of gun-point robberies, and between May and July 1996 almost 100 foreigners were robbed at gun-point, according to a report in the Bangkok newspaper *The Nation*. One of them was Áine Doody (see pp 133).

Motos, cyclos, cars and taxis

Foreigners, for their own safety, are not allowed to use public transport, so your choices for transport are basically motorcycle taxis *(motos); cyclos,* the ubiquitous Asian *rickshaw;* and cars hired for the day (about $25 including driver), although taxis for individual trips can be obtained at large markets and international hotels. Taxis do not cruise the streets, you have to go looking for them. A shortish *moto* or *cyclo* ride in Phnom Penh is about 500-1000 riel; a longer one 1 500-2 000, and you should bargain and agree a price before you start a journey. *Moto* drivers are more likely to be able to find addresses, but you might want to bear in mind that Volunteer Services Overseas (VSO) discourages its volunteers from using *motos,* and requires that volunteers wear a helmet (on pain of being sent home, if caught without one). If you are planning to stay in Cambodia for a while and intend to use motorcycles, bring your own helmet as the locally-made ones are not very safe.

SERVICES

Libraries

There are three libraries in Phnom Penh.

The National Library, 92 Street, is open from 8am to 11am and from 2pm to 5pm. It is used mainly by Khmer students, but there is a small section of English books available for borrowing.

The American Embassy has a reading room with information on law, economics and university studies in the USA.

The French Cultural Centre has a reading room with French material, which can be borrowed once you register with the Alliance Française.

Bookshops

There are a few bookshops in Phnom Penh which stock English language books, as well as teaching books. Two well-known shops are:

Bookazine, 228 Monivong Blvd
International Stationery and Book Centre, 435 Monivong Blvd.

There is also a second-hand bookshop which has a stall with books for sale at supermarkets and at the Ettamogah Pub, as well as at:

Bert's Books, 79 Sisowath Quay. Tel: 023 916 411.

Banks and financial matters

The official currency of Cambodia is the riel. There are notes of 50, 100, 200, and 500. There's a parallel economy using US dollars. A lot of restaurants and bars post prices in dollars, but you can pay in riel if you ask to, and in any case, some of your change is likely to be in riel, because US coins are not used. Thai baht are also readily changed.

Banks are open Monday to Friday 7.30am to 10.30am, and 2.00pm to 4.00pm. Some banks are open on Saturdays 7.30am to 10.30am.

Health

Cambodia is one of the worst countries in South-east Asia in terms of health and health-care facilities. During the Pol Pot regime, most health-care services were totally destroyed and Western medical aid, including Red Cross distribution of medicines, was denied for the specious reason that the drugs might benefit the Khmer Rouge. Today, there are few hospitals or doctors in Cambodia, and medicine is still in short supply, although most Western drugs are now available over-the-counter – including some that are banned and unsafe, so be wary of self-medication. See Chapter 1 for health advice on vaccinations before arriving in Cambodia and for precautions you should take while living in Cambodia.

One other major health consideration that you just don't have to think about in most other countries is the land-mine. Some NGOs, including the UK-based Halo Trust, are involved in mine-clearing, but it has been estimated that between 1990 and 1994, of the 3 000 000 land mines in the country, only 6 000 had been safely removed. In Phnom Penh there is no danger, but if you are outside the capital you should be very careful. Keep to well-worn paths, and if possible, you should go with a guide or a local person who knows the area if you are walking in the countryside. If you come across anything suspicious in the ground, DO NOT GO NEAR IT AND DO NOT TOUCH IT! Keep in mind that one of the biggest threats posed by mines is that, during the rainy season especially, the mines shift and a previously-cleared area can become deadly again.

An Australian Red Cross doctor has said that the one-legged man is Cambodia's most obvious national characteristic. One in every 236 people in Cambodia is an amputee, compared with one in 22 000 in the USA.

The importance of comprehensive medical insurance, including medical evacuation insurance, cannot be stressed enough. Most foreigners who become ill in Cambodia go to nearby Thailand or Singapore for surgery or major medical procedures. The hospital and medical centres listed below offer a reasonable level of care for well-known illnesses. They are able to test accurately for typhoid, dengue fever, and about six common illnesses. But if you are persistently ill and your problem cannot be identified locally, you should not hesitate to seek treatment outside Cambodia, and you should seek that treatment sooner rather than later. Just recently an EFL teacher in Phnom Penh died of complications related to poorly-treated hepatitis. Although he had evacuation insurance, doctors refused to airlift him out because his liver had shut down. When he was eventually airlifted out, he haemorrhaged on the plane and died a few days later in Singapore. There are some countries in South-east Asia where you do not need much insurance or can even squeak by without it. Cambodia is not one of them. Of the clinics and hospitals listed below, both SOS International Medical Centre and Mission Aviation Fellowship offer emergency medical evacuation to Bangkok.

Australian Medical Unit, Corner of 57 and 334 Streets. Tel: 018 810 151/27 877.

Calmette Hospital (Khmer-Soviet Hospital), North Monivong Blvd.

Mission Aviation Fellowship (MAF), #14, 392 Street. Tel: (023) 62 148/ 018 810 470.

Polyclinic Aurora, #58/60, 113 Street. Tel: 60 152.

SOS International Medical Centre, 83 Issarak Blvd. Tel: 912 765.

UN Dispensary, #24, 334 Street. Tel: 018 811 287.

RECREATION

Bars

Since UNTAC packed their bags, Phnom Penh night-life has become more Cambodian orientated. Most pubs have music – usually live Filipino or Cambodian bands, recorded pop, or MTV. Bars and pubs which are popular with teachers and other foreigners include:

The Foreign Correspondents' Club (FCC), 3rd Floor, 363 Sisowath Quay. Fabulous view of the river and its night-life. Films on Sunday nights ($3, non-members)and debates/talks on topical issues on Wednesdays.

Heart of Darkness (a bit difficult to find, so ask someone). It's on Street 51 near the junction with Street 178. Tiny, dark, deeply cool. Pool table, good music. Good place to meet NGO workers or backpackers.

Ettamogah Pub, also called Mannie's. Next door to Lucky Supermarket on Sihanouk Boulevard. An Australian pub; good place to shoot the breeze and drink VB; has satellite TV and sometimes local bands.

Irish Rover, 87 Sihanouk Boulevard. Lovely, friendly Irish pub with a mural of verdant hills on the walls. There is sometimes a sing-along in the evenings.

Films

The Centre Culturelle Française on 184th Street shows French films subtitled in English, and also hosts cultural events, French classes, etc.

The Foreign Correspondents' Club (see above) has English language films on Sunday and Tuesday evenings.

Sports

The International Youth Club (51/96 Streets) has a swimming pool, tennis courts, and a gym. All facilities are available for US$10 a day.

The National Sports Complex (at the junction of Sivutha and Achar Hemcheay Blvds) has a pool, volleyball, gymnastics and boxing facilities.

Some of the larger hotels have swimming pools which you can use, for a small fee, even if you are not a guest there.

Help-lines

Police Liaison for Expatriates		22467 081 811 542
Fire Department:		
	Tuol Sleng	23555
	Sorya	22555

APPENDICES

Appendix 1. Two case histories

Áine Doody

Áine Doody was born in County Claire, Ireland. She studied for a BA at the University of Limerick, where her course in European Studies incorporated a TEFL component. She has also recently received an MSc in politics from the School of Oriental and African Studies in London. Before going to Cambodia as a volunteer, she worked as an EFL teacher in Oman, London and Japan.

She chose volunteering because of her interest in aid and development work, and because, after a number of years in the private sector, she had grown a little disillusioned with private language schools.

Áine is a volunteer with APSO – the Agency for Personal Services Overseas (see Chapter 2: Volunteer recruitment organizations), which is the recruiting agency for United Nations Volunteers in Ireland. She works in the Ministry of Social Affairs and teaches English to the civil servants there. 'The department is highly overstaffed, so the civil servants love learning English – having something to do in their working day is exciting for them. The classes are free and for many of them English is seen as some kind of salvation – a chance to get a real job where their skills will be used, and they will earn enough pay so that they won't have to do an evening job as well.'

Although in the rainy season water pours down her classroom walls, and drips onto her and the students, Áine says that she's very lucky compared to most other volunteer teachers in Cambodia. 'With 30 royal blue metal chairs, a whiteboard, two fans, books and a tape recorder, I'm one of the best supplied teachers I know.'

Compared to working in Japan, Áine said the main difference is that she is much more focused on the students' needs. 'English isn't some sort of hobby here.' she said. 'It's so much more rewarding teaching people who wouldn't normally be able to afford English lessons and who really want to learn. I feel I'm equipping people with a real skill that they can use as their route out of poverty.'

Áine is asthmatic. Ventolin is readily available in Phnom Penh, but Becotide has to be ordered from Bangkok and is very expensive. However, her asthma has cleared up since she came to Cambodia, which she says isn't that unusual, in such a dry climate.

Despite the material hardships, and the emotional difficulties of living in a country with so many amputees and beggars, Áine still loves living in Cambodia; she insists 'The only things I really miss from home are fish fingers!' Áine loves the Khmer attitude to time. She said 'I've forgotten the meaning of the word 'punctuality' – one of the wonderful things about living and working in Cambodia is that no two clocks *ever* tell the same time!'

Conor Boyle

Conor Boyle was born in Guisborough, England, but his family moved back to their native Northern Ireland shortly after he was born. He lived there until he was seven when his family emigrated to Canada. At university he studied history and psychology. He first went to Cambodia as a traveller in 1994 and after returning to Canada to complete a work contract, decided to go back to Phnom Penh in July of the same year. He found some part-time work with the Australian Centre for Education (ACE), the most reputable and longest established private educational institution in Cambodia. After a short time there he realized that teaching was what he wanted to do. 'I was in the right place at the right time. Cambodia was beginning to really take off, the people were excited about the future and the opportunities for "skilled" foreigners were tremendous.' He was given the job of Logistical Co-ordinator and after a year was made Academic Administrator, a position he still holds. 'Basically, from an administrative point of view, I'm in charge of supervising all programmes at the school. I hire new staff and counsel students with their particular educational needs, as well as dealing with the day to day running of the school. I also teach about 15 hours a week.' The school's teaching programmes include General English, English for Special Purposes for government ministry workers, and private Business English classes at company offices in the city.

In June 1996 Conor passed the RSA/UCLES CTEFLA course which he completed at ECC (Thailand) in Bangkok.

As far as other teaching opportunities go Conor said that there are new schools opening all the time, and the demand for qualified teachers is on the increase: 'Teaching in Cambodia has been incredibly interesting. The students all have chunks of their educational background missing as a result of the tragic political situations of the 1970s and 1980s. They know little of the outside world; many have never heard of McDonalds – which is wonderful as far as I'm concerned. They are, however, very keen to learn, they look upon teachers with great respect and they are generally a real pleasure to teach.'

Conor finds Phnom Penh a beautiful, small, slow-paced city. 'In many ways the people, city and country are like a phoenix rising from the ashes and rubble of over 20 years of war and instability. It is very exciting to witness this, as well as perhaps playing a small role in the re-development of Cambodia.' There are, however, a few drawbacks. 'People are extremely poor although they appear to be genuinely content. It takes quite a lot of time as an outsider from the "first" world to come to terms with and to feel comfortable with this overwhelming poverty. Also, unfortunately, as in any fledgling capitalist country, the everyday realities of robbery and violence have set in. But overall this is still a magical and fascinating land to live in.'

Conor said that about every six months he says he'll stay just for six more months. 'But since I've been saying that for over two years, you'd have to take it with a pinch of salt, and also understand that once you've been to Phnom Penh you can be spoiled for life.'

Appendix 2. Useful Khmer words and phrases

As noted above, Khmer is not a tonal language, however it does have many more sounds than English. For example, Khmer has a sound somewhere between the English /b/ and /p/, as well as a sound somewhere between /d/ and /t/. The transcription given below can, therefore, only give an approximation of how the words sound in Khmer.

Numbers

1	*mouy*	11	*doup-mouy*	21	*maphei-mouy*
2	*pee*	12	*doup-pee*	30	*samsup*
3	*bei*	13	*doup-bei*	40	*siisup*
4	*boun*	14	*doup-boun*	50	*hasup*
5	*bram*	15	*doup-bram*	60	*hoksup*
6	*bram-mouy*	16	*doup-bram-mouy*	70	*jetsup*
7	*bram-pee*	17	*doup-bram-pee*	80	*peitsup*
8	*bram-bei*	18	*doup-bram-bei*	90	*kohsup*
9	*bram-boun*	19	*doup-bram-boun*	100	*mouy-rouy*
10	*doup*	20	*maphei*		

Days

Monday	*tha-ngai chan*	Friday	*tha-ngai sok*
Tuesday	*tha-ngai angkea*	Saturday	*tha-ngai sav*
Wednesday	*tha-ngai puot*	Sunday	*tha-ngai atut*
Thursday	*tha-ngai preuo-haou*		

Months

January	*makara*	July	*kakkada*
February	*kumphak*	August	*seiha*
March	*meenear*	September	*kanh-nha*
April	*mesa*	October	*tola*
May	*ou-saphea*	November	*vichika*
June	*me-thuna*	December	*tha-nou*

Times and dates

Today	*t'ngai nih*
Tonight	*jooup nih*
Yesterday	*masel menh*
Tomorrow	*t'ngai saiit*
Next week (formal)	*supada kroie*
Next week (informal)	*atut kroie*
What time is it please?	*eilov nees moung ponmaan?*
When?	*pel na?*

Greetings and small talk

Hello	*joom reab suor/sour sdei*
Good-bye	*lear heouy*
Please	*suom*
Thank you	*ar kun*
Excuse me	*suom tous*
I am sorry	*suom tous*
Yes (used by women)	*jas*

Yes (used by men)	*bat*
No (formal)	*te*
No (informal)	*ahte*
Do you speak English?	*Niak ai ngtyay poasa Anglais*
I'm sorry I don't speak Khmer	*Suom at ai ngtyay paisa Khmer.*
I don't understand.	*Kinyoum át yoou al dtay*

Shopping

Where can I buy...?	*Knoum ai tenh noeu ai nah...?*
How much does it cost?	*Talihi punman?*
Do you have...?	*Niak mien dtay....?.*
Where is the...?	*...ai nah?*
Open	*baouk*
Closed	*bouk*

Appendix 3. Public holidays

7 January	Liberation Day. This holiday was restored, amidst controversy, in 1995 after being scrapped in 1991. It commemorates the 'two aspects' of 7 January 1979: Phnom Penh's liberation by the Vietnamese, and Cambodia's loss of sovereignty to foreign troops.
18 February	Anniversary of the treaty of friendship between Cambodia and Vietnam
17 April	Victory Day
1 May	International Workers' Day
9 May	Genocide Day
19 June	Anniversary of the founding of the Revolutionary Armed Forces of Kampuchea
28 June	Anniversary of the founding of the People's Revolutionary Party of Cambodia
2 December	Anniversary of the founding of the Front for National Reconstruction

Appendix 4. Embassies and consulates abroad

At the moment there are no Cambodian embassies in the West. In the region the closest embassy is in Bangkok at:

193 Sathon Tai Road. Tel: (02) 254 6963, 213 2573.

Selected embassies in Phnom Penh
Not all countries have embassies or consulates in Phnom Penh just now. Some English speaking embassies are listed on the facing page.

Australia and Canada: Villa 11, 254 Street (just north of Victory monument) Tel: (023) 6000, 6001.

UK: #27-29, 75 Street. Tel: (023) 27124.

USA: #27, 240 Street, Tel: (023) 26436, 26438, 26805, 26808, 26810.

Appendix 5. Suggested reading

Cambodia, Footprint Handbooks, Bath, UK/NTC, Chicago, 1997.

Chandler, David, *Brother Number One: A Political Biography of Pol Pot*, Westview Press, CO, 1995.

Haing Ngor, *A Cambodian Odyssey*, Warner Books Inc, New York, 1989.

Kiernan, Ben, *The Pol Pot Regime: Race, Power and Genocide in Cambodia under the Khmer Rouge, 1975–79*, Yale, New Haven and London, 1996.

McDonald, Malcolm, *Angkor and the Khmers*, Oxford University Press, Singapore 1987.

Nayan Chanda, *Brother Enemy: The War after the War: A History of Indo China Since the Fall of Saigon*, Collier Macmillan/Asia Books, 1986.

Osborne, Milton, *Sihanouk: Prince of Light, Prince of Darkness*, Allen & Unwin, 1994.

Ponchaud, F, *Cambodia: Year Zero,* Penguin, 1978.

Shawcross, William, *Sideshow: Kissinger, Nixon and the Destruction of Cambodia,* The Hogarth Press, London, 1994/Simon & Schuster, New York, 1979.

Shawcross, William, *Cambodia's New Deal,* Carnegie Endowment Publication, 1992.

Smyth and Kien, *Courtesy and Survival in Cambodian*, School of Oriental and African Studies, 1991.

Szymusiak, Molyda (Linda Coverdale, trans), *The Stones Cry Out: A Cambodian Childhood*, Jonathan Cape, London, 1986.

Robinson, Daniel and Tony Wheeler, *Lonely Planet Travel Survival Kit Cambodia,* Lonely Planet Publications 1992.

Rooney, Dawn, *A Guide to Angkor*, Asia Books, Bangkok.

Appendix 6. Suggested videos

The Killing Fields, directed by Roland Joffe.

Swimming to Cambodia.

Year Zero and *Year Ten*, two documentaries directed by David Munroe.

7

Vietnam

FACTFILE

History

208 BC	Establishment of independent kingdom in the northern mountains of Vietnam by Trieu Da, a renegade Chinese general.
111 BC	Northern Vietnam conquered by China's Han Dynasty. More than a thousand years of Chinese rule in the north follows, punctuated by revolts and periodic times of independence. In the south, the Hindu-Buddhist state of Funan is established in the Mekong Delta area.
967 AD	Emperor Dinh Bo Linh presides over a period of independence from the Chinese.
1407	China reconquers Vietnam after it has been weakened by a series of wars with Mongol armies.
1428	China recognizes Vietnam's independence after nearly a decade of revolt led by national hero, Emperor Le Loi.
1460	Borders of Vietnam gradually push southward.
1545	Vietnam split for the first time following civil strife.
1802	The country is united under the Nguyen dynasty.
1627	French Jesuit missionary Alexandre de Rhodes adapts the Vietnamese language to the Roman alphabet, foreshadowing increasing French influence and Christian proselytizing.
1843	A permanent French fleet is deployed in Asian waters.
1861	French forces overrun Saigon.
1862	French hegemony established when Emperor Tu Duc signs a treaty conceding them sweeping religious, political, and economic powers. In the following year the French will conquer Cambodia.

1890 Ho Chi Minh is born in central Vietnam. In 1911 he leaves the country, not to return for 30 years.

1945 On 2 September, Ho Chi Minh proclaims an independent democratic government in North Vietnam. He then leads a successful guerrilla war against the French until 1954.

1954 On 7 May the French are resoundingly defeated at Dien Bien Phu. Vietnam is then divided along the 17th parallel with an independent Communist government in the North and a US-backed democracy in the South. The South is the target of guerrilla activity against which the USA eventually responds.

1965–75 US war with Vietnam.

1975 Saigon falls to the Northern communist forces.

1977 Severe drought, cold and typhoon season. Border fighting with Kampuchea (Cambodia). China is accused of supplying military aid to Kampuchea.

1978 Rumours of war with China. China closes borders to Chinese refugees from Northern Vietnam. Vietnam signs friendship treaty with the USSR.

1979 Vietnamese forces occupy Phnom Penh.

1986 The Sixth Party Congress launches *doi moi*, economic reform, and opens the country to limited foreign trade.

1989 Vietnamese troops withdraw from Phnom Penh.

1990 Political relations with China resume.

1994 The USA lifts its trade embargo which had been in place against north Vietnam since the 1960s.

1995 Vietnam joins the Association of South-east Asian Nations.

Geography

Vietnam is a long, thin country with a coastline of more than 3 000 kilometres on the South China Sea and it is about the same size as Japan or California, or about two and a half times the size of England. Neighbouring countries are Laos, Cambodia, and China. The central and northern areas of the country are dominated by mountains and two important rivers: the Red River in the north and the Mekong in the south which form large, fertile deltas. The Mekong is one of the world's longest rivers, stretching over 4 100 kilometres from Tibet, through China, Laos, Cambodia and Vietnam and then into the South China Sea.

Climate

Vietnam's climate is much more diverse than those of other countries in the region, because of its variations in elevation and immense length. North Vietnam has a cold winter from November to January with the winds that blow in from China. During this time humidity is very high and drying clothes can be difficult, if not impossible. From June to October heavy rains and higher temperatures are the norm. Central Vietnam is a transitional zone with light but steady rains all year round. South Vietnam has a more typically South-east Asian climate with a dry season from November to May and a monsoon season from June to October.

Time

Vietnam is 7 hours ahead of Greenwich Mean Time, 12 hours ahead of New York, 15 hours ahead of San Francisco, 3 hours behind Sydney and 5 hours behind Wellington.

The people

The population of Vietnam is estimated to be 70 million, and is increasing at a rate of 2.3% per year. There are 54 ethnic groups in Vietnam, including the Vietnamese themselves (called the *Viet,* or *Kinh*) who make up nearly 90% of the population. The other 53 distinct ethnic groups mainly live in the upland areas.

Politics

The government is communist, but economically Vietnam is increasingly entering the free market. Since 1986 economic reforms have been introduced to encourage foreign investment and trade. In the south, the transformation to a semi-capitalist economy has been quicker and smoother than in north which has a longer history of communism.

Language

Today, thanks to the romanized dictionary compiled by the Jesuit missionary Alexandre de Rhodes, the language is written in *quoc ngu* (pronounced 'kwok noo-oo' with a break in the middle and a falling- and -rising inflection) rather than Chinese ideographs. *Quoc ngu* does not exactly match the spoken language. For example, written Vietnamese does not have an *f, j, w, or z,* although these sounds are common in the spoken language. The way these sounds are rendered in the roman alphabet is at times a bit unwieldy and was a bone of contention for Ho Chi Minh (pronounced 'Ho Chi *Ming*'), who thought the romanized alphabet was useful for national unity and literacy, but insisted there was no reason that the *f* sound should be written with a *ph*, or the *z* sound with a *d*.

There are slight variations between the way Vietnamese is spoken in the north and in the south. Northerners tend to have more clipped accents, and use all six tones, while southerners use only five tones.

Spoken Vietnamese is a six-tone monosyllabic Mon-Khmer language with borrowings from Chinese and Thai. The tones are: rising, falling, level, low rising, high broken, and low broken. The tone you use alters a word's meaning, so, for example, the word *ma* can mean ghost, mother, that, tomb, horse or rice seedling, depending on which tone you use. For more information on tones, see Appendix 2: Useful Vietnamese words and phrases.

Robert Olen Butler in *A Good Scent from a Strange Mountain* (see Appendix 5) includes a good description of misunderstandings that can arise from mis-use of tones. Miss Noi, a Saigon bar-girl who now lives in the USA, says:

> You must understand one thing about the Vietnam language. We use tones to make our words. The sound you say is important, but just as important is what your voice does, if it goes up or down or stays the same or it curls around or it comes from your throat, very tight. These all change the meaning of a word, sometimes very much, and if you say one tone and I hear a certain word, there is no reason for me to think that you mean some other tone and some other word. It was not until everything is too late and I am in America that I realize that something is wrong in what I am hearing that day. Even after this man is gone and I am in New Orleans I have to sit down and try all different tones to know what he wanted to say to those people in Saigon.
>
> He wanted to say in my language 'May Vietnam live for ten thousand years.' What he said, very clear, was, 'The sunburnt duck is lying down.'

Religions

Tam Giao (The Triple Religion)

Vietnamese culture has been nurtured by two religions and two philosophies/moral codes: Buddhism, and Christianity; Taoism and Confucianism. The non-Christian belief systems have merged with popular Chinese beliefs, as well as ancient animism, to form a uniquely Vietnamese conglomerate, called the 'Triple Religion', or *Tam Giao*. The Vietnamese, unless professing Christians, are most likely to call themselves Buddhists. This probably means they are Mahayana Buddhists, when in the pagoda (*chua*), celebrating births, weddings, funerals; Confucian in their thinking about the Vietnamese education system, family, and social hierarchy; and Taoist in believing popular cosmology which includes demons, sorcerers, genies and divinities – and 'hot' *(yang)* and 'cold' *(yin)* foods that must be balanced for health. An older Vietnamese belief, *To Tien*, is a cult of ancestor worship that even pre-dates Confucianism. See Chapter 1: The Chinese.

Christianity

Catholicism was introduced into Vietnam in the 16th century by missionaries from Spain, France, and Portugal; Vietnam has the highest percentage of Catholics (about 10%) in Asia outside the Philippines. There are also small groups of Protestants, Hindus, and Muslims (the Chams, ethnic-Khmers). Visibility of religious practice is increasing now that the government is taking a more liberal attitude to religions.

Cao Dai

A fairly recent religion, *Cao Dai* originated in Vietnam in the 1920s. The Mekong Delta is the centre for this very nationalist religion that may have as many as 2 million adherents. If you can you should visit the colourful *Cao Dai* Cathedral or Great Temple which is in Tay Ninh, about 100 kilometres north-west of Ho Chi Minh City (day trips can be organized from Ho Chi Minh City). *Cao Daism* is based on tenets for a new religion believed to have been dictated to Ngo Van Chieu, a civil servant, by *Cao Dai*, the Supreme Being. It claims to be a synthesis of Buddhism, Christianity, Taoism and Confucianism. Cao Dai saints include Moses, Brahma, Joan of Arc, Victor Hugo and Winston Churchill.

Hoa Hao

Another indigenous sect, *Hoa Hao*, was founded as a reform of Buddhism by Huynh Phu So in 1939. Its followers became involved in military clashes with the Viet Minh in the 1940s. There are about 1.5 million adherents.

Cultural considerations

Buddhism

As Vietnam is mainly a Buddhist country, it is important not to offend Buddhists by behaving inappropriately when you visit a temple, or when you talk to a Monk. See Chapter 1: Buddhism (Cambodia, Laos, Thailand and Vietnam) for further information on cultural considerations while in a Buddhist country.

Covering the mouth

When your students talk, you may see them covering their mouths with their hands. This is not because they are shy or afraid they've got bad breath, but is a traditional gesture used especially when talking to strangers.

Greetings and terms of address

Vietnamese traditionally greet each other with a *wai* (see pp 67-68). In Vietnam, unlike in Thailand and Laos, a handshake is much more common than a *wai*.

Vietnamese use a title such as Ms or Mr before a first name. To use a first name on its own expresses great intimacy or arrogance. For an old woman use *Ba,* for a middle-aged woman use *Bac,* for a young woman use *Chi* or *Em* and for a teenage girl use *Co*. For an old man use *Ong,* for a middle-aged man use *Bac,* for a young man use *Chu* and for a teenage boy use *Anh.*

TEACHING POSSIBILITIES

At the moment the main teaching opportunities are through the limited number of private language schools in Hanoi, in universities and teaching colleges or through volunteer organizations like VSO, or the Peace Corps. For further information about voluntary organizations see Chapter 2: Volunteer Recruitment Organizations. VSO is responding to the increasing demand for English in Vietnam and sent 20 volunteers in 1995 – all English teachers. Placements are in a variety of tertiary-level institutions ranging from universities in Hanoi to provincial teacher training colleges.

Language schools

Hanoi

The British Council, 1813 Cao Ba Quat, Ba Dinh District, Hanoi. Tel: (04) 843 4941, 843 6780. Fax: (04) 4962. E-mail: bchanoi @netnam.org.m. The British Council now has a DTO (direct teaching operation) in Hanoi, currently employing about 11 people, and expanding.

Ho Chi Minh City

ELT Lotus (Special English Course for International Business), 53 Nguyen Du Street, District 1, Ho Chi Minh City. Tel: (08) 251 556. Fax: 330 059.

Minh Hoa Tescan, Language and Computer Services, 20/B-60, 3 Yhang 2 Street, Ward 12, District 10. Tel/fax: (08) 654 977.

The British Council is currently setting up a direct teaching operation in Ho Chi Minh City.

Universities and colleges

Hanoi

Hanoi University for Foreign Study, Km 8, Nguyen Trai Road, Hanoi; contact: Mr. Nguyen Xuan Do, Head of the International Relations Department.

Hanoi University for Teachers of Foreign Languages, Km. 9 Cau Giay Road, Tu Liem, Hanoi.

Danang

Danang Foreign Languages Teachers' College, 17 Le Duan Street, Danang. Fax: (84) 5 123 683

International schools

Hanoi

United Nations International School, c/o The Amsterdam School, Giang Vo, Hanoi. Mr. James Ambrose, Director. Tel: (04) 235 782. Fax: (04) 263 635.

Ho Chi Minh City

International Grammar School, 236 Namh Ky Khoi Nghia Street, District 3, Ho Chi Minh City. Tel: (08) 293 237. Fax: (08) 230 000.

BEFORE YOU GO

Insurance

If you are going to a pre-arranged job or are working for a volunteer organization, you will probably be provided with medical insurance. If you are not going to a pre-arranged job, then take out a health insurance policy, as health care can be expensive, if you want to get as high a standard as you can get at home. See Chapter 1: Health for the addresses of two insurance companies in the UK which have proved popular with English teachers working abroad.

Vaccinations

The only vaccination that is required before going to Vietnam is a yellow fever one if you have been in a yellow fever area in the six days before you arrive in Vietnam. Most doctors also recommend that you are immunized against cholera, diphtheria, hepatitis A and B, rabies, tuberculosis, typhoid, tetanus and polio. See Chapter 1: Health for further information on diseases which are prevalent in Vietnam and for advice about what vaccinations you should have before leaving your home country.

Passport

Make sure your passport is valid for at least six months and that you have at least five empty pages left for all the stamps you will collect in Vietnam.

ARRIVAL AND VISAS

Visas

As Vietnam opens up more and tries to attract tourist and business dollars, getting the necessary visa is slowly getting easier. You should contact the Vietnamese embassy in your home country to get the most up to date information about visas before you leave for Vietnam.

Tourist visa. Tourists visas are now routinely issued for three months (in the UK the fee is about £60) and your visa can also be extended within Vietnam. If you are going to Vietnam looking for work and find it you will probably have to leave the country to change from a tourist visa to a work visa, although in theory it is possible to change within the country. Specify your desired entry point on your visa. This applies particularly if you want to enter Vietnam overland from Cambodia – if you do not have Moc Bai stamped in your passport you will be sent back to Phnom Penh.

Business visa. If you can arrange sponsorship or are going to a pre-arranged job in Vietnam you can apply for a multiple entry Business Visa (£45 in the UK), which will be valid for the length of your contract.

Student visa. You can enter Vietnam on a tourist visa and then within the country change to a student visa. You have to pay tuition fees, have proof that you are a student, and study for a minimum of 10 hours a week to qualify for a student visa. You can apply to the Immigration Police to change your status from a tourist to a student. Most foreigners who apply for student visas are enrolled in a Vietnamese language programme at one of the universities.

Immigration

The immigration officials at the airport have considerable power and have been known to validate people's visas for shorter stays than they had applied for. So even if your tourist visa was issued for three months when you applied for it, as soon as you have cleared immigration check the back of your visa to see how long you've been granted to stay in Vietnam. If you've only been given a one week stay, go back to immigration and politely and pleasantly ask if you can change it. If not, you will have to go to the Immigration Police in Hanoi or Ho Chi Minh City to see if you can extend your tourist visa. Like their counterparts elsewhere in South-east Asia, Vietnamese immigration officials take a dim view of a traveller they consider dirty, scruffy or not properly dressed. A conservative outfit, clean finger nails and a smile will help you enormously at Vietnamese immigration.

Transport from the airport

Hanoi

Noi Bai Airport is about 35 kilometres from the city centre. It costs $2 for the bus, and $3 for the minibus trip into town and it takes about an hour for the journey. A non-metered taxi from the airport into Hanoi will cost about $20.

Ho Chi Minh City

Tan Son Nhat International Airport is seven kilometres from the city centre. A non-metered taxi will cost you about $10, a motorcycle taxi about $3, and a *cyclo* (trishaw) about $2. For all these three types of transports you should negotiate and agree your price before you start your journey.

ACCOMMODATION

Short-term accommodation

In the major cities as well as popular holiday destinations there are cheap hotels and guest houses. For basic accommodation, you will pay between $10 and $15 and for that you will have a single room usually with a shared bathroom. Some hotels also have dormitories which are cheaper than single or double rooms. Accommodation in Ho Chi Minh is better and cheaper than in Hanoi, mainly because the south has been used to accommodating foreigners for many more years than the north has. Some popular hotels and guest houses in Hanoi and Ho Chi Minh are:

Hanoi

Lotus Guest House, 42V Ly Thuong Kiet St, Hoan Kiem District. Tel: (04) 268 642.

The Green Bamboo Cafe, 42 Nha Chung St. Tel: (04) 264 949.

The Trang Tien Hotel, 35 Tang Tien St. Tel: (04) 256 341. Fax: (04) 258 964.

Ho Chi Minh City

Thanh Thanh 2 Hotel, 205 Pham Ngu Lao St, District 1. Tel: (08) 324 027. Fax: 251 550.

Hotel 211, 211 Pham Ngu Lao St, District 1. Tel: (08) 352 253.

Van Canh Hotel, 184 Calmette St, District 1. Tel: (08) 294 963.

Long-term accommodation

As in other countries in the region, other teachers and foreigners are probably the best source for finding out about accommodation. You can also check the ads on notice-boards of the pubs listed below (see p 154) as well as in the weekly *Vietnam Investment Review* newspaper. You might also consider using an English-speaking housing agent to help you find somewhere to live.

Rent is expensive in Vietnam, and you should budget on, at a minimum, between US$300 and $400 a month in Ho Chi Minh, and between $600 and $700 in Hanoi. In Ho Chi Minh, rents in District 1 (the central area) are very expensive. There are a lot of foreigners and teachers who live out beside the airport, where the rents are much cheaper, but travelling to work can take 20 minutes on a motorbike. For some teachers who want to live close to work, the answer is to house-share with two or three other people.

Normally, you have to pay six months' or a year's rent in advance, so it is worth looking around carefully, and checking out plenty of houses and districts before you commit yourself to spending such a large amount of money.

British Council employees are housed in a diplomatic compound with tennis courts about 20 minutes drive from the city centre.

Electricity, gas and water

Electricity is steadily being standardized at 220 volts, 50 cycles with round two-pin or flat three-pin plugs being the norm, although older houses in Hanoi or Ho Chi Minh might still only be on 110 volts.

Electricity in Vietnam sometimes surges, and there are also periods of low power and blackouts. You should therefore have access to some candles or a torch and consider buying a voltage regulator when you arrive here to help protect your electrical goods.

Gas comes in large canisters and is used mainly for cooking. A canister will usually last you two to three months.

Water does not always flow when you turn on the tap in Vietnam so, especially in the dry season, you should fill some buckets or your bath tub, in case of a sudden shortage of water.

On average, your bills for electricity, gas and water will be about US$100 a month.

Household help

Most teachers in Vietnam employ someone to help with their household work. Washing machines are rare in Vietnam (as they are most of South-east Asia), and if you have someone to help in your house she (almost all household help in Vietnam is female) will wash all your clothes by hand, as well as doing the ironing, and cleaning your house. Other teachers can usually recommend someone to you, and her salary is negotiable depending on how often you want her to come to your house, how big your house is, and how many of you live there. Most teachers employ someone to come to their house two or three times a week, and most expats have live-in help.

LIVING COSTS

How expensive is Vietnam?

Vietnam is both expensive and cheap. The cost of rent makes Vietnam one of the most expensive countries in the region, but the cost of practically everything else makes it one of the cheapest. The exception is if you decide to live on imported goods; then your cost of living will be very high. A bowl of noodles at a road-side stall will cost you 30¢, a meal in a basic restaurant will cost $4, and in the Metropole Hotel a meal will cost you more than $20.

Salaries

Most teachers earn between $3 and $10 an hour, with a few earning $20 an hour working for large joint-venture companies. Volunteers are usually given free accommodation and a living allowance of around $350 a month.

Taxes

Income tax

The current income tax position in Vietnam is unclear for two reasons: firstly, legislation is sometimes vague allowing for different interpretations; and secondly, laws on income tax are issued nationally, but enforced locally which means that different tax offices will tax the same income at different rates.

An ordinance on income tax was issued in June 1994, but as yet the supporting decree and circulars have not been issued. This ordinance states that foreigners living and working in Vietnam for more than 182 days within any 12 month period are liable for income tax, which is based on a progressive rate scale, ranging from 10 to 60% depending on your income.

Departure tax

Airport departure tax is currently US$1, payable only in dong, for domestic flights and $8 for international flights.

Supermarket costs

The following prices are in Vietnamese Dong and were taken from a mini market.

Bread (white sliced)	9 000	Cornflakes (box)	31 000
Milk (1 litre)	11 000	Mineral water (1 litre)	10 000
Tea (25 bags)	14 000	Beer (large bottle)	9 000
Instant coffee (50 g)	17 000	Rum (large bottle)	120 000
Cheese (250 g)	19 000	Wine (75 cl)	200 000
Butter (250 gs)	13 000		
Cooking oil (large bottle)	20 000		

EATING AND DRINKING

Vietnamese specialties

Cha Gio (in the South) and *Nem Sai Gon* (in the North) are spring rolls. In Vietnam these rolls are often not deep fried, but cold, fresh, served with a sauce to dip them in and utterly delicious. *Nem rau* are vegetarian spring rolls.

Other Vietnamese dishes include *Bun thang* (rice noodles with egg, shredded chicken and prawns in soup); *Xup rau* (vegetable soup) and *Pho* (noodles served with green vegetables and a soup of prawns or chicken bones with *nuoc nam* – fermented fish sauce).

Drinking

The beer available in Vietnam, as in so many other countries in South-east Asia, is a light, fizzy beer, similar to lager in the UK, or the light beers of Australia and America. The main Vietnamese brands are Castel, Halida, Saigon Export, and Ba ba ba (333). Carlsberg and Heineken are brewed under licence in Vietnam.

You can buy both Russian-imported, and locally-made spirits such as vodka. Vietnamese rice-wine is also popular, but definitely an acquired taste.

TRANSPORT

There are very few buses or taxis in Vietnam yet, so if you are living long-term here, having your own transport is a real bonus. Most teachers and volunteers have either a push-bike (especially volunteers who are out of the main cities), or a motorbike.

Bike

A new Chinese-made bike will cost you about $60. When you first arrive in Vietnam you can hire a bike from most travel agents or hotels in the larger cities for $1 or $2 a day. If you are thinking of using a bike when you come to Vietnam, consider bringing a mountain-bike from home because good quality mountain-bikes are practically unheard of yet here. You might also consider bringing lights, reflectors, a puncture repair kit and a helmet as these biking essentials are either not available yet or are not of a very high standard.

Motorbike

Average prices for motorbikes are $2 500 for a Honda, $2 000 for a Taiwanese Bonus and $650 for a Russian Minsk. The red-tape involved in buying a new motorbike is incredible, as the following advice given to British Council teachers shows.

1. Choose your model and go and buy it – preferably with someone Vietnamese present.
2. Take the documents you are given by the shop at the time of purchase, keep them on you when you ride the bike.

   The shop owner will take one document to the police for them to sign and you have to go back and collect it sometime later from the shop (in a couple of days).
3. Take the bike and go to 86 Ly Thuong (near the old Thai restaurant), where new bike registration is carried out. Again, it's better to have someone Vietnamese with you. The procedure is as follows: Take along
   (a) all your papers
   (b) two letters in Vietnamese (duplicates) signed and stamped saying that you work at the British Council.
   (c) two copies of your passport
4. Take all your papers and 200 000 Dong to the tax office to get the bike registered.
5. Go back to the police registration office (Ly Thuong Kiet) with your passport and all the papers you've now amassed and fill in another two forms.

   You will come away with a pile of papers and one new addition – a small piece of paper to keep and bring in to claim your registration plate when it is ready. (They may tell you 10 days – but it can take up to two months!)
6. Eventually, with patience, on your 'n'th inquiry at the police station your registration plates will be ready and you can finally put them on proudly and be a fully-fledged Hanoi biker – legally!

Heather Swabey, English Teacher, The British Council

Bus

In Ho Chi Minh there are very few bus routes, no published bus map available as yet, and bus stops are not always very clearly marked. Until you know your way around, it is probably wiser to use some of the other transport listed below, and once you know some foreigners, or English speaking Vietnamese, they can help you find out where the buses go. Fares range from 20¢ and 40¢. In Hanoi, although bus routes are often marked with a red line on tourist maps, the service is fairly infrequent. In general most teachers and volunteers in Vietnam rely on their own transport or use a *cyclo* (in Hanoi or Ho Chi Minh) or a *Honda om* (in Hanoi).

Taxi

There are two main taxi companies in Hanoi. As yet there are not many taxis driving around looking for fares, so phoning them is the easiest way to get one.

> **Hanoi Taxi**. Tel: (04) 535 252
> **Taxi PT**. Tel: (04) 535 171.

The situation is similar in Ho Chi Minh where there are few empty taxis out on the roads. Reliable taxi companies include:

> **Vina Taxi.** Tel: (08) 442 170.
> **Airport Taxi.** Tel: (08) 446 666.

Train

Trains run between the major cities in Vietnam, but the journey is often very slow. For example, the fastest train available between Hanoi and Ho Chi Minh City takes over 35 hours. For most journeys you can chose from up to six levels of speed, comfort and price:

> **Saigon Railway Station**, 1 Nguyen Thong Street, District 1. Tel: (04) 230 105.
> **The Hanoi Railway Station,** Tran Hung Dao Street. Tel: (04) 253 949.

Cyclo (rickshaw)

Cyclos can be hired in both Hanoi and Ho Chi Minh City, and they are ideal for short trips around town. Fares start at about 50¢ for a short trip and you should negotiate the price before you travel.

Honda Om (Motorbike taxi)

In Ho Chi Minh City you can hire a motorbike taxi by flagging down a driver as he rides by. If he is not a taxi driver (and most motorbike drivers are willing to be one, even if it's not their usual job), he will soon find someone to drive you wherever you want to go within the city. As for *cyclos,* the going rate for a short *Honda Om* trip starts at about 50¢ and you should agree on a price before you start your journey.

Boat

You can travel along the two major rivers, the Mekong and the Red River, and indeed the many other smaller rivers and tributaries, by boat. The choices you have when travelling by boat are similar in scope to when you are travelling by train in Vietnam; boats come in an amazing variety of shapes, sizes, speeds, comfort and prices.

Plane

Vietnam Airlines is the national airline. It is currently working hard to upgrade its image and has now retired its Russian-built planes in favour of a fleet of Airbuses and Boeings. Vietnam Airlines also operates internal flights and they fly between the major cities regularly. For example, they offer flights between Hanoi and Ho Chi Minh five times a day, seven days a week which cost about US$150, one way.

SERVICES

Libraries

Hanoi. The National Library is at 31 Trang Thi Street (Tel: (04) 252 643). The Army Library is on Ly Nam Street (Tel: (04) 258 101).

Ho Chi Minh City. The Municipal Library is at 34 Ly Tu Trong Street.

Bookshops

At the moment there are very few good bookshops in Vietnam. Unless you want to read *The Quiet American* (which is available *everywhere* in pirated editions), you would do well to bring at least a few paperbacks which you can always swap for more reading material from other teachers when you're finished with them.

Of course, as Vietnam continues to open up to both capitalism and tourism, more and better quality books will become available. For the moment however, the main bookshops are:

Hanoi

The Thong Nhat Book Store, corner of Ngo Quyen Street and Trang Tien Street.

Ho Chi Minh City

Hieu Sach Xuan Thu, 185 Dong Khoi Street, District 1. Tel: (08) 224 670.

Tiem Sach Bookstore, 20 Ho Huan Nghiep Street. A second-hand bookshop.

Banks and financial matters

The Vietnamese currency is the dong. There are notes of 200, 500, 1 000, 2 000, 5 000 and 10 000. US dollars are also widely accepted.

You can open a dong or a dollar account at Ngan Hang Ngoai Thuong Viet Nam (the Bank of Foreign Trade of Vietnam, known locally as Vietcombank) which is the state-owned bank with branches in Hanoi and Ho Chi Minh City.

Most banks are open Monday – Friday 8am to 3pm (and closed for an hour and a half for lunch) and on Saturday from 8am to noon.

Health

Tap water in Vietnam is not safe to drink, so you should boil tap water or buy bottled water for drinking. See Chapter 1: Health for health precautions for Vietnam.

Health care in Vietnam is basic, not because of a lack of trained doctors, but because equipment is very limited. For scheduled operations in Hanoi blood is safety-tested if you are an expat, but in emergencies blood-screening is not guaranteed.

Most foreigners who become seriously ill in Vietnam opt to fly to Bangkok or Singapore for treatment. This means you need to have your own insurance policy before you find work, and you should check what kind of health insurance your school or university has before you accept a job with them.

International SOS Assistance offers medical evacuations. Membership is $200 per year and you can contact them 24 hours a day in Hanoi at 824 2866 and in Ho Chi Minh City at 829 4386.

Hospitals and clinics with English-speaking doctors include:

Hanoi

Swedish Clinic, opposite the Swedish embassy, Van Phuc. Tel: (04) 825 2464

Viet Duc Hospital, 48 Trang Thi. Tel: (04) 825 3531.

Bach Mai Hospital, International Department, Giai Phong. Tel: (04) 852 2004.

Ho Chi Minh City

Emergency Centre, 125 Le Loi, District 1. Tel: (08) 829 2077/829 1711.

Cho Ray Hospital, 201 Nguyen Chi Thanh, District 1. Tel: (08) 855 4137/855 4138.

MEDIA

Television

There is only one TV channel in Vietnam, but it does have English-language news broadcasts usually as the last programme of the evening, sometime between 10 and 11.30pm. The larger hotels have satellite TV where you can see major international sporting events, films and news on the Hong Kong-based network Star TV. The Polite Pub (see below) also has satellite TV.

Radio

Radio Australia, the BBC World Service and Voice of America all broadcast in Vietnam. The reception wavelengths for these three English-speaking stations change throughout the day and night. Full details are listed daily in the *Vietnam News.*

Newspapers

There is only one daily English-language newspaper, *Vietnam News*. Unfortunately, the term 'newspaper' is used very loosely here. The *Vietnam News* is more likely to be full of production statistics, little Vietnamese news and certainly no foreign news. It does, however, give programme details of English-language radio broadcasts. Three more interesting and useful newspapers are the weekly *Vietnam Investment Review*, the monthly *Vietnam Economic Time*s, and *What's On in Saigon. What's On in Saigon* is an expat newsletter, it's free, and you can find it in some of the bars listed below.

RECREATION

Bars and pubs

Bars which are popular with teachers include:

Hanoi
The Pear Tree, 78 Tho Nhuom Street. Tel: (04) 257 812.
Apocalypse Now Bar, 338 Ba Trieu. Tel: (04) 244 302.
The Polite Pub, 5 Bao Khanh Street. Tel: (04) 250 959.
Tin Tin Pub, 14 Hang Non Street. Tel: (04) 260 326.
Gold Cock, 5 Bao Khanh Street. Tel: (04) 259 499 .

Ho Chi Minh City
Apocalypse Now, Thi Sach St.
Hard Rock Cafe, 24 Mac Thi Buoi St.
Saigon Headlines, 7 Lam Son Square, District 1. Tel: (08) 225 014.

The Press Club, The corner of Hai Ba Trung St and Le Duan Boulevard, District 1.
Tiger Tavern, 227 Dong Khoi St. Tel: (08) 222 738

Sports

Hanoi

The Hash House Harriers run every Saturday, and the location for post-run drinks changes weekly. Check noticeboards in pubs above for details.

Tennis courts can be hired for $2–5 at Trung Tu diplomatic quarters, Van Phuc diplomatic quarters, and the Thang Loi Hotel, Yen Phu, West Lake (Tel: (04) 268 211).

The Khuc Hao Sport Club at 1B Le Hong Phong has tennis courts, table tennis, martial arts and aerobics classes (Tel: (04) 232 287).

Ho Chi Minh City

The Hash House Harriers run every Sunday. A bus usually leaves from the Saigon Floating Hotel at 3pm to take runners to the starting point, but check pub notice-boards for details.

Saigon Rugby Football Club welcomes new players, supporters and social club members. Call (08) 225 219 or (08) 222 982 for further details.

APPENDICES

Appendix 1. Case histories

Simon Winetroube

Simon Winetroube from London is a qualified EFL teacher. Before working for the British Council in Hanoi, he worked for two years in Bangkok.

He found that teachers were highly respected in Vietnam and that they were expected to be the source of all knowledge. Sstudents were quick to spot teachers who were not prepared or didn't know what they were doing, but Vietnamese politeness would often stop students saying anything directly to an ill-prepared teacher. He found the Vietnamese people very friendly and soon after he started working was often invited to his students' homes.

He said that a smart, clean appearance was very important although stylish clothes were not as important as they were in other South-east Asian countries.

The cost of living was very low; 'If you live locally it's *extremely* cheap, but if you live the expat life it is pretty expensive. More and more Western goods are becoming available in Vietnam, but medicines, personal hygiene stuff, high-quality large size shoes, and non-Vietnamese spices and herbs, are still difficult to find.'

Simon said he could write a book on his experiences in Vietnam; one of his favourite stories was of when he was teaching and there was a power cut – a fairly common occurrence in Vietnam. His students drove four motorbikes to the door of the classroom and turned on the headlights, so that the class could continue.

The thirst for English language knowledge seems unquenchable just now and the case of a *cyclo*-driver, who, on discovering that Simon was an English teacher, said, 'OK, I take you round sightseeing all day, no charge, but you speak English to me, I want to learn English better,' is typical.

Duncan Fyfe

Duncan Fyfe, 29, has a degree in Chinese and the RSA CTEFLA qualification. Before coming to Hanoi to work with The British Council, he worked in merchant banking and as a teacher with The British Council in Cairo.

Professionally, he finds the biggest difference between teaching in Egypt and teaching in Vietnam to be the level of motivation of the students. 'Many of the Egyptian students were rather lazy. Here, on the other hand, I find teaching very rewarding. Students are mature, have a high sense of political awareness and a good sense of humour. Above all, they are extremely motivated and willing to carry out self-study. Perhaps surprisingly, nothing seems taboo. Teachers are treated like God.'

Duncan's students are mainly government and quasi-government officials from, for example, Petro Vietnam and Vietnam Air. Like the other teachers in the Council's Vietnam Office, he spends part of the year teaching in provincial towns. Secondments are usually for six weeks and often involve teaching party officials in Provincial People's Committees. These secondments away from the Council's headquarters can be challenging as they usually involve teachers designing their own courses. He enjoyed his stay in Hué, but not all of his colleagues have been so lucky. The town of Vinh, for example, has a particularly grim reputation.

He describes his relationship with Hanoi as 'love/hate'. On the down side, he said 'The small number of expats and the difficulty of learning Vietnamese mean that the social circle is incestuous and can get on top of you.' Like many teachers, he has a problem with Hanoi's climate: 'Winter is damp, humid and rainy. The humidity is quite incredible; during rainy spells it is literally impossible to dry clothes, they have to be ironed before you put them on.' He also finds that public sports facilities aren't very good, although there are tennis courts where he lives, and he has also joined a private gym.

On the up side, the social life, while small and occasionally suffocating, is welcoming. Regular hangouts for Council teachers and other younger expats include *The Polite Pub* and the *Apocalypse Now* disco (see above). Duncan rides a Minsk motorbike which is cheap and convenient, even if it would never pass emissions standards in the West (so he will have to sell it when he leaves). Accommodation for British Council employees is in pleasant modern apartments in a diplomatic compound about 25 minutes bike-ride (15 minutes by motorbike) from the Council's offices and the centre of town. Perhaps the most enjoyable aspect of living here for Duncan is that the city is so atmospheric and relatively unspoiled: 'It's very exciting to be living in Vietnam during this period of rapid change.'

Appendix 2. Useful Vietnamese words and phrases

As mentioned above, Vietnamese has a completely different script from English. It is also a tonal language, and has more vowel sounds than English. The following words and phrases have been written as close as possible to how you would pronounce them using English transliterations. The tone is always said on the vowel sound, and in this guide the tones are marked above or below the vowel. I have followed the tone-markings used in the *Lonely Planet Travel Survival* and *Language Survival* books. This will make it easier for you if you are moving between this book and one of the Lonely Planet series. Other guidebooks and language books use other tone-markings, but since the *Lonely Planet Language Survival* books are probably the most well-known and readily available books both in Vietnam and abroad, I have decided to use their system of tone-markings.

Tones are relative to each person's voice range, so a high tone is said in the highest part of your voice range which might be considerably different from someone else's high tone. There are six Vietnamese tones:

- A rising tone is said as if you were asking a one-word question 'coffee?' It begins low and ends at a higher pitch. It is marked – á.
- A falling tone is said as if you were calling someone from far away. It begins at your high or mid tone level and ends lower. It is marked – è.
- A mid or level tone is said in the middle range of your voice and has a flat sound (it neither rises or falls). There is no mark for it – i.
- A high, broken tone starts above your normal voice pitch, falls a little and then rises sharply. It is marked – õ.
- A low, broken tone is said in a low falling tone which ends abruptly. It is marked – ủ.
- A low rising tone starts low, then falls slightly before rising again. It is marked – ạ.

Personal pronouns

Which word you choose when saying 'you' will depend on how well you know your listener, and what age they are:

To a woman, formally, use *ba*
To a woman informally, use *chi*
To a man, formally, use *ong*
To a man, informally, use *anh*
To a younger female or male, use *em*

Numbers

1	*mọt*	11	*muòi mọt*	21	*hai muoi mót (ham mót)*
2	*hai*	12	*muòi hai*		
3	*ba*	13	*muòi ba*	30	*ba muoi*
4	*bón*	14	*muòi bón*	40	*bón muoi*
5	*nam*	15	*muòi nam*	50	*nam muoi*
6	*sáu*	16	*muòi sáu*	60	*sáu muoi*
7	*bảy*	17	*muòi bảy*	70	*bảy muoi*
8	*tám*	18	*muòi tám*	80	*tám muoi*
9	*chín*	19	*muòi chín*	90	*chín muoi*
10	*muòi*	20	*hai muoi*	100	*mọt tram*

Days

Monday	*Thú hai*	Friday	*Thú sáu*
Tuesday	*Thú ba*	Saturday	*Thú bảy*
Wednesday	*Thú tu*	Sunday	*Chú nhạt*
Thursday	*Thú nam*		

Months

January	*Tháng gieng*	July	*Tháng bảy*
February	*Tháng hai*	August	*Tháng tám*
March	*Tháng ba*	September	*Tháng chín*
April	*Tháng tu*	October	*Tháng muòi*
May	*Tháng nam*	November	*Tháng muòi mọt*
June	*Tháng sáu*	December	*Tháng muòi hai*

Times and dates

Today	*Hom nay*
Tonight	*Dem nay*
Yesterday	*Hom qua*
Tomorrow	*Ngài mai*
Next week	*Tuàn tói*
What time is it?	*Mày giò ròi?*

Greetings and small talk

Hello	*Chào* + personal pronoun (see above)
Good-bye	*Chào* + personal pronoun
Please	*Xin mòi* + personal pronoun
Thank you	*Cám on* + personal pronoun
Excuse me	*Xin loi* + personal pronoun
It doesn't matter	*Khong có*
Yes	*Vang*
No	*Khong*
Do you speak English?	Personal pronoun + *có nói tiéng Anh Khong?*
I'm sorry I don't speak Vietnamese.	*Toi khong nói tiéng Viet Nam.*
I don't understand.	*Toi khong hiẻu*

Shopping

Where can I buy...?	*Toi có thể mua...ở dau?*
How much is it?	*Gái bao nhieu?*
I would like to buy...	*Toi muốn mua...*
Where is the nearest...?	*...gàn nhất ở dau?*
What time does it open?	*Máy giờ thì mở của?*
What time does it close?	*Máy giờ thì dóng của?*

Appendix 3. Public holidays

Fluctuating public holidays are marked with an asterisk *.

1 January	*Tet Duong Lich* (New Year's Day)
* Late January – mid-February	*Tet Nguyen Dan* (Vietnamese lunar new year – 1st to 7th days of the first moon)
3 February	*Thanh Lap Dang CSVN* (Anniversary of the founding of the Vietnamese Communist Party)
30 April	*Saigon Giai Phong* (Liberation Day)
1 May	*Quoc Te Lao Dong* (International Workers' Day)
19 May	*Sinh Nhat Bac Ho* (Ho Chi Minh's Birthday)
* June	*Dan Sinh* (Buddha's Birthday) on the 8th day of the 4th moon
2 September	*Quoc Khanh* (National Day)
25 December	*Giang Sinh* (Christmas Day)

Appendix 4. Embassies and consulates

Selected embassies in Vietnam

In Hanoi

Australia:	66 Ly Thuong Kiet St. Tel: (04) 252 763.
Canada:	39 Nguyen Dinh Chieu St. Tel: (04) 265 840.
UK:	16 Ly Thuong Kiet St. Tel: (04) 252 510.
USA (liaison):	8 Doc Ngu St. Tel: (04) 236 050

In Ho Chi Minh City

Australia:	Landmark Building, 5B Ton Duc Thang St, District 1 Trade Office: 4 Dong Khoi St, District 1. Tel: (08) 294 527.
Canada:	203 Dong Khoi St, No 303. Tel: (08) 242 000 Ext. 3320.
UK:	261 Dien Bien Phu St, District 3. Tel: (08) 298 433.

Selected Vietnamese embassies abroad

Australia:	6 Timbarra Cresent, O'Malley, Canberra, ACT 2603. Tel: (06) 286 6059. Fax: (06) 286 4534.
Canada:	695 Davidson Drive, Gloucester, Ottawa, Ontario K1J 617. Tel: (613) 744 0698. Fax: (613) 744 1709.
UK:	12–14 Victoria Road, London W8 5RD. Tel (0171) 937 1912.
USA:	Vietnamese Liaison Office, Washington DC. Tel: (800) 874 5100. Visas are processed by: Travel Documents Inc, 734 15th St NW, Suite 400, Washington, DC 20005. Tel: (202) 638 3800. Fax: (202) 638 4674

Appendix 5. Suggested reading

Bao Ninh, *The Sorrow of War*, Secker and Warburg, 1993.

Brownmiller, Susan, *Seeing Vietnam. Encounters of the Road and Heart*, HarperPerennial, 1995.

Butler, Robert Olen, *A Good Scent From a Strange Mountain*, Minerva 1993.

Karnow, Stanley, *Vietnam: A History*, Pimlico, London, 1991.

Kovic, Ron, *Born of the Fourth of July,* Pocket Books, New York 1974.

Moore, John and Tuan Duc Vuong, *Colloquial Vietnamese*, Routledge, London, 1994.

Nayan Chanda, *Brother Enemy: The War after the War, A History of Indo China Since the Fall of Saigon,* Collier Macmillan/Asia Books, 1986.

Nguyen Xuan Thu, *Lonely Planet Language Survival Kit*, Vietnamese Phrasebook, Lonely Planet Publications, 1993.

Nugent, Nicholas, *Vietnam: The Second Revolution*, In Print, Brighton, UK, 1996.

O'Brien, Tim, *The Things They Carry*, Flamingo, 1990.

Storey, R. and R. Robinson, *Lonely Planet Travel Survival Kit Vietnam,* Lonely Planet Publications, 1995.

Storey, R. *Lonely Planet City Guide Ho Chi Minh City (Saigon)*, Lonely Planet Publications 1995.

Vietnam, Footprint Handbooks, Bath, UK/NTC Chicago, 1997.

Appendix 6. Suggested videos

Born on the Fourth of July
Good Morning Vietnam
Platoon
The Deer Hunter

8

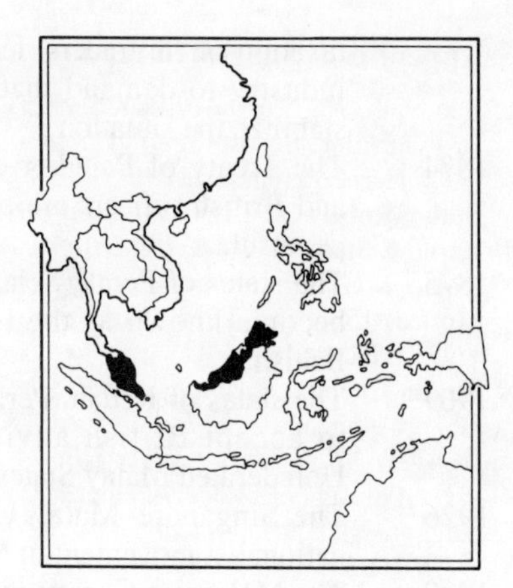

Malaysia

FACTFILE

History

The first Malay immigrants probably came from South China more than 5 000 years ago, forcing the original inhabitants into the interior of the country. Strategically placed between the trading nations of India and China, Malaysia has been influenced by the religions, cultures, arts and traditions of its nearby trading neighbours.

1401 Parameswara, a refugee prince-consort arrives in Malacca from Sumatra. Malacca thrives as a meeting place for traders from China, India and Indonesia.

1430 The ruler of Malacca becomes its first Sultan, and converts to Islam.

1511 The Portuguese arrive in Malacca, and the Sultan escapes to Johor Bahru.

1641 The Dutch arrive on the Malay peninsula.

1786 Sir Francis Light establishes a free port for the British in Penang.

1824 The Anglo-Dutch agreement is signed in London. Indonesia is controlled by the Dutch and Malacca, Penang and Singapore come under British control.

1826 Singapore, Malacca and Penang are combined to form the British Straits Settlements.

1832 Singapore is declared the capital of the Straits Settlements.

1840–70 The tin-rush years. Thousands of Chinese labourers emigrate to Malaysia, many organize into secret societies and fight over the rights to mine the most lucrative deposits. Increasing lawlessness coupled with Malay rulers' harsh taxation of tin-traders, leads British investors in the mining industry to demand that the Colonial Office intervene to stabilize the situation.

1874 The Treaty of Pangkor establishes the Residential system and British officers are posted to key districts in the Malay peninsula.

1875 The states of Perak, Selangor, Negeri Sembilan and Pahang become known as the Federated Malay States under the British.

1909 The states of Kedah, Perlis, Kelantan and Terengganu agree to accept British advisers and become known as the Unfederated Malay States.

1926 The Singapore–Malay Union is set up, the first political-nationalist movement in Malaysia.

1930 The Malaysian Communist Party is established.

1940 The leaders of a left-wing faction of the Singapore–Malay Union which had broken off to establish the Union of Young Malays are arrested by the British.

1941 The Japanese invade North Malaysia on 8 December and dominate the whole country by the end of January.

1941–45 Malaysia is occupied by the Japanese. Nationalist sentiments and independence are encouraged. The Malaysian People's Anti-Japanese Army is established with members coming from the British army, the Malaysian Communist Party and other underground dissident groups.

1945 The United Malays National Organization (UMNO), is established as the main opposition to the returned British colonial power. UMNO also opposes the proposed British plan to create a Malay Union made up of the Federated and Unfederated States along with Penang, Malacca and Borneo.

1948 After negotiations with Malay leaders, the Federation of Malaya is set up in February, dividing the country into 11 states, each with a ruling sultan, and the proviso that the 'indigenous people have a special position' in the new nation. Non-Malays can become Malaysian citizens if they have been resident in Malaya for a minimum of 15 years in the previous 25, sign a declaration of permanent settlement and are able to speak English or Malay. This means that only 3 million of Malaya's 5 million people qualify as citizens. Those who do not qualify are mainly Chinese and Indian.

1948 In June the new leader of the Malayan Communist Party, Chin Peng, calls for armed rebellion. The 12-year civil war or 'Emergency' as the British call it, starts with the murder of three European planters.

1950 The Communists are on the retreat and increasingly losing popular support, mostly because of the climate of fear they introduce in the countryside and also because their appeal is limited to working-class Chinese.

1955 The Alliance Party – a coalition of the Malayan Chinese Association (MCA), and the Malayan Indian Congress (MIC) – wins convincingly in the national election with Tunku Abdul Rahman as its leader. The Alliance calls for independence and the British promise it within two years.

1957 Malaya becomes independent.

1963 Malaya is renamed Malaysia. Singapore joins the Federation of Malaysia. The Federation is made up of Peninsular Malaysia, Sarawak, Sabah and Singapore (at the last minute Brunei pulls out).

1964 Riots in Singapore cause concern in Kuala Lumpur. Lee Kuan Yew considers this 'concern' tantamount to Abdul Rahman's interfering in the internal affairs of Singapore. These tensions increase later in the year, when Lee attempts to unite all Malaysian opposition parties under his People's Action Party (PAP).

1965 Lee Kuan Yew weeps at a press conference announcing Singapore's expulsion from the Federation of Malaysia.

1969 Race riots between Malays and Chinese leave 248 people dead and lead to Abdul Rahman's overthrow. He is replaced by Tun Abdul Razak who shifts Malaysia's foreign policy from being pro-Western to being one of non-alignment. Diplomatic relations with Moscow and Beijing are established. The new government suspends the constitution for over a year. The New Economic Policy is introduced. This is the first of many such policies which are to be introduced in the hope that economic imbalances between the different ethnic groups in Malaysia can be evened out – particularly the differences between the (mainly Chinese) wealthy urban population and the (mainly Malay and Indian) poorer rural population.

1976 Abdul Razak dies and is succeeded by his brother-in-law Dato Hussein Onn. Dr Mahathir Mohamad is named Deputy Prime Minister.

1981 Hussein Onn hands over his leadership to Mahathir.

1989 In an agreement brokered by Thailand, the Malayan Communist Party (MCP) finally agrees to lay down its weapons, almost 30 years after the 'Emergency' is declared over.

Geography

Malaysia is made up of 13 states and a separate capital district of Kuala Lumpur. The country is comprised of Peninsular Malaysia,

Sabah and Sarawak. Sabah and Sarawak were formerly known as North Borneo, and are today also known as East Malaysia. Although very small in population terms (only 14%) Sabah and Sarawak are very important economically, providing the country with pepper, timber, oil and natural gas resources.

Most of the information below is concerned with Peninsular Malaysia, as the major cities (Kuala Lumpur, Penang and Johor Bahru) and most teaching jobs are to be found there.

Peninsular Malaysia is bordered to the north by Thailand and surrounded by the South China Sea and the Straits of Malacca. Singapore and Malaysia are connected by a bridge across the Causeway and the journey between the two countries takes about half an hour.

Climate

Peninsular Malaysia lies just above the equator, so almost all days have 12 hours of daylight, and the sun sets every evening around 6.30pm.

Malaysia has a monsoon season from November to February, and the rest of the year humidity and temperatures are high.

Time

Malaysian standard time is 8 hours ahead of Greenwich meantime, 13 hours ahead of New York, 16 hours ahead of San Francisco, 2 hours behind Sydney and 4 hours behind Wellington.

The people

There are about 18 million people in Malaysia, made up of Malays, Chinese, Indians, and indigenous groups.

Malays

Although the Malays account for 48% of the population, 80% of university openings are reserved for them, 85% of educational scholarships are granted to them, and 80% of government executive jobs are held by them. This seeming imbalance is the result of successive government policies which have been introduced in an attempt to redistribute the country's wealth. It is argued that the Malays arrived first in the country and have, therefore, more rightful claims to its wealth than other groups in Malaysia. It is also argued that under British colonial rule, the Chinese and Indians were favoured over the Malays, and it is time to redress this imbalance. This 'affirmative action' policy sets out to give any *bumiputra* (son of the soil), preferential treatment. Both Malays and *Orang Asli* (see below) are considered to be *bumiputras.*

The first such preferential treatment policy was introduced in 1957 when the newly independent Malaysian government mandated 'special rights for Malays' for 10 years in the hope that rural Malays would become as prosperous as urban Chinese. The most recent policy was introduced in 1991. It was called the 'New Development Policy' (NDP) and it set no deadline for achieving the target of 30% *bumiputra* ownership of Malaysian corporate equity.

Chinese

Chinese Malaysians make up about 38% of the population. Chinese traders arrived here in 7th century but it was not until the 17th century that a sizeable group was established in Malaysia.

Indians

Indian Malaysians make up about 10% of the population. The first Indians arrived here as traders 2000 years ago, although few settled then. By the early 1600s a small community of Indians had settled in Malacca, but it was not until the British colonial era that Malaysia began to have a significant Indian population when indentured labourers from India arrived to build roads and railways and work on the huge rubber plantations.

Orang asli

Orang asli (original or first people) came from the Philippines about 500 000 years ago. *Orang asli* now make up only 1% of the population

Politics

Under the new constitution of 1957 a king is chosen every five years from the nine sultans. There is also a two-tier parliament, with a People's House of elected representatives and a Senate to represent the state assemblies.

The United Malays National Organization (UMNO) is the leading party in the *Barisan Nasional (BN)* or National Front Coalition. The coalition has won every election since 1981, headed by Dr Mahathir Mohamad.

The 1990 election was the first time that the BN coalition looked likely to be toppled. A break-away faction of UMNO, called *Semangat '46* – Spirit of '46 (the year the original UMNO was founded) – seemed on the brink of victory, but on election day the ruling BN coalition won 127 seats out of a possible 180. This gave Dr Mahathir the two-thirds majority needed to change the constitution, if he wanted to. This two-thirds majority has been Mahathir's measuring stick of political success for many years.

Language

The national language is *Bahasa Malaysia* (often shortened to *Bahasa*). It is very similar to Indonesian, and it can be understood in some parts of southern Thailand and even in pockets of the southern Philippines. Like Indonesian, it is written using the Roman alphabet, and unlike English every letter carries the same sound (for example, the letter *c* is always pronounced *ch,* as in chair), so it is quite straightforward to read, once you know the basic sounds. Unlike many of the languages in the region, Malay is not tonal, making it one of the easiest languages to learn in South-east Asia.

Other languages used in Malaysia include English, Mandarin, the Chinese dialects of Cantonese and Hokkien, as well as Tamil and Punjabi.

Religions

The main religion in Malaysia is Islam, although there are sizeable communities of Buddhists, Hindus and Christians.

Islam

The earliest recorded evidence of Islam in Malaysia is an inscription dating from 1303 which was found in Terangganu. This inscription described the penalties for those who did not follow the *adat* – customary law. Although in 1430 Sri Maharaja of Malaccaa converted to Islam, he did not enforce Islam as the religion of his subjects. It was probably the traders on the Arab merchant ships who brought Islam to the people of coastal Malaysia. From there it spread inland, and by the time the Portuguese arrived in the early 16th century Islam had been established as a major religion in Malaysia.

Buddhism

In theory Buddhism is the religion of most Chinese people in Malaysia. In practice, however, the Chinese follow a mixture of beliefs and teachings, combining Buddhism, Confucianism and Taoism.

Hinduism

Hinduism pre-dates Islam in Malaysia. In 1884 the remains of a Hindu shrine dating from the 6th century AD were found at the top of Gunung

Jerai. Today the majority of Malaysia's Indians are Hindus (the remainder are mostly Muslims), although there is also a sizeable Christian minority.

Cultural considerations

Islam

As Malaysia is mainly an Islamic country it is important not to offend Muslims by behaving inappropriately when you visit a mosque, or by the way you dress, or the way you give and receive things. For more information on Islam and ways to avoid offence see Chapter 1: Islam (Brunei, Indonesia and Malaysia).

Gifts

If you are invited to a Malaysian house, it is polite to bring a small gift – something from your home country is always appreciated. Don't be offended if your present isn't opened straight away, or indeed isn't opened during your entire visit. In Malaysia, as well as in most countries in the region, it is considered rude to open a gift in front of the giver.

TEACHING POSSIBILITIES

Most EFL teachers in Malaysia teach at private language schools, but there are also openings at state and private universities, as well as at the international schools. The Centre for British Teachers (CfBT) often recruits for posts at the International Islamic University Malaysia (IIU). You can contact them in Malaysia at:

CfBT Education Services (Malaysia), Sdn Bhd, Lot 308, 2nd floor, Kompleks Pencala, No. 50 Jalan Pencala, 46050 Petaling Jaya, Selangor, Malaysia. Tel: (03) 793 0073/0075. Fax: (03) 793 0069.

Private language schools

Some well-known private language schools in Kuala Lumpur are:

The British Council, 4th floor, Wisma Hangsam (Box 20), 1 Jalan Jang Lekir, 5000, Kuala Lumpur. Tel: (03) 230 6304.

The British Council, Jalan Bukit Aman, (PO Box 10539, 50916 Kuala Lumpur), 50480 Kuala Lumpur. Tel: (03) 298 7555. Fax: (03) 293 37214.

The Bangsar English Language Centre, 3A Jalan Telawi Tiga, Bangsar Baru, 59100, Kuala Lumpur. Tel: 282 3166.

The Language House, 40 Jalan 19/3, 46300 Petaling Jaya. Tel: (03) 755 0412.

Institute Evergreen, 400A Jalan Pudu Raya, 55100, Kuala Lumpur. Tel: (03) 241 5662.

ELS International, 2nd floor MTUC Building, 19 Jalan Barat, 46200 Petaling Jaya. Tel: (03) 756 5468, 756 5578.

The British Council has a number of other DTOs (Direct Teaching Operations in Malaysia:

The British Council, Johor Bahru Language Centre, Unit 14.01, Wisma LKN, 49 Jalan Wong Ah Fook, (PO Box 48, 80700 Johor Bahru), 80000 Johor Bahru. Tel: (07) 223 3340. Fax: (07) 223 3343.

The British Council, 1st Floor, Wing on Life Building, 1 Lorong Sagunting, 88000 Kota Kinabalu, Sabah (PO Box 10746, 88808 Kota Kinabalu). Tel: (088) 222 059/248 055/248 298. Fax: (088) 238 059.

The British Council, Bangunan WSK (Public Finance Building), Jalan Abell, 93100 Kuching (PO Box 615, 93712 Kuching, Sarawak). Tel: (082) 237 704/256 044/256 271. Fax: (082) 425 199. e-mail brcosar@britsar.po.my.

The British Council, 43 Green Hall, (PO Box 595, 10770 Penang), 10200 Penang, Malaysia. Tel: (04) 263 0330. Fax: (04) 263 3589. e-mail: brcopg@britpg.po.my.

International schools

There are a number of international schools in Malaysia which cater to the British and American communities here. These schools recruit qualified primary, secondary and specialist EFL teachers both abroad and in Malaysia:

Kuala Lumpur

International School of Kuala Lumpur, PO Box 12645, 50784, Kuala Lumpur. Tel: (03) 456 0522. Fax: (03) 457 9044.

Garden International School, No. 2A, Jalan Selasih, Taman Ceras, 56100, Kuala Lumpur. Tel: (03) 930 3000.

Penang

Dalat School, Tanjung Bunga, Penang, 11200. Tel: (04) 894 369. Fax: (04) 802 141.

The International School of Penang (Uplands School), Kelawei Road, 10250, Penang. Tel: (04) 361 764.

Sabah

Kinabalu International School, PO Box 12080, 88822 Kota Kinabalu, Sabah. Tel: (088) 31871.

Freelance teaching

Teaching privately will not qualify you for a work permit in Malaysia, so it is almost impossible to live here long-term and teach only freelance. However, if you are on a tourist visa, you might be able to pick up some freelance work, through contacts at back-packer hostels. Especially outside the main cities it is possible to trade English lessons for free accommodation and food. For most teachers however, the main source of private students is likely to be from a school. Once you have a job, students will probably approach you for lessons outside school.

BEFORE YOU GO

Insurance

Medical treatment is much less expensive than in nearby Singapore, but you would still do well to have some kind of health insurance, particularly if you arrive in Malaysia on a tourist visa. Once you find a job, most schools will help with some, but not necessarily all, health-care costs.

Vaccinations

Officially the only vaccination requirement is a yellow fever certificate if you have recently been in an infected zone. You should also contact the Malaysian Embassy and your local doctor for suggested vaccinations to have before going to Malaysia. See also Chapter 1: Health for advice on pre-departure health precautions.

Passport/visa

All visitors need a valid passport. If you are British, Irish, Australian, New Zealander or Canadian you do not need a visa to enter Malaysia as a tourist. If you are an American you do not need a visa if you are staying in Malaysia for less than three months. Most tourists are given a two-month visa when they arrive in the country and your visa can be extended for a further three months at the immigration department in Kuala Lumpur, Johor Bahru or Penang.

ARRIVAL AND VISAS

Visas and work permits

If you are going to a pre-arranged job, your employer will take care of your work permit, and will probably start the process before you arrive. If you arrive on a tourist visa and then find a job, you will have to leave Malaysia to change from a tourist to a work visa. Most teachers take a short trip either to Singapore or Thailand for this.

Immigration

Malaysian immigration officials, like their counterparts in the rest of South-east Asia, take a dim view of dirty, untidy people wanting to enter the country. Wear a conservative set of clothes, and women, cover your shoulders.

Transport from the airport

Subang International Airport is about 22 kilometres from the city centre. Taxis operate on a coupon system and cost around 35 ringgit for the trip into the city. The number 47 bus leaves from the Kelang terminal on Jalan Sultan Mohamed. The journey into town takes between 45 minutes to an hour and costs about 2 ringgit. A new international airport is planned for 1998, after which Subang will be used for domestic flights.

ACCOMMODATION

Short-term accommodation

In the major cities as well as popular holiday destinations there are cheap hotels and guest houses. Here for between 20 and 30 ringgit you can get a single room usually with a shared bathroom. Some hotels also have dormitories which are much cheaper than single or double rooms. These cheap hotels usually cater for back-packers and the lack of privacy may get on your nerves, but in the short-term they are great places for just getting your bearings in a new city. They are usually centrally located, which is useful for when you are doing the rounds of the schools. A list of some hotels and guest houses in the larger cities is given below.

Kuala Lumpur
Travellers' Moon Lodge, 36 Jalan Silang. Tel: (03) 230 6601.
Kuala Lumpur Youth Hostel, 21 Jalan Kampung Attap. Tel: (03) 230 6870.
Meridian International Youth Hostel, 36 Jalan Hang Kasturi. Tel: (03) 232 1428.
Coliseum Cafe and Hotel, 98-100 Jalan Tuanku Abdul Rahman.
Sunrise Travellers' Lodge, 89B Jalan Pudu Lama. Tel: (03) 230 8878.

Johor Bahru
Malaya Hotel, 20 Jalan Meldrum. Tel: (07) 221 691.
Hawaii Hotel, 21 Jalan Meldrum. Tel: (07) 226 332.

Penang
Eng Aun, 380 Chulia Street. Tel: (04) 612 333.
Swiss Hotel, 431 Chulia Street. Tel: (04) 620 133.

Long-term accommodation

In Malaysia houses are generally rented by the month. Most contracts are for a year and you have to pay a refundable two to three month deposit. Other teachers can give you good advice on which areas are popular with teachers. Most teachers in Kuala Lumpur like to live near a bus route or close enough to their school to be able to afford to pay for a taxi each day.

Housing agents can also help you find an apartment. They work on a commission basis, which only has to be paid, usually by the house-owner, when they find you a place you want to rent.

Newspapers also carry adverts for houses. *The New Straits Times, The Star, The Sun,* and *The Malay Mail* are all English language newspapers which carry housing ads. *The Malay Mail* has house ads for the Klang Valley, an area of about a 80 kilometre radius around Kuala Lumpur.

Telephone, gas, electricity, water and sewage

Telephone bills should be paid by the month. It costs about 75 ringgit to have a phone installed. International calls are listed by date, number called and duration of the call. A number of local calls are free with the remainder being charged at about 13 cents a call. Rental per month is about 20 ringgit and the total bill is subject to a 5% tax. If you do not pay your telephone bill on time, you will be disconnected and will have to pay another 50 ringgit to be re-connected.

Off-peak times for cheap rate calls are: South-east Asia (6pm Sunday – 7am Monday); North, Central and South America (6pm Saturday – 9am Monday); Europe, The Middle East and Africa (6pm Saturday – 12 noon Monday).

Gas in Malaysia is used for cooking, usually on a small two ring stove with a grill. A large gas bottle will usually last a single person for about three months. It is a good idea to have two gas canisters in your house so that you will not be caught short if your bottle suddenly runs out. A 12-kg canister of gas will cost around 15 ringgit, but your first purchase will also include a fairly hefty returnable deposit of 50 ringgit.

Electricity bills should be paid by the month. An official comes to your house to read the meter and then a bill is sent to your house.

Water bills should be paid every three months. Your meter is read and the bill slipped under your door.

Sewage bills should be paid every six months. This service is very cheap – only about 2-3 ringgit every six months.

Telephone, electricity, water and sewage bills all have *Tarikh akhir bayaran* – a 'pay by' date on them and should be paid at a post office.

LIVING COSTS

How expensive is Malaysia?

Malaysia is one of the cheaper countries in the region. Imported goods are expensive, but rent, food and transport are generally very cheap, especially compared to neighbouring Singapore.

Salaries

Teachers' salaries start from around 3 000 ringgit a month and after rent and taxes you will be left with about 2 000 ringgit.

Taxes

Income tax. Income tax and health insurance is usually between 17 and 20% of your monthly salary, although if you are working illegally on a tourist visa you will not be have to pay tax.

Departure tax. Departure tax is 20 ringgit for international flights.

Supermarket costs

There are plenty of supermarkets in Kuala Lumpur and some supermarket prices are listed below (in ringgit). It is also worth bearing in mind that supermarkets are not always the best value for money in Malaysia and that many of the prices listed are much lower in local shops or markets:

Bread (small sliced loaf)	2.20	Tea (50 tea bags)	5.60
Beef (100 g)	1.40	Instant coffee (200 g)	10.30
Milk (1 litre)	2.90	Beer (640 ml)	7.50
Sugar (1 kg)	1.80	Imported Gin (750 ml)	95.00
Eggs (10)	2.25	Malaysian Gin (750 ml)	20.00
Rice (1 kg)	3.00	Cigarettes (20 Marlboro)	3.20

EATING AND DRINKING

Eating in Malaysia is a delight. You will be quite spoilt for choice here.

Etiquette

Like Singapore, Malaysia has three main ethnic groups which have slightly different eating customs. If you are eating with Chinese people you should use chopsticks if you can, or a knife and fork (for information on how to use chopsticks, see Chapter 1: Using chopsticks). When eating with Muslim Malaysians and Indians you should use your right hand, or a fork and spoon. Eating with your hand is slightly more complicated than it sounds. Cup your fingers, scoop the food off your plate, then (and this is the difficult bit) turn your hand round so that your thumb is nearest your mouth, put your thumb behind the food and then flip it into your mouth. Putting your fingers in your mouth, sucking on your fingers, or getting your fingers messy, past the knuckles, are all considered very uncouth.

Malaysian specialties

Nasi, or rice, is the mainstay of any meal in Malaysia, whether the dish is Malay, Indian, or Chinese. Like most other people in the region Malaysians believe that you haven't eaten properly if you haven't eaten rice with your meal.

Malay food

Spices are very important in Malay cooking, so if you like your food mild, take care with those small red or green chillies. Traditional Malay ingredients are rice, chillies, garlic, onions, peanuts, chicken, prawns, crab, and fish.

Some well-known Malay dishes include: *satay* (barbecued beef or chicken, served with a hot peanut sauce); *laksa* (spicy soup made with thin noodles and fish stock); *mee rebus* (boiled wheat noodles served with a thick spicy sauce); and *mee Siam* (Thai-style rice noodles) served with a thin, hot, spicy sauce.

Chinese food

Popular Chinese dishes in Malaysia include: *Char kway teow* (fried noodles with eggs, cockles and chilli) and *yong tow foo* (beancurd and vegetables stuffed with fish).

Indian food

Among the widely available dishes are *tandoori* (chicken or fish, marinated in yoghurt and cooked in a special clay oven); *naan* (bread baked with nuts, garlic or onions) and *banana-leaf curry* (hot vegetable curry served on a banana leaf).

Drinking

The beer available in Malaysia is a light, fizzy beer, similar to British lager, or the light beers of Australia and America. The two Malaysian brands are Anchor and Tiger. Malaysian-brewed Guinness is popular, especially with Chinese Malaysians who often believe that the dark brew has special medicinal qualities – proof indeed that 'Guinness is good for you!'

You can buy both imported and locally made spirits, such as gin. Malaysian-made spirits are much cheaper but have a lower alcohol content than imported brands.

TRANSPORT

Malaysians drive on the left-hand side of the road, in right-hand drive cars.

Bus

There are two types of city buses in Kuala Lumpur – large blue buses and small pink minibuses. For the large buses fares depend on the distance travelled, while the pink buses have a flat-rate fair of 60 sen. Unfortunately, there is no bus map available, so you will have to find out from other travellers or teachers, or have a few adventures yourself to find out the bus routes.

Taxi

Metered taxis in Kuala Lumpur have a flag fair of 1.50 ringgit for the first two kilometres, and 20 sens for every further 200 metres. Surcharges include: 1 ringgit for a call-out taxi; 2.50 ringgit waiting charge for every 15 minutes; 50% surcharge between midnight and 6am and 20 sen per person if there are more than two people.

Some taxi companies include:

Comfort Radio Taxi Service: 733 0507.
Koteksi: 781 5352.
Selangor Radio Taxi: 293 6211.

Train

Peninsular Malaysia has two train routes; the west coast service which runs between Singapore and Thailand, via Kuala Lumpur, and the east coast service from Gemes (in the south) to Kota Bahru. Trains in Malaysia come in many different classes, speeds, and prices. At the bottom end of the scale there are Ordinary Trains, and Mail Coaches which stop at every station and are often very crowded, and cooled only by open windows and fans. At the top end of the scale is the Orient Express with a one-way ticket between Kuala Lumpur and Singapore costing about £490/US$750. In the middle there are the

Ekpres Sinaran and the *Ekpres Rakyat* trains which offer air-con sleeping berths, and stop at only a limited number of stations.

Boat

If you want to get away from it all at the weekends or during holidays, the islands off the east and west coasts of Peninsular Malaysia offer sun and sand and some beautifully quiet beaches. On the west coast, north of KL, you can get to the islands of Pangkor from Lumut by boat. On the east coast, boats leave Mersing for Tioman island between noon and 2pm daily, depending on the tides. The cost can range from 15 to 30 ringgit and can take between two and five hours. Other islands near Tioman are Sibu, Tinggi, Rawa, and Besar and all can be reached by boat from Mersing. Further north, you can get to the islands of Redang from Marang, and to Perhentian Besar and Perhentian Kecil islands from Besut.

Bike and motorbike

Having your own transport in Kuala Lumpur for most teachers means having a bike or motor-bike. The classified ads section of the English language newspapers, *The New Straits Times, The Star, The Sun,* and *The Malay Mail*, as well as teachers who are leaving are good sources for second-hand bikes.

Car

Cars are quite expensive in Malaysia and not many teachers can afford to run one. If you are interested in a second-hand car, try the classified ads in the English language newspapers (see above).

Plane

The national airline is Malaysia Airlines System (MAS), which flies internationally to America, Australia, New Zealand and Europe. Internally both MAS and Pelangi Air fly to the major cities and some of the islands off the coast of Malaysia.

SERVICES

Public phones

Phones which use phonecards are increasingly common these days. You can buy phonecards in post offices, hotels and some shops. For phones which use coins you need 10 or 20 sen coins. For most public phones you have to press a release button when the other person answers.

You can make international calls from most *Kedai Telekom*, large telephone exchanges. They have direct dialling and a meter to show you how much your call costs while you are making it. When you finish your call you get a computer printout with the length of time and cost of your call on it. You can also use international phonecards to make overseas calls. International phonecard machines are plentiful in most shopping malls.

Libraries

The National Library is on Jalan Tun Razak (Tel: (03) 292 3144) and the British Council Library is on Jalan Bukit Aman (Tel: (03) 298 7555). The British Council Library costs 35 ringgit a year to join, and you need to show your passport and proof of your address in Malaysia.

Bookshops

There are plenty of good bookshops in Kuala Lumpur which stock English language teaching books and novels, including: Bookazine, 8 Jalan Batai, Damansara Heights, MPH Bookstores and Berita Book Centre in Bukit Bintang Plaza, Jalan Bukit Bintang and Times The Book Shop in Yuah Chun Plaza.

Penang is a good place in which to stock up on second-hand books as it has so many travellers passing through from Thailand for visas.

Banks and financial matters

The Malaysian currency is the ringgit, or dollar (sometimes written as M$) and it is divided into 100 sen, or cents. There are coins of 5, 10, 20, 50 sen and one ringgit and notes of 1, 5, 10, 20, 100, 500, 1 000 and the rarely seen 10 000 ringgit.

Banks are open 9am to 3pm Monday to Friday and on Saturdays are open until lunch-time (12 noon or 1pm). To open a bank account, all you need to show is your passport. Most banks have ATMs now, which are on-line 24 hours a day, seven days a week. A cash card takes about two weeks to arrive after you have applied for it.

Health

Tap water in Kuala Lumpur is generally safe to drink, but especially at the beginning of your time in Malaysia, it might be better to boil tap water or to buy bottled water. See Chapter 1: Health for precautions you should take for Malaysia. For 24-hour emergency care, hospitals recommended by teachers include:

Assunta Hospital, Petaling Jaya. Tel: (03) 792 3433.
Pantai Medical Centre, Jalan Pantai (off Jalan Bangsar). Tel: (03) 757 5077.
Pudu Specialist Centre, Jalan Pudu. Tel: (03) 242 9146.

MEDIA

Television

There are two TV channels which broadcast English language news daily. Channel 1 shows world news from CNN at 7.30pm, and Channel 3 shows Malaysian news at 7pm.

Radio

The BBC World Service, Radio Australia, and Radio Moscow can be picked up in Malaysia. These services are transmitted on different wave lengths at different times of the day, and there is usually a timetable available in the English language newspapers.

Newspapers

The New Straits Times, The Star, The Sun, and *The Malay Mail* are English language newspapers available in Kuala Lumpur, and you can buy newspapers from other countries in most of the international hotels in the city. *The New Straits Times* is a broadsheet which generally reflects the views of the government, while the others are tabloids, featuring racier stories.

RECREATION

Music

Most pubs have live music with local bands usually playing cover versions of middle-of-the-road rock songs. Most bars listed below have live music at least a few nights a week.

Bars and discos

Pubs in KL which are popular with teachers include:

Ban Tai, Jalan Ampang, opposite Micasa Hotel (live jazz at weekends).
The Bull's Head, on the corner of Central Market, off Jalan Hang Kasturi.

Coliseum Hotel, 98 – 100 Jalan Tunku Abdul Rahman.
The Hard Rock Cafe, Concord, 2 Jalan Sultan Ismail (live rock bands at the weekend).
London Pub, Lorong Hampshire, off Jalan Ampang, behind the Ming Court Hotel.

Discos which are popular with teachers include:

Boom-Boom Room, Leboh Ampang.
De Camp, Jalan Tun Razak.
Fire, Lorong P Ramlee (behind the Shangri-La Hotel).

Cinema

Hollywood blockbusters with Malaysian subtitles are shown in all the main cinemas in Kuala Lumpur, although increasingly films are dubbed in Malay, Cantonese or Tamil. Film listings are shown in the daily newspapers *The Straits Times, The Star,* and *The Malay Mail.* Tickets cost about 7 ringgit.

Sports

There are public swimming pools, and facilities for tennis, squash and badminton in most residential areas in Kuala Lumpur. Tennis, squash and badminton courts cost about 6 ringgit an hour to hire. The Bangsar Sports Complex on Jalan Bangsar (Tel: (03) 254 6065) has good swimming and sports facilities. It is open 8am to 10pm and costs 8 ringgit for adults and 4 ringgit for children.

Help-lines (Kuala Lumpur)

Emergency	999
Directory	103
Information	108
Airport	776 1014

APPENDICES

Appendix 1. Case history

Jane Butterworth

Jane Butterworth worked in Hong Kong and Singapore before going to Malaysia to work in a university. She was recruited in England through the CfBT (the Centre for British Teachers). She taught students who were going abroad to study, and so was mostly involved in teaching English for Academic Purposes (EAP).

Although most foreign female teachers in Malaysia are not expected to cover their heads, because Jane was working in an Islamic University she always had to wear a head-scarf when she was working. Other than that, there were few restrictions placed on her while she was working in a Muslim environment and country.

She shared a large flat with another teacher – sharing was the norm, she said, for most teachers. She rarely cooked in her house because there were so many cheap restaurants in Kuala Lumpur. 'There was a fabulous choice of cuisine. In a week, I usually ate a Malaysian, Chinese, and an Indian meal, often from street hawkers, and the occasional Burger King splurge'

The easy access to the beautiful beaches of the east coast is one of the great advantages of living in Malaysia. 'It was so simple to hop on a bus and in a couple of hours, there you are, lying on a deserted beach, or bobbing in the South China Sea.'

As in Indonesia, *jam karat*, or rubber time, is the norm in Malaysia and after the hectic pace of life in Hong Kong Jane said she found the easy-going Malaysian lifestyle and laid-back attitude to punctuality very relaxing.

Jane, like most foreigners, found Malay an easy language to learn, although getting past the intermediate plateau proved difficult. Still, she was very pleased with how successfully she could communicate and would highly recommend that new teachers learn as much Malay as possible. 'I could have got by without speaking much Malay but I would have missed out on the small daily contacts you can have with people if you understand their friendly chit-chat.'

Appendix 2. Useful Malay words and phrases

Numbers

1	*satu*	9	*sembilan*	40	*empat puluh*
2	*dua*	10	*sepuluh*	50	*lima puluh*
3	*tiga*	11	*se-belas*	60	*enam puluh*
4	*empat*	12	*dua-belas*	70	*tujuh puluh*
5	*lima*	13	*tiga-belas*	80	*lapan puluh*
6	*enam*	20	*dua puluh*	90	*sembilan puluh*
7	*tujuh*	21	*dua puluh satu*	100	*se-ratus*
8	*lapan*	30	*tiga puluh*		

Days

Monday	*Hari Isnin*	Friday	*Hari Jumaat*
Tuesday	*Hari Selasa*	Saturday	*Hari Sabtu*
Wednesday	*Hari Rabu*	Sunday	*Hari Minggu*
Thursday	*Hari Khamis*		

Months

January	*Januari*	August	*Ogos*
February	*Februari*	September	*September*
March	*Maret*	October	*Oktober*
April	*April*	November	*November*
May	*Mai*	December	*Disember*
June	*Juni*		
July	*Juli*		

Times and dates

Today	*Hari ini*
Tonight	*Malam ini*
Yesterday	*Kelmarin*
Tomorrow	*Besok*
Next week	*Minggu depan*
What time is it?	*Pukul berapa?*
When?	*Bila*

Greetings and small talk

Good morning	*Selamat pagi*
Good afternoon (early)	*Selamat tengah hari*
Good afternoon (late)	*Selamat petang*
Good night	*Selamat malam*
Good-bye (said by the person going)	*Selamat tinggal*
Good-bye (said by the person staying)	*Selamat jalan*
How are you?	*Apa Khabar?*
I'm fine	*Baik*
Excuse me/I'm sorry.	*Ma'af saya.*
It doesn't matter	*Tidak apa-apa*
Can you speak Malay?	*Kamu bisa becara Bahasa Malay?*
Yes	*Ya/ boleh* [Yes, can be done]
No	*Tidak/Bukan*
Can you speak English?	*Kamu bisa becara Bahasa Inggris?*
I can't speak Malay.	*Saya tidak bisa becara Bahasa Malaysia*
I don't understand.	*Saya tidak mengerti.*

Appendix 3. Public holidays

Public holidays vary from state to state in Malaysia. Each state's Sultan's birthday is a public holiday for that state. The holidays listed below are based on the holidays in Kuala Lumpur. Fluctuating dates are marked with an asterisk.

*1 January	New Year's Day
*Late Jan/early Feb	Chinese New Year
1 February	Federal Territory Day (Kuala Lumpur and Labuan only)
*Early/mid April	*Hari Raya Puasa*, the end of *Ramadan*, the Muslim fasting month
1 May	Labour Day
6 June	His Majesty the King's birthday
31 August	Independence Day
*November	*Deepavali*, the Hindu festival of lights
25 December	Christmas Day

Appendix 4. Embassies and consulates

Selected embassies in Malaysia

Australia: 6 Jalan Yap Kwan Sweng. Tel: (03) 242 3122.

Canada: 7th floor, Plaza MBS, 172 Jalan Ampang. Tel: (03) 261 2000.

New Zealand: 193 Jalan Tun Razak. Tel: (03) 248 6422.
UK: 185 Jalan Ampang. Tel: (03) 248 7122.
USA: 276 Jalan Tun Razak. Tel: (03) 248 9011.

Selected Malaysian embassies abroad
Australia: 7 Perth Ave, Canberra, ACT 2600. Tel: (06) 273 1543.
Canada: 60 Boteler St., Ottawa, Ontario K1N 8Y7. Tel: (613) 237 5182.
New Zealand: 10 Washington Ave, Brookly, Wellington. Tel: (04) 852 439.
UK: 45 Belgrave Square, London, SW1X 8QT. Tel (0171) 235 8033.
USA: 2401 Massachusetts Ave NW, Washington, DC 20008. Tel: (202) 328 2700.

Appendix 5. Suggested reading

Burgess, Anthony, *A Malayan Trilogy: Time for a Tiger, The Enemy in the Blanket and Beds in the East*, Penguin, UK, 1972.

Finlay, Hugh, and Peter Turner, *Lonely Planet Travel Survival Kit Malaysia, Singapore and Brunei,* Lonely Planet Publications, 1982.

Maugham, W. Somerset, *Maugham's Malaysian Stories*, Heinemann, London and Singapore, 1969.

Malaysia and Singapore, Footprint Handbooks, Bath, UK/NTC, Chicago, 1997.

Othman, Zaharah, and Sutanto Atmosumarto, *Colloquial Malay*, Routledge, London, 1995.

Appendix 6. Suggested videos

South Pacific (filmed on location on Tioman island).

9 Singapore

FACTFILE

History

Today, Singapore is officially known as The Republic of Singapore, but in the 7th century Singapore was known as Temasek, 'people of the sea' in Sanskrit. It was an inhospitable, pirate-infested island which was the trading centre of Sumatra's Srivijaya empire. In the 13th century, after a Sumatran prince claimed to have seen a lion on Temasek, it became known as Singapura or Lion City. Although lions have never since been sighted and it is more likely that the prince spotted a tiger, the name has somehow remained. In the following century Singapura was fought over by Java, Siam (Thailand) and China. It was finally abandoned by each faction and reclaimed by the jungle until the early 1800s.

In 1811 Singapore was resettled by 100 Malays led by their local chief, the Temenggong, and eight years later Sir Stamford Raffles of the British East Indies Company landed on the island. He reached an agreement with the Temenggong to found a settlement for the British (along with Malacca and Penang in Malaysia) and for the next century Singapore boomed as a free port.

The British were confident of their military superiority in the region and they made Singapore their naval power base in Asia. In 1942 the Japanese invasion of Singapore took the British completely by surprise. The Japanese had landed in Malaysia, at Kota Bahru, and, in a matter of days, had commandeered all available bicycles and had ridden down to Singapore.

By the end of the war an estimated 100 000 civilians in Singapore had died, including 50 000 Chinese who were killed for being 'too Western'. Almost 30 000 Allied prisoners-of-war were held in Changi prison in Singapore, where many died of starvation, torture and disease. Other prisoners were force-marched to Thailand to work on the infamous Bridge over the River Kwai where many more died.

Although the Japanese were eventually defeated, the fact that they had successfully dominated the whole of South-east Asia at one point during the war and had repelled all the colonial rulers proved to be influential in helping Japan become an important political model for many of the countries in the region; Asians, not Westerners, had ruled during the war. Furthermore, in their efforts to create the East Asian Co-Prosperity Sphere, the Japanese had encouraged each nation they conquered to shake off their former colonial rulers. The Japanese defeat was the beginning of independence struggles in almost all the countries in South-east Asia, and Singapore was no exception. After the Japanese surrender was signed, the idea that the Britain would continue its colonial rule of old seemed completely absurd.

After the war, the Straits Settlements (Singapore, Penang and Malacca) and the Malayan sultanates attempted to form an independent federation. However, this union was short-lived, as fears of Malays dominating the Chinese in the Malayan sultanates became apparent, and fears of the Chinese dominating the Malays in the Straits Settlements surfaced. A British compromise was reached, whereby Singapore would become one country, and a crown colony (with a predominantly Chinese population), and the Straits Settlements of Penang and Malacca would join the other nine Malaysian states to form the Federation of Malaysia (with a mainly Malay population).

As a first step towards independence, municipal elections were held in 1949, but only English-speaking people were allowed to vote in them. In 1954 the People's Action Party (PAP) was formed. The PAP was an anti-imperialist party which brought together, for the first time, people of British and Chinese backgrounds. In 1959 Chinese people were allowed to vote in the elections for the first time and the PAP, led by Lee Kuan Yew, gained an overwhelming victory. Lee Kuan Yew became Prime Minister (a post he was to hold for more than 30 years) and he campaigned constantly for full independence. He also planned to take Singapore into a new federation with Malaysia, which had been independent since 1957.

In 1963 the Federation of Malaysia was formed, but as before, ethnic tensions between Singaporean Chinese and the Malays proved to be too divisive. Singapore withdrew from the federation less than two years later.

Singapore did not become fully independent until 1965. With no natural resources it seemed unlikely that Singapore would become a financially stable country in the near future. But Lee Kuan Yew had other ideas, and within a few years of independence Singapore was being called an 'economic miracle'. Singapore was built up as a free port and a financial and shipping centre. Lee Kuan Yew achieved this economic success mainly by being ruthless with opposition and enemies. The Internal Security Act (in place to this day) allows anyone the government suspects is a threat to the nation to be detained without trial.

Lee Kuan Yew finally retired as Prime Minister in November 1990, although he remains chairman of the PAP and is Senior Minister without portfolio in the cabinet of the new Prime Minister, Goh Chok Tong.

Geography

Singapore is an archipelago made up of over 50 islands although only a few of these islands are actually inhabited. The most well-known ones, apart from Singapore itself, are Sentosa and St John's. Both of these islands are popular tourist destinations and St John's can be reached by boat, while Sentosa can be reached by cable-car and by bus over the new bridge.

Singapore itself is an island state of only 633 square kilometres. This figure is constantly changing, however, as Singapore continues to reclaim more and more land from the sea.

Climate

Singapore lies about 100 kilometres north of the equator, so each day is almost exactly the same length and temperature. Singapore has a tropical climate with average daily temperatures of 25–30°C (75–87°F) and nights which are slightly cooler. November to January is the monsoon season, so be prepared for heavy, sudden but quickly dissipating showers.

Time

Singapore standard time is 8 hours ahead of Greenwich Mean Time, 13 hours ahead of New York, 16 hours ahead of San Francisco, 2 hours behind Sydney and 4 hours behind Wellington.

The people

There are just under three million people in Singapore, made up of three main ethnic groups – the Chinese (76%), the Malays (15%) and the Indians (6%). The remaining 3% is made up of Eurasians, Europeans and other foreigners.

The Chinese emigrated to Singapore in the late 19th and early 20th century from mainland China. Today their descendants make up separate groups within the Chinese community in Singapore. Hokkiens from Southern Fukien province are the largest group. Teochews from the Swatow region of Kwangtung, the second largest group, were traditionally fishermen. The third group is the Cantonese from Hong Kong who are often found in arts, crafts, food and the restaurant industry. Hakkas and Hainanese, traditionally worked as manual labourers, although Lee Kuan Yew is a Hakka. The fifth group of Chinese-Singaporeans are the Peranakans or Straits Chinese.

Politics

Today Singapore is governed by Goh Chok Tong and the People's Action Party. Goh has promised to bring in a more 'people-orientated' government in the next 25 years, but as yet, there is little evidence that Goh's style of government will be much different from his predecessor, Lee Kuan Yew's.

Languages

There are four official languages in Singapore: Malay, English, Chinese and Tamil. English is the language of administration and business, and it is unlikely that you will meet any Singaporeans who can't speak some English. Most Singaporeans are conversant in English and one of the other official languages. This means that you are unlikely to have a lot of Singaporean students. Most language schools teach students from the rest of South-east Asia who come to Singapore because it is the nearest English-speaking country.

Religions

Singapore is a secular state which practises tolerance of all faiths. The main religions in Singapore are Buddhism, Taoism, Islam, Christianity and Hinduism. About 60% of Singaporeans are Buddhists or Taoists, 15% are Muslim, 13% Christian, and 4% Hindu. Most of the Chinese are Buddhists and Taoists; the Malays are mainly Muslims; some Chinese, Malays, Indians and most Europeans are Christians; and most Indians in Singapore are Hindu.

In the late 1980s the government introduced the Maintenance of Religious Harmony Act which made proselytizing illegal, banned teaching religion in schools, and also banned any mixing of politics and religion.

Cultural considerations

Singlish

There is a special language in Singapore that combines direct translations from Chinese and Malay mixed with English to form

Singlish. Because of the effects of direct translations from Chinese you may think that the Singaporeans are being very rude. In fact they only sound rude to you because you may not be used to the intonation and such abrupt phrasing. (This phenomenon is similar to the way that many people think that Germans, when they speak English, are rude when actually the judgment is based upon tone of voice rather than content.) In Chinese, it is considered polite to include both 'yes' and 'no' options in an offer, as if to say that either possible answer is anticipated as satisfactory. But when this idea is translated directly into English it may sound rude, for example 'Drink now, want or not?' 'Come to my house, can or cannot?'

Singlish uses only one question tag – *is it?* – which you may find either amusing or annoying: 'You're a teacher, is it?', 'Do you like this, is it?' This is similar to French which also only uses one question tag – *n'est-ce pas*?

Kiasu

Kiasu (from Hokkien) means being afraid of being left out or of failing. To outsiders this can be interpreted as rudeness or greed. When you see Singaporeans piling their plates to dizzying heights at a restaurant buffet, or pushing to be at the front of the queue, don't lose your temper (you'll only lose face), instead count to ten slowly and then think *Kiasu!* Even McDonald's has caught onto the concept of *Kiasu,* using it as the basis of an advertising campaign by putting a quiz about what is and isn't *Kiasu* on their hamburger trays. Some Singaporeans are quite proud of being *Kiasu,* thinking of it as their own particular economic drive.

Small change wallets

While you are waiting at a bus-stop you may feel tempted to tell the old person beside you that they have some silver sticking out of their ears. Don't! You may be a bit disconcerted, but some Singaporeans, particularly older people, are very happy to keep their small change in their ears!

TEACHING POSSIBILITIES

Singapore is not a good destination for unqualified teachers. To be eligible for a work visa, you have to be a graduate and a qualified teacher. The kind of person who would like to hang out in Singapore for a few months and find some casual teaching work to finance further travel around South-east Asia is precisely the kind of person the Singapore government does not want in its country.

Singapore is an excellent country to work in if you are interested in living in Asia for a few years, but want to acclimatize yourself slowly to life in the East. English is one of the official languages in Singapore, you can buy Western food and clothes and see Western films and at the same time you can also eat with chopsticks, watch dragon-boat racing and visit mosques, and Hindu and Buddhist temples.

Going to a pre-arranged job

The main school which recruits abroad is inlingua. In Britain, unqualified teachers can take their two-week course (cheaper and shorter than the RSA/UCLES CELTA) and will then almost certainly be offered work in their school in Singapore. Most other schools in Singapore now recruit their staff locally, but it is still worth writing to the schools listed below before you leave your home country.

Private language schools

Most teachers find work in private language schools. Going along to the schools listed below with your CV will probably gain you an interview with the Director of Studies. Usually you will be asked to give a demonstration lesson, and if successful, you will be offered either full-time or part-time work. Do not worry if you are after a full-time contract and are not offered one right away. Often, showing that you are keen, teaching a few hours a week, and being available for cover work when other teachers are absent is the most usual way for new teachers to move from part-time status to full-time. Below are some of the best known English language schools in Singapore.

ATT, 19 Tanglin Road, #08-01, Tanglin Shopping Centre, Singapore, 247909. Tel: 235 5222. Fax: 738 1257.

Brighton, 51 Anson Road, Anson Center, #05 – 53, Singapore, 199748. Tel: 221 7608. Fax: 221 7135.

The British Council, 30 Napier Road, Singapore, 258509. Tel: 473 1111. Fax: 472 1010. e-mail:britcom@britcom.org.sg

The British Council, Holland Village Centre, 362 Holland Road, Singapore 278696. Tel: 4694263. Fax: 4632970. e-mail britcoun@britcoun.org.sg

The British Council, Tampines Centre, Temasek Polytechnic Campus, 21 Tampines Avenue 1, School of IT & Applied Science, Block 8, Level 4, Room IT 8 4-19, Singapore 5297. Tel: 7839209. Fax: 7834509. e-mail britcoun@britcoun.org.sg

ILC, Cuppage Centre, 55 Cuppage Road, #08 -21, Singapore, 229467. Tel 736 1707. Fax: 336 6554.

inlingua, 41 Sunset Way, Singapore 597071. Tel: 463 0966. Fax: 467 5483.

Language Systems Pte, Ltd, 1 Sophia Road, Peace Centre, #07 -01/04, Singapore 228149. Tel: 336 4222. Fax: 337 4854.

State and private schools and universities

Some teachers find work in state and private schools or universities once they arrive in Singapore. For teaching posts in primary or secondary schools contact

Ministry of Education, Teacher Recruitment Unit, Kay Siang Road, Singapore.

National University of Singapore, The Personnel Department, 10 Kent Ridge, Kent Ridge Crescent, Singapore 119260.

In the UK you can apply for teaching work at the National University of Singapore through their London office:

The Singapore High Commission, Students Department, 16 Kinnerton Street, London, SW1X 8ES. Tel: 0171 235 4562.

International schools

There are a number of international schools in Singapore which cater mainly for the British and American communities here. If you are qualified, either as a primary, secondary or specialist EFL teacher, you can contact them at:

American College, 25 Paterson Road, Singapore 238510. Tel: 2359537, Fax: 7325701.

Australian International School, 37 Emerald Hill Road, Singapore 229313. Tel: 7338411. Fax: 7331983.

Canadian International School, 5 Toh Tuck Road, Singapore 596679. Tel: 4671732. Fax: 4671729.

Dover Court Preparatory School, Dover Court, Singapore 139644. Tel: 775 7664. Fax: 777 4165.

International School (Singapore), 21 Preston Road, Singapore, 109355. Tel: 475 4188. Fax: 273 7065,

Singapore American School, 60 King's Road, Singapore, 268125. Tel: 466 5611. Fax: 469 5957.

Tanglin Schools, Portsdown Road, Singapore, 139294. Tel: 778 5577/7780771. Fax: 777 5862.

United World College Of South-east Asia, Pasir Panjang, PO Box 15, Dover Road, Singapore. Tel: 775 5344. Fax: 7785846.

Winchester School, 8 Winchester Road, Singapore 117782. Tel: 2739522. Fax: 2727410.

Freelance teaching

Teaching private students will not qualify you for a work visa in Singapore, so it is practically impossible to teach only privately and live here. However, after you have found a job with a language school, it is easy to find outside work to supplement your income. Most schools frown on this practice, but in reality there is little the school can do about it.

> The school I worked for had it written into the contract that I was forbidden to teach privately. Every teacher signed the contract and practically every teacher I knew had at least one private student. The boss either didn't know or chose to pretend he didn't know that all the teachers were also working outside the school. Either way, it was a great source of extra money for me.
>
> *Anna Groom, England*

BEFORE YOU GO

Insurance

If you are going to a pre-arranged job your employer will look after your health care and a private health insurance plan is unnecessary. However, if you do not have a job pre-arranged, then health insurance is a very good investment as health care in Singapore is expensive.

Vaccinations

You must have a certificate of vaccination against yellow fever if you have recently been in any of the infected countries (South America and most of Africa). Other than that, there are no other vaccinations or health precautions you have to take.

Passport/visa

To enter Singapore as a tourist you must have an onward ticket out of Singapore and proof of funds for your two-week stay in Singapore.

ARRIVAL AND VISAS

Visas and work permits

If you arrive in Singapore without a pre-arranged job and enter the country as a tourist with an onward ticket and sufficient funds, you will be given a two-week social visit pass at the airport. You do not need to apply for a visa before you leave for Singapore if you come from one of the following countries: Australia, Canada, Ireland, New Zealand, South Africa, the UK or the USA.

Without a work permit you will either have to apply to the Immigration Department if you want to stay longer or make a trip to Malaysia every two weeks to renew your tourist visa. If you apply to the Immigration Department you will need proof of funds, an onward ticket and a better reason for wanting to stay than 'Looking for work'.

If you choose to extend your time in Singapore by leaving the country, keep in mind that the Singapore customs take a dim view of anyone with too many suspicious tourist visa stamps in their passport. If the authorities suspect you have been working while on a tourist visa you can be deported immediately.

There has been considerable press coverage recently of an American youth who was sentenced to six strokes of the cane because he vandalized a car. A case which has had less publicity but which you should take note of was of a young man who received a similar punishment for overstaying his tourist visa.

After you have found a job your school will usually help you to apply for an employment pass. This involves filling out very detailed forms requesting particulars of all your immediate family, your complete education and employment history, as well as your signature to a declaration that says 'I undertake not to be concerned in any political or other activity ... which would make me an undesirable or prohibited immigrant under the Immigration Act.' Prohibited immigrants include anyone suffering from a contagious disease, anyone advocating opposition to the Singapore Government or anyone who is a drug addict, drug user or drug trafficker. You will also need certified copies of your birth certificate or passport, your university degree and TEFL qualification and a recent medical fitness certificate. Your medical certificate can be issued by a doctor in Singapore who should sign it stating that your chest x-ray was clear.

Immigration

As in other Asian countries, a conservative set of clothes, the correct documentation and a polite manner will speed you through immigration. If you are arriving on a tourist visa, do not tell the officials that you are planning to use your time in Singapore to look for work, as they could immediately deport you.

The airport

If you are catching the bus into town from the airport you will need the exact fare and there are banks at the airport where you can change money.

Local calls are free from the airport if you use the red phones which are available after you come through immigration.

Transport from the airport

The 16E bus leaves from Basement 2 of terminal 1 and goes close to Bencoolen Street and to Orchard Road. It costs S$1.20 (air-conditioned) and S$0.90 cents (non-AC) and you need the exact change. The journey into town takes about half an hour. There is also an Airbus connecting Changi with the major hotels in the centre of town (you do not have to stay at one of the hotels to use this bus service).

Taxis leave from outside the Departure Hall. Taxis from the airport are subject to a S$3 surcharge which is not shown on the meter. The fare to Orchard Road is about S$15 and the journey takes about 20 minutes.

ACCOMMODATION

Short-term accommodation

The main area for cheap 'crash-pads' is in Bencoolen Street. Crash-pads are residential flats which have been converted into very small bedrooms and dormitories and although they are officially illegal, the government seems to turn a blind eye to them.

Bencoolen House, 27 Bencoolen Street, 7th floor (Tel: 338 1206)

Goh's Homestay, Hong Guan Building, 173/175 Bencoolen Street, 6th floor.

Hawaii Guest House, Hong Guan Building, 173/175 Bencoolen Street, 2nd floor (the lift is at the back of the building)

Latin House, 46 Bencoolen Street, 3rd floor (Tel: 339 6308).

Peony Mansions, 46-52 Bencoolen Street, 6th floor, door 50E (the lift is at the back of the building).

Long-term accommodation

Finding long-term accommodation in Singapore is not quite the headache it is in other Asian countries. For example, you don't have to pay a year's rent in advance, as you do in Indonesia. It is usual to pay only a one or two months' rent in advance, and this deposit will be returned to you at the end of your lease. Private accommodation for rent and accommodation agencies are advertised in *The Straits Times*. If you go through an agent, it is usual for the owner to pay the agent's fee, rather than you. Going through an agent is often a good idea initially, because the agent will pick you up and drive you to see different apartments. This is also a good way to see what is available, and also to see different parts of Singapore that you might not have considered living in. In general though, most teachers find their accommodation through other teachers. Usually, established teachers know of rooms to let in a teacher's flat, or can recommend an agency to you. Most Singaporeans live in Housing Development Board (HDB) flats, which are in government-built apartment blocks. Although technically they are not allowed to, unless they have a special permit, many Singaporeans rent out their HDB flats to foreigners. The government regularly issues warnings that they are going to clamp down on this practice but, in reality, it continues without too much bother to either flat-owners or tenants.

Rent in Singapore in, for example, a shared flat with three people sharing is between S$800 and S$1 000 per person. Cheaper rents are available if you are prepared to live outside the city-centre. With the MRT up-and-running, living out in Yishun in the north of Singapore is not the hardship it used to be.

Telephone. Most rented accommodation comes with a telephone which can be used for international direct dialing.

Water, electricity and gas. Tap water is safe to drink, electricity is 230-250 volts, 50 cycles AC, and gas is piped into houses. Bills for utilities are paid monthly at banks or post offices. If you are renting an HDB apartment (see above), your house-owner will usually show you your monthly bills, collect your money, and then pay the bill for you at the bank, since legally you should not be living in an HDB flat.

Household help. In most countries in the region teachers can afford to hire household help. Singapore is the exception to the rule because employing a maid is too expensive. Few Singaporeans want to work as maids so most household help comes from abroad, particularly from the Philippines. As well as paying a maid around $400 a month, you would also have to pay an additional tax of $300 a month for employing foreign household help. It is possible to hire part-time domestic help but few teachers do.

LIVING COSTS

How expensive is Singapore?

Although Singapore is certainly more expensive than most of its neighbouring countries in South-east Asia, it is still cheaper than the major cities in the West. It is certainly cheaper if you live as the Singaporeans do and not as the expats do. A fully-Westernized lifestyle is available in Singapore and in many ways its very availability can lead some teachers to two common misconceptions. First, because Singapore and its people are so Westernized, some visitors think that 'Culture Shock' does not exist here. When the sky-scrapers look the same as back home and the people speak English, are dressed in Levis, eat fast food and watch the latest block-busters from Hollywood, it is easy to assume that, therefore, their culture and world-view must be the same as yours. Nothing could be further from the truth. Second, because everyday products are on the supermarket shelves, it can easily be assumed that they should be as affordable in Singapore as they are at home. Oreo cookies, Heinz Ploughman's Pickle, or a can of Victoria Bitter are all imported goods and are much more expensive in Singapore than they are in New York, London or Sydney.

Most teachers in Singapore have a comfortable life. It is certainly true that the recent rising accommodation prices have made life in Singapore less financially attractive than it has been in the past. However, compared to the cost of living in the West, the money you get in Singapore will go a lot further. Food and drink are not expensive if you choose where you spend your money, as meals in a hawker centre can cost as little as S$3.

Salaries

Full-time teachers' salaries start from around $2 000 a month. Ater rent and taxes you will be left with around $1 200 which if not blown on drinking in clubs and pubs or eating in expensive restaurants, can go quite far.

Taxes

Income Tax. There is no Pay As You Earn scheme in Singapore, instead you pay your tax bill at the end of the year (31 December). Tax on your income depends on how much you earn and also on how many days you work in any one financial year. A yearly tax bill is 2–15% for most teachers.

Central Provident Fund. Until recently there was a savings scheme called CPF (Central Provident Fund). This was a non-taxable saving scheme to which you contributed 22.5% and your employer 18.5% of your salary each month. When your left Singapore you could collect the lump sum. At the end of an 18-month contract, teachers could expect to receive about $15 000.

Unfortunately, suddenly, in 1995, the government announced that CPF for foreign workers was to end the following day! They later relented and introduced a three-year grace period for companies to phase out this scheme. Most private EFL schools elected to drop out of CPF immediately, so if you are a new teacher to Singapore, you will not be entitled to join one of the world's best savings schemes. Now, instead of the employer's CPF contributions, schools like ATT, for example, offer new teachers a 10% gratuity at the end of their contracts.

Fines. Singapore is infamous for its fines and the following table gives you an idea of what is considered unacceptable behaviour and how much it will cost you if you are caught doing it.

$ Singapore	Misdemeanour
50	Jaywalking – crossing a street within 50 metres of a pedestrian crossing.
50	Not using car seat-belts.
95	Not flushing a public toilet.
300	Smoking inside any public building.
315	Eating or drinking on the MRT.
625	Littering.

Supermarket costs

There are plenty of supermarkets in Singapore and Cold Storage, a popular supermarket with teachers and other foreigners, has a number of branches throughout the island. A sample shopping-basket of goods is given below. Unlike many other countries in South-east Asia, supermarket costs in Singapore are the same or even lower than in small local shops (prices are in S$).

Bread (small sliced loaf)	1.40	Rice (1 kg)	1.60
Beef (100)	1.40	Tea (50 tea-bags)	5.00
Milk (1 litre)	2.60	Instant coffee (200 g)	6.90
Sugar (1 kg)	1.00	Beer (750 ml)	4.60
Eggs (10)	0.60	Cigarettes (20 Marlboro)	4.50

EATING AND DRINKING

Eating is a joy in Singapore, the choice is enormous, the variations seem endless, and eating out can be incredibly cheap.

Etiquette

When eating Chinese food you should use chopsticks, or a knife and fork. When eating Malay or south Indian food you should use your right hand or a spoon and fork. Eating with your hand is slightly more complicated than it sounds. Putting your fingers in your mouth, sucking on your fingers or getting your fingers messy, past the knuckles, is a sign of bad manners. Try to cup your fingers, scoop the food off your plate, then (and this is the difficult bit) turn your hand round so your thumb is nearest your mouth, put your thumb behind the food and then flip it into your mouth.

Restaurants

The cheapest place to eat at in Singapore is at a hawker centre (or food centre). Here for as little as S$3.00 you can taste some of the best

Singaporean dishes. You can find hawker centres all over Singapore, often on the ground floor of large HDB (Housing Development Board) flats or near markets. In a hawker centre you will see hundreds of small stalls and fixed round tables and stools. You can sit at any table, you do not have to sit at a table in front of the stall where you order your food. When your food is ready the stall-holder will bring it to your table, and you pay then. Drinks are also available at hawker centres – tea, coffee, beer, and a wonderful selection of freshly-made fruit drinks.

Singaporean specialties

Every dish seems to be a Singaporean specialty – everything from Indian curry to Chinese dim-sum and Malay satay. Some of the most popular dishes are: beef *kway teow* (a beef broth served with flat noodles and liver or tripe); *char siew fun* (steamed rice with barbecued pork and slices of cucumber); *banana leaf curry* (as the name suggests, curry served on a large banana leaf, instead of a plate); and *nasi lemak* (rice cooked in coconut milk with anchovies, egg, cucumber and chili paste).

Drinking

Singapore-brewed beers are Tiger and Anchor. Both are light, fizzy beers (like lager for British beer-drinkers) and very pleasant. Tiger is probably the best beer made in South-east Asia.

Most spirits are available in Singapore – imported gin, vodka and whisky, as well as *saké* from Japan. In image-conscious Singapore, the colour of your whisky label is very important – ordering a bottle of Johnny Walker black label in a restaurant or pub shows everyone that you've arrived!

Wine is becoming increasingly popular here, and good wines from Europe, Australia and America are available in most supermarkets at a price.

Cheap venues. The cheapest place for a bottle of cold Tiger beer is in a hawker centre. Another cheap drinking option is in small tea or coffee houses, which also serve beer.

Medium-priced venues. The pubs listed below (bars and discos) that are popular with teachers and other foreigners, while being a lot more expensive than hawker centre, are certainly not out of the reach of most teachers. Most of these pubs have happy hours (often for two or three hours in the early evening) with half-price beer, making them even more affordable for teachers.

Expensive venues. The most expensive drinking places in Singapore are the luxury hotel bars. Here a band, usually from the Philippines, plays cover-versions and beers cost S$10-15 a glass, exclusive of tips and tax. A Singapore Sling at Raffles will cost you about S$15.

TRANSPORT

Singaporeans drive on the left-hand side of the road and generally drive right-hand-drive cars.

MRT

The Mass Rapid Transport (MRT) is an underground train service. Fares start from S$0.60 and you buy plastic tickets from machines inside the station. Inserting your ticket at the barrier automatically opens it. When you finish your journey the barrier opens again and retains your ticket, which is later removed to be recycled. You can buy a 'Transit Link farecard' or a 'stored-value' card for S$12 or S$22, including a S$2 deposit which is refundable when you return your card to the station. These cards can also be used on the buses.

Bus

Singapore has a very good bus service. Fares start from S$0.50 cents and you need the exact fare. You pay as you enter and take a ticket from the machine behind the driver. You can also use a 'stored-value' card (see above) which you insert into a machine on the right of the bus as you enter. Press in your fare amount and the machine automatically deducts it from your card.

Taxi

Taxis in Singapore are safe, reliable and are all metered. Surprisingly, although the island is small, taxi drivers often have difficulty finding addresses so it is worth knowing, if possible, exactly where you want to go before getting into a taxi. When taxi drivers are going home after changing shifts they put a red destination card on their dashboard and will pick up passengers who are going only in that direction. Taxi fares start at S$2.20 with the following charges which might not be shown on the meter: a 50% surcharge between midnight and 6am; a S$2.20 surcharge for taxis booked by phone and a further S$1 for every additional hour in advance; a S$3 surcharge for journeys from Changi airport; a S$1 surcharge for journeys from the CBD (Central Business District) between 4pm and 7pm weekdays and noon to 3pm on

Saturdays; and a S$3 surcharge if you are the first driver's passenger going into the CBD between 7.30am and 10.15am Monday to Saturday, or 4.30pm and 6.30pm Monday to Friday.

Train

There are no internal trains in Singapore, however, Singapore and Malaysia are connected by rail. Trains depart regularly throughout the day for Johor Bahru and Kuala Lumpur.

To Johor Bahru it costs S$1.50 (single) and the journey takes just 45 minutes. To Kuala Lumpur it costs S$34 (second class single) and the journey takes seven hours. For further information contact the Singapore Railway Station on 222 5165.

On the famous Orient Express the journey to Kuala Lumpur costs a mere £1 270/US$1 905 for the presidential suite. For further information contact the Eastern and Oriental Express Company on 227 2068.

Boat

Boats and ferries in Singapore are mostly for tourists these days. Tours up and down the river cost from as little as S$3.00 to $85 for an evening dinner cruise.

You can travel by boat to Batam or Bintan (two Indonesian islands) from the World Trade Centre. The journey takes about 30 minutes (Batam) or one hour (Bintan) and costs S$26 return to Batam and S$27 to Bintan. See below (sports) for information on hiring boats for water skiing.

Car

Cars are very expensive in Singapore and few teachers can afford them. A new car costs about S$95 000 including 150% government tax and a 41% custom tax. Even before you buy a car you have to buy a Certificate of Entitlement (COE). These certificates are auctioned every month and can cost from S$40 000 to S$100 000. Road tax is S$1 500 a year, with an additional 10% added on for each year of the car's life. When cars are 10 years old they have to be sold to the government for scrap. So if you fancy buying a cheap, second-hand banger, you can see why Singapore might not be the place to do it.

Plane

Singapore Airlines (SIA) is the national carrier which flies to destinations within South-east Asia as well as to all major international airports.

If you are flying to Malaysia, buy only a single ticket in Singapore. Each one-way ticket costs $132, but if you buy your ticket for the Malaysia–Singapore part of the journey in Malaysia, you can pay in Malaysian dollars, which makes it much cheaper than the Singapore–Malaysia part of the trip.

SERVICES

Public phones

From public phone-boxes local calls cost 10 cents. However, more and more public telephones now use phonecards. You can buy phonecards, in denominations of S$2, S$5, S$10, S$20 and S$50, from post offices. You can use your phonecard to phone abroad or you can phone direct from the General Post Office and some other larger post offices in Singapore.

Libraries

Libraries in Singapore have a good selection of English books. The National Library on Stamford Road costs S$10 to join. You need your passport, entry permit and proof of your address in Singapore to join. Your National Library card gives you access to books in the National Library and eight other branch libraries.

Bookshops

There are lots of bookshops in Singapore with large selections of EFL books, novels and non-fiction English language books. In most shopping centres there is a branch of one or more of the three main bookshops – Times, MPH or Wordshop. Centrepoint shopping centre on Orchard Road has large branches of both Times and MPH bookshops. Second-hand books are available on the second floor of the Holland Road Shopping Centre.

Banks and financial matters

The Singapore currency is the dollar (made up of 100 cents). There are coins of 1 ,5, 10, 20, 50 cents and one dollar. There are notes of 1, 2, 5, 10, 20, 100, 500, 1 000 and 10 000 dollars.

Banks are open Monday to Friday 10am to 3pm and usually open either all day or mornings only on Saturdays. Cash withdrawal machines are open 24 hours a day, seven days a week and your cash withdrawal card can also be used in some supermarkets and department stores, as can all the major credit cards.

Health

Tap water is safe to drink anywhere in Singapore. Diseases such as cholera and typhoid (prevalent in nearby Malaysia and Indonesia) which are caught from drinking contaminated water are unheard of now in Singapore, although dengue fever is still a health risk.

Singapore has excellent medical facilities. Doctors are listed under 'Medical Practitioners' and dentists under 'Dental Surgeons' in the Yellow Pages. Most schools have health care insurance for their full-time teachers and teachers usually pay for treatment when they visit the doctor and then are reimbursed by the school later. A central doctors' practice is:

Singapore Medical Centre, 19 Tanglin Road, #06 38/39, Tanglin Shopping Centre, Singapore 247909. Tel: 7341311

MEDIA

Television

The government controls all broadcasting in Singapore. There are three channels on Singapore TV, with most TVs able to receive a further three channels from Malaysia. Locally made programmes are in English, Chinese, Malay and Tamil. Imported programmes, mostly American sit-coms and dramas, are also regularly broadcast.

Radio

Radio stations broadcast in English from 6am to midnight and play a mixture of US, British and Asian pop music.

The BBC World Service has great reception in Singapore and can be heard 24 hours a day on 88.900 VHF.

Newspapers

There are two daily English language newspapers – *The Straits Times* (a morning broadsheet) and *The New Paper* (an afternoon tabloid). Newspapers from abroad are available in bookshops and large hotels. *The Times* (from London or New York) will cost you about S$10.

RECREATION

Music

Singapore is beginning to feature as a regular stop on the Asian tour route for well-known bands and singers. Michael Jackson's recent

Asian tour included a Singapore date (before he cancelled the concert and went into hiding when certain allegations broke) but the cost of a ticket for a superstar's concert makes it a special night out for teachers in Singapore. If you can afford them, tickets are available from Tangs department store and Centrepoint Shopping Centre in Orchard Road.

Some pubs have live music, usually bands playing cover versions of heavy metal, rock, jazz or country and western. Some popular bars with live music are Saxophone, Anywhere and Ginivy's (see below for addresses and telephone numbers).

Bars and discos

Pubs which are popular with teachers include:

The Front-page Pub, 9 Mohd. Sultan Road. Tel: 235 7013.
The Next Page Pub, 15 Mohd. Sultan Road. Tel: 235 6967.
Elvis Place, 1A Duxton Hill. Tel: 227 8543.
The Yard Lounge, 294 River Valley Road. Tel: 733 9594.
Saxophone Bar and Restaurant, 23 Cuppage Road. Tel: 235 8385.
Hard Rock Cafe, 50 Cuscaden Road, #02 – 01. Tel: 235 6256.
The Third Man, 11 Stamford Road, #01 – 02. Tel: 334 1985.
Anywhere, Tanglin Shopping Center, Tanglin Road. Tel: 734 8233.
Ginivy's, #02 – 11 rear block, Orchard Towers, 400 Orchard Road.

Discos which are popular with teachers include:

Fire, #04 -19 Orchard Plaza, 150 Orchard Road. Tel: 235 0155.
Zouk, 17 – 21 Jiak Kim Street. Tel: 738 2988.
Warehouse, 332 Havelock Road. Tel: 732 9922.
Top Ten, 5th floor, Orchard Towers, 400 Orchard Road. Tel: 732 3077.

Cinema

All the latest Hollywood films come to Singapore. Tickets cost around S$8.00 and listings are shown in all the daily papers. Cinemas are seriously air-conditioned so you should take a sweater with you as the sudden change in temperature might come as a bit of a shock to the system.

Theatre

The Drama Centre in Fort Canning Rise and the Victoria Theatre in Empress Place both regularly feature productions of musicals, ballets and plays. Increasingly Singaporean plays are being produced as well as foreign productions.

If you fancy yourself as a bit of a thespian, you can join an amateur drama group which puts on four shows a year in English, including a Christmas pantomime. The Stage Club is open to anyone who is interested in acting or working back-stage and costs S$40 a year to join:

The Stage Club, 41 Malcolm Road 308276. Tel: 251 1380, 255 1181.

Sports

Swimming, tennis, badminton and squash

There are public swimming pools which cost about S$2 and public tennis, badminton and squash courts which cost about S$4. A lot of teachers join the YMCA on Orchard Road, S$52 for the first year and S$36 for each subsequent year which gives them access to the roof-top swimming pool for S$1 a swim and the use of squash and badminton courts and gyms, each for S$4. Especially if you have a split-shift timetable, an afternoon swim is an ideal way to spend a couple of hours, rather than staying in school or going back home, before returning relaxed and refreshed for your late-afternoon or evening classes.

Water-skiing

You can rent skis, a boat and a driver for S$60–70 an hour. Often a group of teachers gets together at the weekend and hires a boat for an afternoon. For more information contact:

Seashore Boating Centre, Track 24 Ponggol Road. Tel: 482 0888.
William Water Sports, Ponggol Point. Tel: 282 6879.

Sailing and windsurfing

You can hire sailboards or small laser boats and have sailing lessons, if you need them, from S$20 an hour at:

The East Coast Park Sailing Centre, 1210 East Coast Park Way. 449881 Tel: 449 5118.

Help-lines

Police	999
Ambulance	995
Fire Brigade	995
The Samaritans	1800 221 4444
Alcoholics Anonymous	338 2791

APPENDICES

Appendix 1. Case history

Catherine Nightingale

Catherine Nightingale, from Oxford, graduated from Manchester University in 1986 with a degree in English language and literature. She completed a one-week TEFL course with Linguarama in Manchester before going to Italy to work on an archaeological excavation site. In Italy, when her money ran out, she found teaching work and stayed there for one and a half years. After teaching in Italy she worked in France for a year.

She was recruited in England for a private language school, inlingua, in Singapore on an 18-month contract and although she left Singapore after only a year, she insists it was more boredom with teaching than boredom with Singapore that made her end her contract early.

She found Singapore a very safe place for a woman on her own; 'It was wonderful to walk about at two in the morning and know that I wasn't in any danger at all.'

Not knowing Asia also made Singapore an ideal country for Catherine. 'It was an easy country to go to first in Asia. On the surface it's a gleaming, modern city where everything and everyone works and that very reliability is comforting if it's your first time in Asia.'

She said that what she most enjoyed about Singapore was its food, 'cheap and various and it meant I never had to cook at home'; its proximity to Malaysia, 'I could go away to a beautiful beach for the weekend without spending a lot of money or time travelling there'; and its cheap sports facilities, 'I even learned to water-ski, something I would never have done in Britain.'

When she scratched Singapore's surface she said she found a wide variety of religions and cultures; 'Every other day there was a festival, and in places like Little India there were pockets of very strong cultural expression.'

After she finished working in Singapore she traveled for six months in Indonesia, Malaysia, Thailand, Hong Kong and China, and returned to Britain on the Orient Express from Beijing. Her trip around Asia was paid for from her CPF savings (see p 193) which she also used to finance further study when she returned to London.

She graduated from University College, London, in Archaeological Conservation and now works for the Science Museum in London. 'I don't regret for a minute the time I spent in Singapore and would recommend it to anyone who wants to go to Asia but is a bit apprehensive about going to a country very different from their own. Singapore is a great place from which to start a love affair with Asia.'

Appendix 2. Useful Singaporean words and phrases

English is one of the official languages in Singapore so you can easily make yourself understood without having to learn Mandarin, Malay or Tamil (the other three official languages). See Chapter 8: Malaysia, Appendix 2 for useful words and phrases which you can use in Malaysia and Indonesia as well as Singapore.

Appendix 3. Public holidays

Fluctuating dates are marked with an asterisk *

1 January	New Year's Day
* Late January/ early February	Chinese New Year
* Early/mid April	*Hari Raya Puasa*
* April	Good Friday
1 May	Labour Day
* Early May	*Hari Raya Haji*
* Mid May	*Vesak* Day
9 August	National Day
* Late October	*Deepavali, Hindu Festival of Lights*
25 December	Christmas Day

Appendix 4. Embassies and consulates

Selected embassies and foreign missions in Singapore

Australia: 25 Napier Road, Singapore 258507. Tel: 737 9311.

UK: 325 Tanglin Road, Singapore 247955. Tel: 473 9333.

Canada: 80 Anson Road #14-00, IBM Towers, Singapore 079907. Tel: 225 6363.

Ireland: 541 Orchard Road #08-02, Singapore, 238881. Tel: 732 3430.

New Zealand: 391A Orchard Road #15-06, Ngee Ann City Tower A, Singapore, 238873. Tel: 235 9966.

South Africa: 331 North Bridge Road #15-00, Odeon Towers, Singapore, 188720. Tel: 339 3319.

USA: 27 Napier Road, Singapore 258508. Tel: 476 9037. Fax: 476 9080.

Selected Singapore embassies abroad

Australia: Singapore High Commission, 17 Forster Cresent, Yarralumla, Canberra, ACT, 20600. Tel: 273 3944.

Canada: Singapore Consulate, c/o Russel and Du Moulin, 1075 West Georgia St, Vancouver, BC, V6E 3G2. Tel: 224 7386.

New Zealand: Singapore High Commission, 17 Kabul St, Khandallah, Wellington. Tel: 792 2076.

UK: Singapore High Commission, 9 Wilton Crescent, London, SW1X 8SA. Tel: 235 8315.

USA: 1824 R Street NW, Washington DC 20009-1691. Tel: 667 7555.

Appendix 5. Suggested reading

Bloodworth, Dennis, *The Tiger and the Trojan*, Times Books, 1986.

Barber, Noel, *The Singapore Story*, Fontana, 1986.

Clavell, James, *King Rat,* Coronet, London, 1996.

Farrell, J.G., *The Singapore Grip*, Fontana, London, 1979.

Finlay Hugh, and Peter Turner, *Lonely Planet Travel Survival Kit Malaysia, Singapore and Brunei,* Lonely Planet Publications.

Theroux, Paul, *Saint Jack*, Penguin, 1976.

Turner, Peter, and Tony Wheeler, *Lonely Planet City Guide Singapore,* Lonely Planet Publications.

Wise, Michael, *Travellers' Tales of Old Singapore,* In Print, Brighton, UK, 1996.

10

Brunei
(Brunei Darussalam)

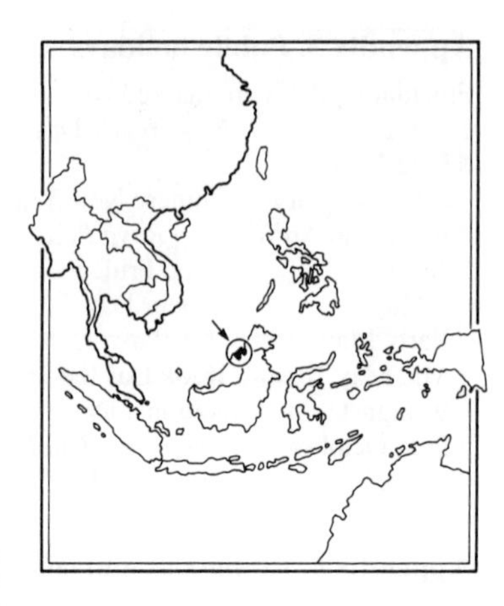

FACTFILE

The official name for Brunei is the Islamic Sultanate of Brunei, or Brunei Darussalam. Brunei is made up of two tracts of land bounded on three sides by the Malaysian state of Sarawak and to the north by the South China Sea. Most of the towns are located on the narrow coastal strip; the rest of the country is mainly tropical rainforest.

History

During the 16th century Brunei's rule extended to the north-west coast of Borneo and the southern islands of the Philippines. Around this time Spain attempted to subdue the sultanate, and, although it was unsuccessful on the mainland, Spain did manage to colonize the Philippine islands, which had previously belonged to Brunei.

At the end of the 16th century the Dutch set up the Dutch East India Trading Company and colonized all of nearby Indonesia, but Brunei managed to remain independent.

In 1886 the Sultan asked Britain for protection in an attempt to stop James Brooke, the British Rajah of Sarawak, from encroaching further on Brunei's territory.

The first British Resident arrived in 1906 and British presence was felt until 1979, when a five-year friendship and cooperation agreement with Britain was signed. This agreement set out a timetable for Brunei's independence and in 1984 Brunei became fully independent.

Oil was first discovered at Seria in 1929, and in 1963 the first offshore deposits were found. The oil crisis of the 1970s and the Arab oil boycott of 1973 ensured that Brunei became one the world's wealthiest nations. In fact, the Sultan is believed to be the richest person in the world.

> 'A few years ago he built the biggest palace in the world. It has 1 788 rooms, 5 swimming pools, 257 toilets, 44 staircases and 18 lifts. The dining room can seat 4 000 people. There are 564 chandeliers with 51 490 light bulbs. A servant is employed full time to change bulbs – about 200 a day. The total cost of the palace was $400 million.'
>
> *Headway Pre-Intermediate EFL coursebook*

Today Brunei is one of the few countries in the world which has no foreign debt. Citizens pay no personal tax and have access to free education and free health care. Per capita income is over US$22 000.

Geography

Brunei is one the world's smallest nations; it has only 5 770 square kilometres of land. More than 80% of Brunei is still covered by jungles and forests.

Climate

Brunei lies within the tropical zone and, like most of the countries in South-east Asia, has two seasons – dry and hot and wet and hot. The rainy season is generally in November and December and the dry and slightly cooler season is from April to July. Temperatures can range from 22°C (71°F) at night to 32°C (90°F) during the day.

Time

Brunei Standard Time is the same as Singapore and Malaysia, 8 hours ahead of Greenwich Mean Time, 13 hours ahead of New York, 16 hours ahead of San Francisco, 2 hours behind Sydney and 4 hours behind Wellington.

The people

There are about 260 000 people living in Brunei; about 65% of them (around 63 868) live in the Brunei–Muara district, which contains the capital, Bandar Seri Begawan. The population is made up of 65% Malays, 20% Chinese and 15% indigenous Dayaks and Europeans.

Politics

Brunei is ruled by an absolute monarch, His Majesty, Sultan Haji Hassanal Bolkiah Mui'zzaddin Waddaulah. He is the country's prime minister and defence minister, and rules by royal decree. There is only one legal political party – the National Democratic Party.

In December 1962 a mass uprising broke out against the proposed integration of Brunei into the Federation of Malaysia. Although Brunei did not in the end join the Federation, the political party behind the rebellion, The Brunei People's Party, was outlawed and its leaders jailed or forced into exile.

Six of these prisoners were released in January 1991, mostly, it has been suggested, because of political pressure from the UK.

Brunei is also a member of ASEAN, the Assosciation of South-east Asian Nations.

Languages

The official language of Brunei is Malay, but other languages widely spoken include Chinese and English. This means it will be easy for you to make yourself understood, but it also means that there are few job opportunities available to you as a teacher.

Religions

The main religion of Brunei is Islam, although there are some Chinese Buddhists and Christians as well.

Cultural considerations

Islam. As Brunei is mainly a Muslim country, it is important to respect Islamic traditions, religion and customs. See Chapter 1: Islam (Brunei, Indonesia, Malaysia and Singapore) for further details of appropriate behaviour in a Muslim country.

Alcohol. Unlike the two other Islamic countries in South-east Asia (Malaysia and Indonesia), Brunei has banned alcohol for Muslims and alcohol is difficult to obtain for non-Muslims. In January 1991 prohibition was introduced by the Department of Religious Affairs. This ruling made it illegal to sell or give alcohol to a Brunei Muslim. All bars in Brunei were closed down, or became places which sold only alcohol-free beer (Swan and Lowenbrau) and alcohol-free wine (Californian Ariel Blanc).

Non-Muslims can still bring in their duty-free allowance of alcohol which amounts to two bottles of wine or spirits and 12 cans of beer.

Face. See Chapter 1: Cultural considerations. As elsewhere in the region, showing anger, or any other strong emotion, is considered inappropriate. The all-purpose Asian smile is much in evidence in Brunei and saving and losing face is as important here as it is in other parts of South-east Asia.

Electricity. Appliances in Brunei use 230 volts, 50 cycles. Most plugs are three-pin, 13 amp.

TEACHING POSSIBILITIES

It is unlikely that you will find casual teaching work if you just show up in Brunei. However, there are three main possibilities for work that you could consider before arriving here.

The Centre for British Teachers regularly recruits for teachers in Brunei. You can contact them at:

The Centre for British Teachers (CfBT), Quality House, Chancery Lane, London, WC2A 1HP. Tel: (0171) 242 2982. Fax: (0171) 242 0474.

The second possibility, if you are a qualified primary teacher, is to apply to the international school:

International School Brunei, Box 2187, Bandar Seri Begawan, Brunei Darussalam. Tel: (02) 30608.

Finally, if you are a qualified EFL teacher with at least two years' experience, the British Council has an English Language Centre and a Direct Teaching Operation (DTO):

The British Council, Hong Kong Bank Chambers, Jalan Pemancha, PO Box 3049, Bandar Seri Begawan 1930. Tel.:(02) 2227480/227531. Fax: (02) 241769

The British Council, English Language Centre, No 45 Simpang 100, Jalan Tunku Link Gadong, Bandar Seri Begawan, 3192. Tel: (02) 448 988. Fax: (02) 448 988.

ARRIVAL AND VISAS

Visas

British people do not need a visa for visits up to 30 days. Canadians do not require a visa for a visit up to 14 days. If you are American, Australian, Irish, New Zealander or South African, you will have to apply for a visa, which you can do in your home country. However, if your home country does not have a Brunei Darussalam embassy or diplomatic mission, you can get a visa from British consulates, or from the Immigration Department when you arrive in Brunei. If you are travelling in the region and then decide to go to Brunei, remember that you cannot get a visa from the two Malaysian neighbouring states of Sabah or Sarawak.

If you have a pre-arranged job to go to in Brunei, your employer will look after your work visa for you.

Transport from the airport

As Brunei has a per capita GNP of over US$22 000, cars are a way of life for most people in Brunei. The public transport system is almost non-existent so you are unlikely to find a bus to take you from the airport to the centre of town.

Brunei International airport is about 12 kilometres from the centre of Bandar Seri Begawan (BSB). The taxi fare costs B$20–30 and takes about 20 minutes.

ACCOMMODATION AND LIVING COSTS

Short-term accommodation

Most hotels in Bandar Seri Begawan cost B$100 or more per night. Brunei does little to encourage budget travellers or people coming here in the hope of finding work. There are only two reasonably priced hostels in BSB, costing about B$10 a night.

Pusat Belia Youth Centre, Jalan Sungai Kianggeh. Tel: (02) 23936. Priority is given to people who have a youth-hostel or student card, although if there is space available, it will be given to non-members.

Government Resthouse, Jalan Sungai Kianggeh. Tel: (02) 223571. The resthouse is officially reserved for government officials, but often Western visitors are given rooms if there are any available.

Long-term accommodation

Rent in Brunei is very expensive, but most teachers are given free or subsidized accommodation. There are housing agents who will help you negotiate with house-owners, as it is quite difficult to negotiate for yourself. But usually the school you are working for will take care of finding you a house.

Supermarket costs

Prices in this list are in Brunei dollars.

Item	Price	Item	Price
Bread (1kg)	3.50	Milk (1 litre)	3.83
Butter (250 g)	2.36	Mineral water (1 litre)	1.12
Cheese, cheddar (500 g)	9.82	Potatoes (1kg)	3.83
Coffee:		Rice (1kg)	1.50
ground (500 g)	13.45	Steak (1 kg)	21.00
instant (250 g)	14.00	Sugar (1 kg)	2.43
Cooking oil (1 litre)	7.07	Tea bags (250 g)	7.81
Eggs (12)	2.58	Cigarettes (20)	1.59

EATING

The food in Brunei is similar to that of neighbouring Malaysia. The main difference is that the meat available in Brunei is flown in from a government-owned cattle ranch in Australia and the quality is very good.

Brunei specialties

Traditional dishes include: *Cucur ubi* (sweet potato fritters); *Kalupi* (steamed sweet cakes, individually wrapped, made from cassava or rice); and *Kueh koci* (rice flour dumplings with a sweet coconut filling, wrapped in banana leaf).

Drinking

As mentioned above, alcohol is banned for Brunei Muslims, and as a visitor you are only entitled to consume the alcohol you bring into Brunei as your duty-free allowance.

SERVICES

Banks and financial matters

The currency in Brunei is the Brunei dollar which is managed by Singapore because Brunei does not have its own Central Bank. Both currencies are interchangeable as the Brunei dollar is linked to the Singapore dollar. There are coins of 1, 5, 10, 20 and 50 cents, and notes of 1, 5, 10, 50, 100, 500 and 1 000 dollars. Banks are open from Monday to Friday from 9am until 3pm and on Saturday mornings from 9am until 11am.

Health

Health-wise Brunei is one of the safest countries in which to live and work in South-east Asia. Malaria, cholera and smallpox were eradicated in the late 1970s and there are currently no vaccinations that are required before you visit Brunei.

One of the best hospitals in Brunei is the RIPAS Hospital in Bandar Seri Bagawan which has English-speaking doctors.

MEDIA

Newspapers

There is one daily English-language newspaper – *The Borneo Bulletin*. Newspapers from Singapore and Malaysia are also available daily.

RECREATION

Sports

Sports facilities are quite good, especially if you enjoy water sports. As for night-life, well, there's always Singapore. There are no public bars or nightclubs (see above on alcohol restrictions).

Help-lines

Police:	222333/223901
Ambulance:	223366
Fire brigade:	222555

APPENDICES

Appendix 1. Useful Malay words and phrases

The official language of Brunei is Malay. For useful words and phrases see Chapter 8: Malaysia (Appendix 2: Useful words and phrases).

Appendix 2. Public holidays

Fluctuating dates are marked with an asterisk *.

1 January	New Year's Day
* Late January/early February	Chinese New Year
23 February	National Day
* March	Anniversary of the Revelation of the Koran
* 2 days early April	*Hari Raya Aidil Fitri (Puasa)*
31 May	Armed Forces Day
15 July	The Sultan's birthday
* Late July/early August	*Hari Raya Haji*
25 December	Christmas Day
26 December	Boxing Day

Appendix 3. Embassies and consulates

Selected Brunei embassies abroad

There is no embassy in Canada, Ireland or New Zealand.

Australia: High Commission of Negara Brunei Darussalam in Australia, 16 Bulwarra Close, O'Malley, ACT, 2606, Canberra. Tel: (62) 290 1801/ 290 1802. Fax: (62) 290 1832.

UK: High Commission of Negara Brunei Darussalam, 19 Belgrave Square, London, SW1X 8PG. Tel: (0171) 581 0521. Fax: (0171) 235 9717.

USA: Embassy of the State of Brunei Darussalam, Watergate Suite 300, 3rd floor, 2600 Virginia Avenue NW, Washington DC 20037. Tel: (202) 342 0159. Fax: (202) 342 0158.

Selected embassies and consulates in Brunei

Australia: Australian High Commission, 4th floor, Teck Guan Plaza, Bandar Seri Begawan 2085. Tel: (02) 229 435. Fax: (02) 221 652.

UK: British High Commission, 3rd floor, Hong Kong Bank Chambers, Bandar Seri Begawan 2085. Tel: (02) 222 231. Fax: (02) 226 002.

USA: Embassy of the United States of America, 3rd floor, Teck Guan Plaza, Bandar Seri Begawan 2085. Tel: (02) 229 670. Fax: (02) 225 293.

Appendix 4. Suggested reading

Bartholomew, J, *The World's Richest Man; The Sultan of Brunei*, Viking London.

Finlay, Hugh, and Peter Turner, *Lonely Planet Travel Survival Kit Malaysia, Singapore and Brunei*, Lonely Planet Publications.

11

Indonesia

FACTFILE

The official name for Indonesia is The Republic Of Indonesia.

History

The earliest record of inhabitants in Indonesia was discovered in 1891. 'Java Man', as he has come to be known, is thought to have lived on Java about 1.7 million years ago. He was a hunter-gatherer who lived in open caves and is thought to have been the first creature to know how to use fire.

Between the 2nd and 15th centuries Indonesia was ruled by various religious kingdoms – some ruling over a few islands while others divided the country into sultanates. Hindu, Buddhist, and Islamic religions each influenced the region as did the cultural, artistic, political, economic and agricultural ideas from Malaysia, India and the Middle East.

Between 1512 and 1949 European colonists from Portugal, Britain and the Netherlands ruled Indonesia, with the Dutch re-naming the islands the United Dutch East India Company. Indonesia was the famous 'Spice Islands' which the Dutch colonized in the 17th century and ruled until independence was declared on 17 August 1945.

During the Second World War Indonesia was occupied by the Japanese and was included in Japan's East Asia Co-Prosperity Sphere. The Japanese encouraged *Bahasa Indonesia* as a national language and created an armed Indonesian homeguard.

After the Japanese left Indonesia, the Dutch, with British help, returned to Indonesia. But Indonesia had become politicized during the war, and with a national language to unite its people and arms left from the Japanese, Indonesia fought against the Dutch and British and won its independence. More than four years after it had first been declared, Indonesian independence was officially recognized by the world, on 27 December 1949.

Since independence, Indonesia has had only two leaders – Sukarno and Suharto. Sukarno was president until 1967 when he was gradually stripped of his power after the failed 1965 'coup'. This coup gave Suharto, a little-known general, a reason to punish the supposed communist conspirators who were said to be behind the coup. Increasing evidence now suggests that it was actually Suharto himself who was one of the main instigators of the staged 1965 coup. During the coup, six top army generals were murdered and in the aftermath of the coup Suharto took control of the army and government, and oversaw the killing of thousands of suspected communists.

Golkar, the military-backed coalition of functional groups (which prefers not to be called a political party), has won every election in recent history, against the only two permitted opposition parties. Natural resources such as oil, tin and copper, coupled with huge investment from abroad have made Indonesia one of the fastest growing economies of South-east Asia. The standard of living for most Indonesians has increased during Suharto's reign. However, this is not to say Suharto is not without his enemies. Fundamentalist Muslims have their grievances. Separatist groups in Aceh and Irian Jaya oppose Suharto's rule and would like to be independent of Indonesia. The East Timorese who have been occupied since 1975 and who have had proportionally more of their citizens killed under Suharto than Pol Pot killed in Cambodia are still fighting against genocide.

In 1996 the death of Suharto's wife (reminding Indonesians of their leader's own mortality) was followed by widespread rioting in support of Megawati Sukarnoputri, the leader of the opposition PDI party and Sukarno's daughter.

Geography

Indonesia is made up of almost 14 000 islands, yet only one island – Java – is home to more than half of Indonesia's 170 million people. Not all the islands are named and less than 1 000 of them are inhabited. The main islands are Java, Sumatra, Kalimantan, Sulawesi, Bali, Maluku, Irian Jaya and Nusa Tenggara (the name for the islands east of Bali).

Indonesia is on the 'ring of fire' with between 70 and 80 active volcanoes, the most famous is Krakatau, about 90 miles southwest of Jakarta, which erupted in 1883 killing more than 35 000 people. Krakatau continues to claim lives today. An EFL teacher from Jakarta was killed recently when she was hiking there with some friends.

Climate

Indonesia lies within the tropical zone and has two seasons – dry and hot, and wet and hot. From November to May, rainfall and humidity increase markedly, while during much of the rest of the year, winds blow from Australia bringing drier weather. The equator crosses the islands so Indonesia has fairly consistent temperatures, with a mean of 25–28°C (78–82°F), and days of almost consistent 12 hours of darkness and light.

Time

Indonesia is divided into three time zones: Sumatra, Java and West and Central Kalimantan are on Western Indonesian Time; Bali, Nusa Tenggara South and East Kalimantan and Sulawesi are on Central Indonesian Time; Irian Jaya and Maluku are on East Indonesian Time. The time zones are seven, eight and nine hours ahead of GMT respectively.

The people

Over the centuries people have emigrated to Indonesia from China, Polynesia, Malaysia, Laos, Vietnam, Cambodia, India, the Middle East, Portugal and Holland.

With between 170 and 190 million people (depending on which source you read) Indonesia has the fifth highest population and is the 14th largest political unit in the world. It has hundreds of different ethnic groups and more than 250 languages. However, one language, *Bahasa Indonesia*, and a single political system 'guided democracy', tries to unite this very diverse nation. The political slogan, *Bhinneka Tunggal Ika* (Unity in Diversity), perhaps best sums up how this nation of very different religions, beliefs, languages and cultures sees itself as one people.

Politics

Since independence Indonesia has only had two presidents. Indonesian politics is based on the state ideology *Pancasila* which was introduced by Sukarno in 1945. These five principles were originally designed as a way to unite a large, diverse country, its people and their differing beliefs and traditions. However, in reality, each political group since 1945 has claimed its own interpretation of the *Pancasila*.

The five principles of the *Pancasila* are:

(1) *Faith in God* – all Indonesians must believe in Allah, Vishnu, Buddha or the Christian God, it does not matter which God, as long as each person believes in a God.

(2) *Humanity* – Indonesia must take its place in the family of nations.
(3) *Nationalism* – all ethnic groups must unite.
(4) *Representative government* – consensus must be achieved through deliberation among representatives. This is perhaps the most difficult principle for non-Indonesians to grasp, the idea of talking until everyone has had their say and a compromise is reached which pleases everyone. In the West, a show of hands or a vote seems the fairest and quickest way of resolving any dilemma, but for Indonesians, Westernized democracy means that 51% of the people oppress the other 49%.
(5) *Social justice* – a just and prosperous society will provide adequate food and clothing for all.

Language

Indonesia has more than 250 different dialects, but *Bahasa Indonesia* is officially the national language. Although the roots of *Bahasa Indonesia* date back to the 12th century, it was not until relatively recently (the 1950s), that is was adopted as the national language.

Bahasa Indonesia is a deceptive language. At first glance it seems remarkably straightforward, but the more you learn the more you realize you still have to learn. Be that as it may, there are certainly some aspects of it that make it a lot easier to learn that practically any other language in Asia. It is written using the Roman alphabet and, unlike English, each letter carries the same sound value (for example, the letter i is always pronounced like the ee in see). And, again unlike English, the syllables in each word are equally stressed.

In Jakarta and the other main cities you can get by with English, but any Indonesian you can learn will pay off handsomely, as Indonesians are pleasantly surprised by anyone who makes the effort to speak their language.

Consider doing a self-study course before you leave for Indonesia; it is not necessary to spend a lot of money on a course with tapes because, as outlined above, the pronunciation of Indonesian is very straightforward. In Indonesia, if you have the time and money an excellent school for language learning is in the charming city of Yogyakarta:

Yogyakarta Indonesian Language Centre, YILC, Jalan Rajawali, Gand Nuri No. 6, Yogyakarta, 55281. Tel: 0274 – 88409.

Religions

The main religions in Indonesia are Islam, Buddhism, Hinduism and Christianity. Islam first came to Indonesia in the 7th century from the Middle East and Indonesia is now the biggest Muslim country in the world (80% of Indonesians declare themselves Muslim). The islands of Bali and Lombok are mainly Hindu, the islands of Flores and Ambon, and the north of Sulawesi are mainly Christian, while the Chinese-Indonesians, mainly on Java, are Buddhists.

For more information on Islam and Buddhism see Chapter 1: Major religions in South-east Asia.

Cultural considerations

Islam

As most Indonesians are Muslim, especially on Java where almost all the population is Muslim, a healthy respect for Allah is advisable. Although in reality many Indonesians do not pray five times a day, do not attend the Mosque on Fridays, or fast during *Ramadan* (the fasting month), they still consider themselves to be Muslim. There is no term in Indonesian for being a 'lapsed Muslim' (as in 'lapsed Catholic').

During *Ramadan,* however, respect for Islam does not include, for non-Muslims, abstinence from drink, tobacco, sex, or food. In fact, if you eat in front of fasting Muslims they gain more merit from watching you and rejecting the temptation to eat with you than from not seeing you eat at all. During *Ramadan* very strict Muslims will allow no liquid to pass their throats and so will spit rather than swallow their own saliva. Comments on what you might regard as this lack of hygiene would obviously be inappropriate.

It is part of the Indonesian *Pancasila* that every Indonesian must believe in God (be it the Hindu, Islamic or Christian God). So, when Indonesians ask you what religion you are, an answer 'I don't believe in God' is incomprehensible. Unless you want to be part of a discussion that might go on for days, or are content to be ostracized for your radical politics, it's probably better to answer whatever religion is familiar to you from childhood.

Most public holidays have some religious significance, and the most important events in the Javanese Islamic calendar are *Ramadan* and *Idul Fitri.* For further information on *Ramadan* and *Idul Fitri* see Chapter 1.

Respect for the government

Outwardly Indonesians have great respect for their government, perhaps because recent history has taught them that opposition can bring death. Between 1965 and 1968 some 700 000 people were killed because they were suspected communists and more recently opposition to Indonesian rule in East Timor has met with brutal demonstrations of power. Foreigners in Indonesia should be very wary of criticizing the government.

Animism, ghosts and solitude

Animism is the belief that all objects have some hidden powers. Although animism is mainly practised in the outer islands, you can still see remnants of these beliefs in Java and Bali, where aspects of Islam and Hinduism incorporate animism, for example, in ceremonies held to bless animals or new houses.

Most Indonesians are very frightened of ghosts, the dark, black magic and solitude. Every evening a man from the neighbourhood-watch team walks around the local area beating a wooden pole against railings, fences, etc to frighten off burglars, ghosts and other unwanted visitors.

If you live alone, Indonesians will often feel sorry for you, and regularly ask if you are lonely or frightened being by yourself. If you say you like living alone, you will often be called 'brave'.

Rubber time

Punctuality is not as important as it is in the West. Indonesians view most arrangements taking place in *jam karat* (rubber time) and being fashionably late is a way of life for most Indonesians.

Terms of address

There are two main terms of address which you should use in Indonesia. With people your own age and friends, use first names. With people who are older than you and officials and bureaucrats, use *Ibu* for women and *Bapak* or *Pak* for men.

Showing respect for elders

Respect is shown by dipping as you pass someone, so that you are not above them. Bend your knees slightly, lower your shoulder, lead with your right arm out in front of you and say *Permisi* (Excuse me). Generally children defer to adults, students to teachers, women to men and subordinates to superiors. The fun starts if you are a woman and a teacher trying to walk passed a seated student who is a much older, male, top-ranking civil servant.

TEACHING POSSIBILITIES

The beginning of the academic year, September, seems to make little difference to the amount of teaching work available – there is no especially good time to arrive in Indonesia looking for English teaching work. However, most language schools close twice a year for

> I was disconcerted to find the Rector of my college lowering his shoulder when he passed me. He was not deferring to my younger age or my inferior position on the staff, but to my native-speaker 'foreign-expert' status. I felt uncomfortable by what was to me unjustified respect. Reluctantly I reconsidered my status and the responsibilities and demands it carried.
>
> *Francis O'Brien (England)*

one to two weeks at Christmas and at *Idul Fitri* (the end of *Ramadan,* the Muslim fasting month). The date for both *Idul Fitri* and *Ramadan* are set according to the moon's cycle (354 days), so they change every year. However, the fluctuations are small, a week to 10 days every year. A good rule of thumb for the 1990s is that *Ramadan* will be around March and *Idul Fitri* will be the first or second week in April.

The days of an English speaker arriving in Jakarta without a teaching qualification and being inundated with work offers are mostly over. There are certainly jobs for unqualified teachers but the schools that are willing to take you on will probably be fairly unscrupulous and the pay will be very low.

Places to teach in vary from private language schools and your own living room to huge government departments and multi-national corporations. Hourly rates range from around 30 000 to 50 000 rupiah, depending on whether you are working for yourself or working part-time for a language school.

You may be on the full-time staff of a school, and receive many fringe benefits such as a housing loan, medical insurance and paid holidays in addition to a guaranteed income. Alternatively, you may opt for higher rates of hourly pay in a part-time position without the benefits.

There are several English language newspapers in Indonesia: *The Indonesian Times, Indonesian Observer* and *The Jakarta Post.* The biggest of these is *The Jakarta Post,* a daily newspaper which runs a job vacancies column, on the second-back page. Usually these teaching jobs are for the Jakarta area only, but sometimes there are ads for jobs in other cities as well. Indonesian language newspapers sometimes run ads for English teaching jobs, so it is worth keeping an eye on them. The major Indonesian language newspapers are *Kompas* and *Surat Pembaruan* (Jakarta), *Pikiran Rakyat* (Bandung), and *Surabaya Pos* (Surabaya).

The best way to find a list of language schools is through the Yellow Pages telephone directory, listed in English under 'Language Schools'.

Going to a pre-arranged job

Many schools no longer need to recruit from abroad because there is a large pool of qualified teachers in Indonesia looking for work.

However, it is still worth applying from your home country if you are interested in setting up a job before you leave. For further information see the schools and organizations listed in Chapter 2: Finding a job in South-east Asia.

Arriving without a job

Most teachers now working in Indonesia found work after they arrived here. Initially teachers find some part-time work, perhaps with two or three schools, and after they have proved willing, one of those schools will offer a full-time contract.

Private language schools

The majority of teachers in Indonesia work for private language schools. Most language schools are open from Monday to Friday, from 9am to 9pm and offer classes for children, teenagers and adults. Most classes meet twice a week for about three to four hours per week, usually in 100 hour blocks. For teachers, a 24 to 28 hour teaching week is the norm, with most schools expecting you to put in a 40-hour week (teaching, preparing your lessons, marking and administering tests, etc). If you get a full-time contract with a language school they will arrange and pay for your work permit – KIMS (*Kartu Izin Menetap Sementara*). A school that offers you a part-time contract will usually process your papers, with you covering the costs, either completely or 50/50 with the school.

Some English schools in the main cities are given below:

Jakarta

BBC International, Jalan Sinan Sedayu 12, Rawamangun, Jakarta Timur. Tel: (021) 489 9292. Fax: (021) 472 1815.

British Council, Jalan Jeneral Sudirman 71, Jakarta, 12190. Tel: (021) 2524126. e-mail: bc.jakarta@bc-jakarta.sprint.com

EEC, Jalan Let. Jend. S. Parman 66 Slipi, Jakarta 11410. Tel: 591 144, 548 6296.

EEP, Jalan Wiljaya V111/4, Jalan Selatan. Tel: (021) 770 812.

ELTI, Grand Wijaya Center, Blik H, Kebayoran Baru.

IALF, Cipta Building, Jalan HR Rasuna Said, Kav c-10, Kuningan, Jakarta 12G20.

ILP, Jalan Panglima Polim 1X/2, Kebayoran Baru, Jakarta.

TBI, S Widjojo Center, Jalan Rasuna Said, Jakarta 12920. Tel. (021) 512 044.

Bandung

BBC International, Jalan Dipatiukur 80. Tel: (022) 250 491.

EEP, Jalan Lombok 43, Bandung. Tel/fax: (022) 708 254.

ELSI, Jalan Dipati Ukur 89, Bandung. Tel: (022) 250 1293. Fax: (022) 250 248.

TBI, Jalan RE Martadinata 63, Bandung, 40145. Tel: (022) 441 465. Fax: (021) 421 9138.

Triad English Centre, Jalan Purnawarman 76, Bandung, 40116. Tel: (022) 433 104.

Surabaya

ACCESS, Jalan Kayoon 2, Lantai II, Surabaya. Tel: (031) 523 181. Fax: (031) 511 856.

Australian Institute of English, Jalan Diponeggoro 25, Surabaya. Tel: (031) 576 486.

British Council, English Study Centre, Jalan Cokroaminoto 12A, Floor 3, Surabaya 60264. Tel: (031) 589 958. Fax; (031) 589 957.

ILP, Jalan Jawa 4, Surabaya. Tel: (031) 520 509.

Institute of Business, Management and Technology, Jalan Cokroaminoto 12 -A, Surabaya. Tel: (031) 575 061. Fax: (031) 515 252.

Professional Training Services, Wisma BII, 5th Floor, Jalan Pemuda, Surabaya. Tel: (031) 510 006.

TOPSII, Jalan Embong Malang 73F, Surabaya. Tel: (031) 513 732.

Bali

IALF, Jalan Kapten Agung 19, Denpasar. Tel: (0361) 25 243.

State and private schools and universities

You cannot work for state schools or universities unless you are Indonesian or are a foreigner working on a diplomatic visa. Voluntary Services Overseas (VSO) teachers usually work on diplomatic visas as do teachers associated with the British Council. Work in universities is usually on an unpaid, voluntary basis, while working in a language project in private university requires serious qualifications – a PGCE or an MA – and usually at least five years' teaching experience.

International schools

Private primary and secondary schools (catering mostly for expatriate children) also want qualified primary or high school teachers, and occasionally qualified EFL teachers. You can contact the international schools at:

Jakarta

British International School, PO Box 310, KYB, Jakarta. Tel: (021) 5480858. Fax: (021) 549 4899.

Jakarta International School, PO Box 79/JKS, Jakarta, 12430. Tel: (021) 769 2555. Fax: (021) 769 7852.

Bandung

Bandung Alliance School, Jalan Gunung Agung 14, Bandung 41142, Java. Tel: (022) 818 844.

Bandung International School, Jalan Drg. Suria Sumantri, PO Box 132, Bandung. Tel: (022) 856 15.

Freelance teaching

Working from home does not qualify you for a work permit, however that is not say that freelance teaching is completely out of the question. Rather, once you are established in a language school which has processed your work visa, you can then work freelance to earn extra money. Often students at school will approach you for private lessons for them or for family or friends and once you are settled in an area and word gets around that you are a teacher, your neighbours can also be a good source of private business. In Jakarta the going rate for private teaching is about 50 000 rupiah an hour. In other cities it is between 30 000 and 40 000 rupiah.

BEFORE YOU GO

Insurance

Take out a travel insurance policy which includes health-care cover in case you become ill before you find a job. It is also useful to have a health insurance policy even after you find work as the health care cover your school offers might not be as comprehensive as you would like.

Vaccinations

See Chapter 1: Health for information on vaccinations and also on what health precautions you should take before and after arriving in Indonesia.

Passport/visa

Make sure you have a passport valid for at least one year and a business visa, if you are going to a pre-arranged job. If you have no work lined up you can get a tourist visa at your home Indonesian Embassy, or wait until you arrive at immigration in Indonesia (see below for more visas).

ARRIVAL AND VISAS

Visas

There is a range of visas, depending on the purpose of your visit, the length of stay, and your nationality. It is very difficult to obtain a clear and complete picture of the situation on visas for two reasons. Firstly, because the granting of a visas is often at the discretion of an individual civil servant, it is not 100% guaranteed that if you follow certain procedures that you will always obtain the visa you want; and secondly, because of corruption. It has been estimated recently that in Indonesia as much as 30% of the government's budget is lost through corruption (*The Jakarta Post*, 23 December 1993), and there is no reason to believe that the Immigration Department civil servants are somehow immune from this graft.

Most schools have their own contact in the Immigration Department and if any 'contribution' is made you will not have to do it directly. It is more likely that when you go to the Immigration Department an Indonesian school representative will present the paperwork along with a 'gift' to help the application process.

There are five main types of visas which are likely to be relevant to you:

DINAS visa. This is a diplomatic visa, which is only issued to foreign diplomats or VSO (Voluntary Services Overseas) workers.

Social/Budaya (Social/Cultural) visa. This visa is issued if you have Indonesian friends who can sponsor you, or if you are interested in studying an aspect of Indonesian culture. Your social sponsor must produce a letter taking responsibility for you which you should take to your home Indonesian embassy. If you wish to study Indonesian culture you should be able to produce an acceptance letter from the institution where you plan to study.

Business visa. If you are going to a prearranged job, your school will usually ask you to apply in your home country for a business visa which will be converted into a work visa three to six months after you arrive in Indonesia.

Tourist visa. Most teachers who arrive in Indonesia without a job initially enter the country on a tourist visa. If you are from Australia, Britain, Canada, New Zealand or the USA you do not need a visa in your passport before you enter the country. You will usually be issued with a two-month tourist visa when you arrive in Indonesia. You should be able to produce an onward ticket out of Indonesia, have a passport that is valid for at least six months and proof of sufficient funds for your two-month stay.

Work visa. It is not possible to apply for a work visa either in your home country or when you arrive at Indonesian immigration. You must enter the country on one of the four visas above and then apply to change to a work visa.

After you find a job, your school will usually process your papers at the local Immigration Department and your tourist visa will be changed to a business one. After between three and six months your business visa will be changed to a work visa. Officially on a business visa you can work but not earn, and officially you are employed as some kind of unpaid consultant. However, in reality most teachers do earn and everyone turns a blind eye to your income until a work visa is processed. Recently the government has been threatening to clamp down on organizations which have foreign employees earning while on business visas, but in general it is employers and not employees who are fined for this violation.

To change from a business to a work visa you usually have to leave Indonesia and apply at an Indonesian Embassy outside Indonesia. For most people this means a trip to Singapore (the nearest and cheapest place to fly to). Remember that, as you leave Indonesia, you should not tell the immigration officials that you have been earning while on a business visa.

The Indonesian Embassy in Singapore is at 7 Chatsworth Road (Tel: 737 7422) and is open Monday to Thursday 8.30am – 5.00pm. You can lodge applications between 8.30am and 12am and collect your visa one to two working days later, between 3.30pm and 5.00pm. If you pay an express fee, you can collect your visa on the same day.

To apply for a work visa you need a copy of a telex that the Immigration Department in Jakarta has sent to the embassy in Singapore, confirming that you are eligible for a work visa. You also need a passport that is valid for at least a year and four passport photographs.

After you return to Indonesia with a work visa stamped in your passport, you should report to your local Immigration Department within five days to start your application for a KIMS (work permit). You will have every digit fingerprinted a number of times, and have your photograph taken. You will then be issued with the vital KIMS. This is a small laminated card that entitles you to live, work, and earn in Indonesia for a year.

Renewing your KIMS the following year is much more straightforward and increasingly these days does not entail a trip to Singapore as your KIMS can be extended for up to three years in Indonesia.

Immigration

If you are entering Indonesia as a tourist remember that, even if you comply with the regulations as outlined above, you are not immediately entitled to a tourist visa. An immigration official who decides that you 'may endanger the country's security, peace and stability as well as the public health and morals' can refuse you a tourist visa. Wear a conservative set of clothes. For women, you should cover your shoulders and the tops of your arms, and if you are wearing a skirt, make sure that it covers at least down to your knees. For men, a long pair of trousers and a shirt and tie is the norm. Show a polite and patient manner and don't forget that a smile works wonders. This encounter will get you into good practice for your many future meetings with Indonesian officialdom.

Transport from the airport

There is a Damri public bus which leaves from outside the arrivals hall of Jakarta international airport. The trip to Gambir Railway station takes about an hour and costs 3 000 rupiah. From the railway station it is about a ten-minute walk to Jalan Jaksa – the main street for cheap accommodation. Private taxis operate from the airport but unless you are a very hard bargainer you will probably end up paying over the odds. Metered taxis are also available, but check before you go too far that the meter is running: '*Tolong pakai argo*' (Please use the meter). The trip to Gambir railway station takes about the same time as the Damri bus and will cost about 25 000 rupiah, excluding toll-fares which you also have to pay.

ACCOMMODATION

Short-term accommodation

In all the major cities as well as popular holiday destinations there are *losmen* – small, family-run guesthouses. Here for about 10 000 – 15 000 rupiah a night, you can get a single room and breakfast of strong black *kopi* (coffee) and often toast and fruit. *Losmen* usually cater for the budget traveller and the lack of privacy may get on your nerves, but in the short-term they are great places for just getting your bearings in a new city. A list of some *losmen* is given below.

Jakarta

Jalan Jaksa is the main area for cheap accommodation in Jakarta. One losmen is very much like another in this street, so if the first one you try is full or you don't like it, don't worry, there are plenty more down the road.

Norbeck Hostel, Jalan Jaksa 14. Tel: (021) 330 392.
Djody Hostel, Jalan Jaksa 27.
Hotel Karya, Jalan Jaksa 32 – 34. Tel: (021) 320 484.
Djody Hotel, Jalan Jaksa 35.
Wisma Delima Youth Hostel, Jalan Jaksa 5. Tel: (021) 337 026.

Bandung

All these *losmen* are close to the railway station, a very short *becak* (trishaw) ride, or a 5–10 minute walk.

> **Hotel Nugraha**, Jalan H Mesri 11. Tel (022) 436146.
> **Hotel Guntur**, Jalan Oto Iskandardinata 20. Tel (022) 507763.
> **Losmen Sakadarna**, Jalan Kebonjati 50/7B. Tel (022) 439897.

Surabaya

> **Wisma Ganesha**, Jalan Taman Prapen 34A. Tel: (031) 818 705.
> **The Bamboe Denn,** Jalan Ketabang Kali 6A. Tel: (031) 413 33.

Denpasar

> **The Bali Hotel,** Jalan Vetern. Tel: (0361) 225681, 225685.
> **Adi Yasa,** Jalan Nakula 11.

You can also rent a room by the month in a *kos.* A *kos* is a single room attached to a larger family house. Usually there will be 5 to 10 other students or single workers living in the same *kos* and all of you will have access to a small communal kitchen. Living in a *kos* can be an excellent way to meet Indonesians, to start learning the language and also a chance to give yourself a breather before you commit yourself to renting a house.

Long-term accommodation

In Indonesia houses are rented by the year, so it is worth spending time firstly, deciding if you want to stay in Indonesia and secondly, choosing a house carefully before you part with your money.

Newspaper ads in the English language press are almost exclusively aimed at expats on huge salaries, and houses advertised for more than US$1 000 a month are not uncommon. House agents are similarly geared to finding huge mansions for exceptionally rich foreigners and initially might find it difficult to comprehend that you really want a small, reasonably-priced house and that you cannot afford the marble-floored, white-elephants they keep taking you to view. Do not despair, it costs nothing to look at the houses an agent takes you to see, you only have to pay the agents' fee if they find you a house you agree to rent, and you may find seeing how the other 2% live shocking, amusing, or both. Keep trying though, because if you say *'terlalu mahal, terlalu besar'* (too expensive, too big) often enough, house-agents will eventually take you seriously. If an agent does find you a house, the usual fee is one month's rent which either you pay or, more usually, the house owner pays.

Probably the best way to find a house is to ask other teachers. They often know of houses to rent, or at least can tell you the likely areas where foreigners can easily find accommodation.

Find an area that you want to live in and spend a few days asking locals *'Ada rumah dikontrakan dekat disini?'* (Are there any houses to rent near here?). If there are any empty houses the locals will take you to have a look and will often contact the owner for you. Bear in mind that although it is unlikely that you will be asked to pay for this help it is common practice to offer some money to the person who took you to the house, if you eventually rent it.

House rents are negotiable, so do not be put off when the owner initially asks for what seems like a ridiculous price. You can bargain about the rent, the furniture, the length of the lease, installing a telephone or practically anything else you can think of. For more hints on bargaining see pp 8–9.

Once you have seen a house that you like, it is a good idea to visit it again at Mosque time. The *muezzin* (call to prayer) happens five times a day and you could very easily be driven mad, if the Mosque loudspeaker seems to be directly connected to your bedroom window.

When you have rented and are settled into a new house you should visit and register with the RT (pronounced air tay), the *Rukan Tetangga*, a locally elected chief who is in charge of neighbourhood security. This is a simple process of writing your personal details (date of birth, nationality, profession, etc) in his *orang asing* (foreigners or strange people) book and/or giving him a copy of your passport. Remember too that if you have friends to stay for more than two days they should also register with the RT.

Telephone, electricity, water and gas

Private phones are much less common in Indonesia than they are in the West, and even less common in cities outside Jakarta. If you have a phone in your house, you will probably still have to go through the operator for intercity and international calls.

Electricity in Indonesia is usually 110 volts, 50 cycles AC, but increasingly, especially in rented houses, is 220–240 volts, 50 cycles AC. Converters are cheap and easily available. North American TV sets cannot be used to receive Indonesian TV programmes. However, most other appliances from abroad will work with a converter, if a little more slowly and less efficiently than at home.

Water in rented houses is unlikely to be the pull-it-up-yourself-from-the-well type, which is the norm for most Indonesians, but rather, *air ledeng* (running water). Especially during the dry season (October to March), it is a good idea to keep your *mandi* (bath) full, in case there is a water shortage. In the rainy season pipes sometimes become blocked so a full *mandi* all year round is always a good idea.

Paying phone, electricity and water bills is a rather complicated process involving going to either the main office (for water and electricity bills) or to a designated bank (for telephone bills), before a certain day each month which changes for each service and from city to city. While the water and electricity bills are delivered to your house, you only receive an itemized run-down of your calls after you have paid your phone bill. It is a long and tedious process, which you can certainly do yourself every month, but which your *pembantu* (household help) will usually do for you, if you ask.

For cooking, gas is used. A large gas bottle will usually last a single person for about two months. It is a good idea to have two gas canisters in your house so that you will not be caught short if your bottle suddenly runs out. You can get a replacement bottle, either by putting a note in your front window *'gas kosong'* (gas empty), which a gas dealer will see as he drives around your area, or by ringing or going to your local gas agent who will usually be happy to deliver the new gas canister and take back the empty one.

A 12 kg canister of gas will cost around 10 000 rupiah, but your first purchase will also include a fairly hefty deposit of 50 000 – 100 000 rupiah, depending on the time of year. It is more expensive around *Idul Fitri* – see p 18. This deposit is refundable when you finally return your last gas bottle, not necessarily to the place where you bought your first one, before you leave Indonesia. Unfortunately, again the amount of your refund depends on the time of year. Too bad for you if you buy your first canister during *Idul Fitri* (March – April) when all prices go up and sell your last one in the middle of October.

Household help

Most teachers in Indonesia have some kind of household help (*pembantu*). You can arrange for someone (a woman usually, but a male *pembantu* is not completely unheard of in Indonesia) to come to your house to do washing and ironing and household cleaning. How much you pay for household help depends on the number of days she/he comes to your house, the size of your house, the amount of work you want her/him to do, how much you earn, and your bargaining powers. Most teachers pay about 50 000 rupiah a month.

LIVING COSTS

How expensive is Indonesia?

Salaries

Indonesia is one of the cheaper countries in South-east Asia. A newly qualified Indonesian teacher working in a government school can expect to take home about 100 000 rupiah (£35) a month, so a private language school salary of around 2 000 000 rupiah a month seems quite enormous in comparison. Rent accounts for about 500 000 – 750 000 rupiah. After tax and rent you will be left with about 1 500 000 rupiah, which in Indonesia goes a very long way.

In Indonesian cities in general, and in Jakarta in particular, there is no shortage of ways to spend your money. Practically anything you want from back home is available, albeit at an incredibly high price.

Most teachers in Indonesia live very comfortably and are still able to save part of their salary. If you want a back-home lifestyle, then probably the best advice is to stay at home, or get out of TEFL. The foreigners in Indonesia who can afford a completely Westernized way of life are expatriate businessmen and women who have been sent to Indonesia by their firms and who are paid back-home salaries, given free accommodation and a 15% hardship allowance!

As a teacher, you are never going to be able to afford to live the expat life, but, compared to the majority of Indonesians, you will be very rich indeed. During a year's stay in Indonesia, most teachers can usually afford to rent a house by themselves, own most consumer durables and take holidays both inside and outside Indonesia.

Eating and drinking costs are very cheap in Indonesia, especially if you eat and drink as Indonesians do. As it is mainly a Muslim country, pork and alcohol are not usually on the menu of most *warung* – small road-side food stalls – but bacon and beer are still very cheap and easily available, especially in Chinese-owned shops, restaurants and supermarkets.

Taxes

There are three main kinds of personal tax – income, local and departure tax.

Income Tax. This varies according to your salary and also depending on the school's tax category; generally tax is 10–15%. Many schools find it to their advantage to pay your tax for you and then later to claim a tax refund on the money, so you will often not have to concern yourself directly with paying income tax.

Local Tax. This is paid to the RT (*Rukan Tetangg*a, the head of neighbourhood security). Local tax varies from area to area and, within one area, from house to house depending on family size and income. As a rich foreigner you will be expected to pay more than most of your neighbours – somewhere between 5 000 and 15 000 rupiah a month.

Departure taxes. There are of two kinds – airport departure tax and *fiskal* exit tax. Airport departure tax is 17 000 rupiah on international flights. *Fiskal* is an exit tax which must be paid by anyone with a KIMS who has been earning in Indonesia for more than six months. It is a flat-rate sum of 250 000 rupiah and you pay it at the airport after checking-in but before going through immigration. Remember, if you have been working on a business visa for six months and then leave for Singapore to apply for a work visa, you should not pay *fiskal* because officially you have not been earning during those six months.

Supermarket costs

A shopping basket of items at a supermarket is given below. It is worth bearing in mind that Indonesian supermarkets are not always the best value for money and that many of the prices listed below are much lower in the local shops or markets. Prices are in rupiah.

Bread (small sliced loaf)	1 500	Tea (50 tea-bags)	2 080
Beef (100 g)	1 050	Imported coffee (200 g)	6 215
Milk (1 l)	3 350	Indonesian coffee (200 g)	1 650
Sugar (1 kg)	1 350	Beer (750 ml)	3 000
Eggs (10)	2 520	Vodka (750 ml)	31 250
Rice (1kg)	1 460	Cigarettes (20 Marlboro)	1 300

EATING AND DRINKING

The mainstay of the Indonesian diet is rice. Indonesians consider that if they have not eaten rice during a meal, then they have not eaten properly. Spices are also very important in Indonesian cooking and those small green chillies that leave you weeping can look deceptively like green beans, so be careful! Traditional ingredients are rice, noodles, soya beans, tofu, chillies, garlic, onions, tomatoes, spinach, bean sprouts, carrots, peanuts, chicken, beef, mutton, lamb, prawns, crab and fish.

If you go into a *warung* or restaurant and do not understand anything on the menu, or anything that the owner tells you is on offer, do not worry, it is very unlikely that by mistake you will order something that, to Western sensibilities, seems quite repulsive. Indonesians do not eat monkey brains or horses. Certainly, *Bataks* (people from North-central Sumatra) do eat dogs, but the chances of you being served up canine flesh in a restaurant in Jakarta are slim. The only strange dishes you might be presented with are animal intestines (but really, how different is heart from liver?) and fish, or prawn heads (where all the goodness is, you will be told).

Etiquette

As Indonesia is predominantly Muslim, the most important rule of eating etiquette is remembering to use only your right hand for eating and giving or accepting food (or anything else for that matter). Your left hand is considered unclean because it is the one used for washing yourself after using the toilet. Most Indonesians eat with their right hand and/or a fork and spoon. Food does not come in separate courses but instead is put in the centre of the table and you just help yourself.

If you are eating in an Indonesian house, remember that an empty plate means that you want more, so if you do not like the food on offer, do not clear your plate thinking that that will be the end of it. It is polite to wait until you have been invited to eat by your host/hostess, or if you are the host/hostess, to invite your guests to eat, simply by saying *'Selakan'* (Please).

Restaurants

There are three main kinds of restaurants in Indonesia: *warung, rumah makan* and Westernized restaurants. A *warung* is a small road-side eating stall with a canvas roof and rough-and-ready wooden tables and benches. Here for as little as 1 000 rupiah you can taste some of the best cooking in Indonesia. A *rumah makan* (literally eating house) is a slightly more up-market version of a *warung*. This is a permanent, indoor structure with marginally more expensive prices and a bigger variety of dishes. Westernized restaurants include fast-food outlets like McDonald's, Wendy's, Pizza Hut, and Burger King, where you will pay about the same price as in the West for a cheeseburger or a pizza; and also places that cater to a particular nationality – Japanese, Korean, Italian, etc, which are expensive because of the plush surroundings, imported ingredients and often foreign chefs as well.

Eating out cheaply

The cheapest way to eat out is to stop someone with a food barrow. These *kaki lima* (five legs – the three on the barrow and the two on the man) wander the streets calling out their menus. A high-pitched whistle signals the arrival of the *putuh* (steamed rice with coconut and brown sugar) seller, and the sound of the tap of a metal spoon against a plate is the *mi goreng* (fried noodles) man. *Kaki lima* cook on the spot, come complete with plates and cutlery and when your order is ready you can just eat your food on the side of the road. If you still believe what your mother told you about it being rude to eat on the street, then you can wait at home for the sound of the *kaki lima* man and when he has cooked up your food, you can ask for a *bungkus* (a carry-out) and take it home to eat.

As mentioned before, a *warung* or *rumah makan* is also a good bet for a cheap meal. Usually where there is one *warung* there will be at least one other and up to 20 more near it. Each warung specializes in one or two dishes, for example: *bakso* (meat ball soup); *mi goreng* (fried noodles); *kare udang* (prawn curry in coconut milk) or *ayam goring* (fried chicken). Order what you want and then wait five or ten minutes while you watch your meal being prepared. Indonesian *teh* (tea) or boiled water is usually served while you wait and it's free. There are large jars filled with peanut biscuits or *krupuk* (prawn crackers) on each table, which you can help yourself to while you wait for your food and pay for when you have finished your meal.

The following are Indonesian specialties: *gado-gado* (a cold dish consisting of lettuce, bean sprouts, potatoes and rice covered in a peanut sauce and served with prawn crackers); *satay* (a wooden skewer of meat of fish cooked over a charcoal fire and served with a peanut sauce); and *kepiting goreng sause tiram* (fried crab in oyster sauce).

Confectionery and snacks

Indonesians like their food to be colourful and sweet – so do not be too surprised if you are offered green, blue or yellow bread or sponge cakes, and desserts made from raw sugar and carnation milk. For those who do not have a sweet tooth, the fruit available in Indonesia is exotic and abundant. It ranges from the humble apple to the notorious *durian* (definitely an acquired taste and smell), and from many different kinds of bananas to delicious mangosteens, *rambutans,* green coconuts and mangoes.

Drinking

The three principal forms of alcohol drunk in Indonesia are beer *(bir),* spirits (the most popular being whisky) and *arak.*

Beer

The beer is mostly lager; both Indonesian-made and imported beers are available in the major cities. The two main brands of Indonesian beer are *Anker* (Anchor) and *Bintang* (Star). Both have a reputation for causing rough hangovers but since they're much cheaper than imported beer, both are still very popular with teachers in Indonesia. Imported beers available include Fosters, Castlemaine XXXX, Budweiser, and, increasingly, bottles and cans of English bitter and Irish Guinness in large supermarkets. A few bars now have Guinness on draft.

Spirits

Both Indonesian-made and imported spirits are available. Indonesian-made Mansion House whisky, vodka and gin are very cheap, but are not perhaps made from the finest ingredients. Imported spirits are by comparison very expensive.

Arak

This is distilled rice wine or brandy. It is either clear or red and is very strong. It is usually drunk with some kind of mixer and, like the other Indonesian-manufactured drinks mentioned above, delivers a powerful hangover to the uninitiated.

Cheap venues

As Indonesia is a Muslim country, the idea of going out for an evening solely to drink alcohol, although by no means forbidden, is regarded as a rather strange practice. For this reason, perhaps, the number of cheap drinking places are very few. In a *warung* – a small road-side eating stall – you can usually order warm(ish) beer, by itself or with food. But to get *mabok* (drunk or 'dizzy') – on large bottles of lukewarm *Anker* or *Bing-tang* beer would neither be a drinking delight, nor endear you to most of the locals. If you want a cheap night's drinking, probably the best idea is to buy some beers (3 000 rupiah for a large bottle of local beer), put them in the fridge for a while and then invite a few friends round for a party.

Medium-priced venues

Pubs cater for the young, middle-class trendies and foreigners, and a glass of local draft beer costs between 3 000 and 5 000 rupiah. Pubs usually have live music, and most bands do excellent cover versions of one particular kind of music (rock, heavy metal, reggae, folk, etc). In pubs you usually sit at tables and are served by the barstaff. You pay for your drinks at the end of the evening and your bill normally includes a 10% service charge.

Expensive venues

The international hotels all have expensive bars which cater for very rich Indonesians or expats. Here a glass of draft beer will cost you between 5 000 and 10 000 rupiah and the music will be quieter and more urbane. Your bill at the end of the evening will include a 21% service and government charge.

TRANSPORT

Bus

Buses are very cheap, but often dangerously overcrowded. Sitting beside an open-window is not always easy as Indonesians live in fear of catching *masuk angin* ('cold-wind entering' one's body) and would rather you did not open any windows on the bus. Even if you manage to open a window it is not that pleasant in a traffic jam. Car and bus emissions are unregulated here, as in most of Asia, and Jakarta in particular suffers from bad air pollution.

Taxi

Taxis are cheap, safe and reliable. Most taxis now have meters, but around airports, bus and train stations private taxis operate, so make sure you agree your price before you start your journey.

Long distance share taxis operate between some of the major cities in Indonesia. A reliable company is 4848, which has a 24 hour office at Jalan Prapatan 34 (Tel: 348048), near Jakarta's Gambir railway station. At the office you wait until the required number of people show up (usually four to six) and then the taxi will take you from Jakarta to, for example, Semerang and drop you off wherever you want to go in the city.

Train

There are trains which run frequently between the major cities on Java. Each journey can vary enormously in price depending on how much comfort you want. For example, the journey from Bandung to Jakarta ranges from 5 000 to 21 000 rupiah, from a basic wooden seat in a compartment with one or two small electric fans, to an airline-like chair in a car with air-conditioning. The most expensive seats are in first class (*kelas eksekutif*).

Becak

In places other than Denpasar and Jakarta *becaks* are an everyday form of transport. These bicycle trishaw do have semi-fixed prices, which vary from area to area. In the tourist cities of Solo and Yogyakarta *becaks* are more expensive, but still cheap, and can be hired for the day. But in other cities, *becaks* are ideal for short trips, as the drivers can nip in and out of traffic, although you might not always want to look!

Bajaj

A bajaj is a two-seater, three-wheeled, two-stroke engine car and in Jakarta a *bajaj* is a fast way to move around the city. The *bajajs* in Indonesia are imported from India after the Indians are finished with them and they are very noisy and smoky, but like *becaks* are often faster than buses or taxis.

Bike

You will be amazed at how many people can actually get on one bicycle. Whole families on bicycles, or riders loaded down with baskets of food or wriggling animals are common sights in Indonesia. Every household it seems has at least one bike.

Mountain bikes are popular with teachers in cities other than Jakarta. The cost varies enormously, starting as low as 300 000 rupiah. 3 000 000 rupiah will get you a very good quality bike, which you can re-sell or take back home with you when you leave Indonesia. If you think you might buy a bike, bring a reliable lock with you. Light panniers are difficult to find in Indoneisa, so if you want to go on a long tour, bring one. You can take a bike on the plane to Bali free, but don't forget to let the air out of your tires before your bike is loaded.

Motorbike

Motorbikes are also popular with teachers. New motorbikes keep their value well so selling your bike when you leave Indonesia means that you can go home with quite a lot of money (2 – 3 million rupiah). See below (cars) about how to get a driving licence.

Car

New cars are very expensive compared to bikes or motorbikes, and most teachers cannot afford to buy one. However, if you buy a second-hand car you can run it fairly cheaply as petrol is not nearly as expensive as it is in the West. To get a driving licence you have to go to the traffic police station, take a written test (for a small fee you can get an already completed test paper), show proof of identity and be photographed and fingerprinted. A year's licence for a motorbike, SIM–A (*Surat Izin Mengemudi*) costs 50 000 rupiah; it is 100 000 rupiah for car SIM – C (car licence).

Boat

Between the islands you can travel by anything that floats – from very cheap, small boats to enormous, luxurious ships. *Pelni* is the main shipping company and they offer up to five classes (first to fourth class and economy) with regular sailings to all the main islands.

Plane

Garuda is the Indonesian flag carrier. Internal carriers include Merpati, Sempati, Bouraq, and Mandala. Flights are available to some otherwise inaccessible places and of course to all major cities. Internal flights are reasonably cheap, for example Jakarta to Yogyakarta costs about 141 000 rupiah and takes one hour.

SERVICES

Public phones

Public phones take either 50 or 100 rupiah coins for a local call. Phones which use phonecards are increasingly common these days. You can buy phonecards in large bookshops or in a *wartel* (telephone exchange). You can make international phone calls using a phonecard, or in a *wartel,* where you can dial directly and a meter shows you the cost of your call as you are making it.

Libraries

There is a British Council library at S Widjojo Center, Jalan Sudirman 71, Jakarta, 12190 (Tel. 252 4126). The British Council is stocking fewer novels and more textbooks these days.

Bookshops

International hotels stock English language novels in their bookshops and the backpacker areas of Jakarta (Jalan Jaksa) and other tourist areas (Solo, Yogyakarta, and Denpasar) have good second-hand bookshops. Some well-known bookshops in Jakarta include:

Gunung Agung Bookstore, Jalan Kwitang 6.
Gramedia, Jalan Gajah Mada 109.

Banks and financial matters

There are coins of 5, 10, 25, 50, and 100 rupiah (the 5 and 10 rupiah coins are fairly uncommon these days), and notes of 100, 500, 1 000, 5 000, 10 000, 20 000 and 50 000. Banks are open from 8.30am–2.30pm Monday–Friday and from 8.30am–12.30pm on Saturdays and there are ATMs open 24 hours a day. Credit cards can be used for large purchases, in department stores, and in the large international hotels and restaurants. Indonesia is mostly a cash society, cheques are rarely used, and your salary will either be paid in cash or paid directly into your bank account. Opening an account is a simple matter. You usually need only a small deposit and your passport. As Indonesians deal mostly in cash, a cheque account is of little use. Instead, open a savings account and earn some interest on your money. Many teachers keep their savings in a foreign currency bank account, and opening a dollar account is as straightforward as opening a rupiah account.

Health

For pre-arrival health advice see Chapter 1: Health. Should you not have time to get yourself immunized completely before you leave your home country, most hospitals or doctors' clinics will be able to give you the required injections after you arrive in Indonesia.

Indonesia has both state-owned and privately-run hospitals. Government hospitals are cheap, but often have very long queues for outpatients and few doctors who speak English. Private hospitals are slightly more expensive with marginally shorter queues and usually at least a few doctors who speak English.

The hospital listed below is private but it will deal with emergencies and will give vaccinations to non-members for a small fee:

Medical Scheme, Setiabudi Building, Jalan H Rasuna Said, Kuningan, Jakarta. Tel. 51597.

MEDIA

Television

Indonesian TV has between one and four channels depending on where you are in the country. All channels carry a lot of programmes from the USA, and some from the UK, Canada, Australia and even from South America (dubbed Mexican soap operas). Foreign programmes have Indonesian subtitles, so you can watch re-runs of LA Law and learn some Indonesian at the same time. Some pubs and most hotels in Jakarta have satellite TV now.

Radio

There are hundreds of radio stations in Indonesia playing a mixture of Western and Asian pop music and Indonesian *dangdut* music. English language radio stations include programmes from the BBC World Service and the Australian Broadcasting Corporation, although reception varies depending on where in Indonesia you are; cities having much better reception than outlying rural areas.

Newspapers

The main English language daily paper in Jakarta is *The Jakarta Post.* Newspapers from abroad are available from the newsagents in the large hotels, although they are expensive. So, if you need your fix of the *New York Times, USA Today* or *The Sunday Times*, don't worry, the Jakarta Hilton can help you out.

RECREATION

Music

Jakarta is not yet a regular spot on the Asian tour list for internationally known bands, except occasional heavy metal ones. Famous people do play in Jakarta but they tend to be has-beens (like Neil Sedaka) who perhaps cannot get a booking anywhere else and who find that they are now better suited to the quiet, well-heeled audiences of the Jakarta Sheraton. That is not to say you will be without live music in Indonesia; music is everywhere in Indonesia. There is live music in the pubs, discos, restaurants. Blind buskers provide it on the trains, buses and at traffic lights, and every man Jack and his guitar can play you a mean Stairway to Heaven.

Indonesian music

Traditional Javanese music is called *gamelan* – an orchestra made up of *gender* (xylophones), gongs and drums, *rebab* (two-stringed violins), *suling* (wooden flutes) and accompanied by very high, nasal singing.

You can hear *gamelan* music at traditional parties, circumcisions, weddings, funerals or when it is used to accompany *wayang* shows. These shows can be *wayang kulit* (two-dimensional shadow-puppets), *wayang golek* (three-dimensional puppets), *wayang topeng* (masked actors) or *wayang orang* (symbolic dances with and without masks), and can last all night.

Bars and discos

Jakarta

There are a lot of bars in Jakarta where you can meet foreigners and any *losmen* cafe or bar in Jalan Jaksa is a good bet for meeting back-packers or new teachers. Bars which are popular with teachers included:

Memories, Jalan Jaksa.
Romance, Jalan Jaksa.
Asmak, Jalan Jaksa.
Angie's Cafe, Jalan Jaksa.
Green Pub, Jakarta Theater Building, Jalan M.H. Thamrin.
Captain's Bar, Mandarin Hotel, Jalan M.H. Thamrin.
George and Dragon, Jalan Teluk Betung 32.
The Sportsman's Bar, Blok M.
The Tavern, Hyatt Aryaduta Hotel, Jalan Prapatan 44/48.
Elvis, Artha Loka Building.

Discos which are popular with teachers include:

Tanamur, Jalan Tanah Abang Timur 14.
Ebony, Kuningan Plaza, Jalan Rasuna Said.

Bandung

Popular bars for teachers are:

The Laga, Jalan Terusan Pastur.
The Lingga, Jl Cemara.
Tizzi's, Jalan I. H. Juanda.

Denpasar

Denpasar changes constantly so it is difficult to recommend bars, as any bar that is popular this week could suddenly become unpopular, close down or move. Practically any bar in Denpasar will have foreigners in it, and asking around in a few will lead you to the ones that are currently popular with teachers.

Discos

There are two kinds of discos in Indonesia – Western discos with mostly English language music, strobe lighting and high prices, and *dangdut* discos with Indonesian pop music, not too many lights and very cheap entrance fees. *Dangdut* music is the music of the *orang kecil* (literally the little people, or working class people). It sounds like a mixture of traditional Indian and pop music and tells tales of poverty, social injustice and, of course, unrequited love.

> When I first arrived in Indonesia I kept hearing one, particular song, *Sakit Gigi* everywhere I went. Even before I understood the words, I found myself singing along to this *dangdut* song every time I heard it on the bus, in the shops, on the radio. It wasn't till I started having Indonesian lessons that I discovered that I'd been singing perhaps the most romantic line of all times: 'I'd rather have toothache than a broken heart from you'.
>
> *Francis O'Brien, England*

Cinema

All the major Hollywood blockbusters come to Indonesia, sheer bliss if you are a Sylvester Stallone fan. Tickets costs about 6 000 rupiah. English language films have until recently been subtitled in Indonesian, but increasingly now films are being dubbed into Indonesian.

Theatre

Western-styled theatres are uncommon in Indonesia except for a few playhouses in Jakarta doing locally-written works. English language plays are practically unheard of but there is still plenty of drama to be seen in traditional Indonesian theatrical performances. *Wayang* performances are an ancient Indonesian art form based on the Hindu epic poems, *Mahabharata* and *Ramayana*. Full performances last about 12 hours.

Sports

Every morning all across Indonesia people do their exercises together. School, hospital and office front yards are filled with people participating in organized, regimented group exercises.

The national sport in Indonesia is badminton. You will see people playing it everywhere – indoors, outdoors, and even in Post Offices! The recent Olympic achievements of the Indonesian badminton team gave the sport another boost, so make sure you pack your shuttlecock.

Other popular sports include football, basketball and volleyball for school and university students. Tennis and golf are reserved for older and richer Indonesians, and expats.

Swimming

There are public swimming pools which are very cheap at 1 000 rupiah a day. Some large international hotels have fitness centres but membership is quite expensive. One-day gym membership costs about 30 000 rupiah. Often you can use a hotel's pool (and towels and hot showers) for around 3 000 rupiah a day.

Cultural activities

Indonesia is famous for its batik, designed material produced by dying material after covering different parts of it with hot wax. It is a fascinating process to watch or participate in. Although Yogyakarta is the most famous centre for batik, it is possible to study it in all the major cities and in many *kampung,* small villages, too. Indonesians check the quality of a piece of batik by looking at both sides of the material. The same colour strength of design on each side of the piece is a sign of a good batik.

Other leisure activities

Indonesians constantly visit one another and generally hang out with their friends in their spare time. Being by yourself is considered very strange and Indonesians will constantly ask you if they can *'main main'* (literally play play) at your house, or if you will come round to *'main main'* at their place. Cruising shopping centres is a popular pastime for groups of young people at the weekend, as it seems to be throughout South-east Asia.

Help-lines (Jakarta)

International phone inquiries	102
Operator	101

APPENDICES

Appendix 1. Case histories

Rachel Wijaksono

Rachel Wijaksono was born in County Durham, England. She studied English Language and Literature at Oxford University and, after graduating in 1987, studied for the UCLES/RSA CTEFLA. She then went to North India for a year to work as a volunteer English and Music teacher in a girls' school in Simla.

In 1989, through Voluntary Services Overseas (VSO, see p 43), she worked in the English department of an IKIP – a teacher training college – in Kediri, West Java, for two years. She met Agung while she was working in Kediri and they were married in her father's small Anglican church in Kilburn, Yorkshire in the winter of 1992. 'We wore traditional Javanese wedding clothes and a lot of thermal underwear.' She gave birth to their son, Rian, in 1994.

In Indonesia she has worked as a teacher, senior teacher and is currently the Director of Studies in a private language school, The British Institute, a Bell-affiliate school in Bandung, Java. She says that she had no idea when she arrived in Indonesia in 1989 that years later she would be married to an Indonesian, with a small child and still living happily in Asia.

The benefits of living in Indonesia include the endless variety of food, the tropical climate and the constant excitement of living in a foreign country. 'It's demanding living here' she says. 'It's not all sunshine and exotic fruit, yet there's always something new to learn, be it as small as a new Indonesian word, or as big as a challenge to one of my dearly held opinions. For instance, before I left England I believed that was a "true" price for everything and that I should pay the same price as everyone else, whether they were richer or poorer than me. But, after a few years of day-to-day bargaining with people who earn a twentieth of my income, I now think that an adjusted price (adjusted to the buyer's income) is much more just. I don't talk about a 5 pence 'rip-off' anymore, and my blood pressure's a lot more healthy as a result. I feel that these years in Indonesia have made me slightly plumper and more willing to see someone else's point of view.'

Natalie Burwell

Natalie Burwell was born in Newport News, Virginia, USA. She majored in Religion at the College of William and Mary in Virginia. In 1990 she went to England and worked for two years as a volunteer, first with severely emotionally disturbed adolescents and then with adults with learning difficulties in London.

She completed the RSA/UCLES CTEFLA at Bell, London, and wanted to find work in South-east Asia because of her interest in religions. She found out about a school in Indonesia, and they actually sent her a contract to sign. However, the monthly salary mentioned on the contract was half what the EFL Guide and other sources had said to expect, and there was a clause saying that the school would keep her passport for the duration of her time there. In the end, she decided to go to Indonesia by herself and find work once she got there.

'Just going to Indonesia on spec was scary at the time – and even a bit scary in retrospect when I think of myself sitting in a grungy guesthouse with the beginnings of (as it turned out) a common cold, thinking, "This is typhoid. Does that fried rice look funny? I don't have a job yet. I'm history." But the bad things that could have happened didn't, and now, going to a country myself to arrange work seems like normal practice.'

She found a job – first a six-month half-time contract that entailed lots of overtime, and then a full-time contract – at The British Institute, a private language school in Bandung. The school provided health insurance, a housing loan, and took care of visas and work permits.

'If you're going to volunteer your services in Asia, that's one thing, but if you are looking for paid work and it's your first job, you shouldn't just think in terms of survival. There are some excellent schools that emphasize teacher development and that have good facilities. If you are on the scene, you quickly learn the reputation and "personality" of different schools. Surviving by teaching in Asia is easy, but the kind of school that will lock up your passport will make life miserable for you.'

Natalie worked in Bandung, West Java for about three years. When asked about the attractions of living and working in Indonesia, she mentioned the motivated students, generally supportive teaching community, and the lifestyle that was possible there:

'Renting a whole house for a year cost about $1 200; and I mean a three-bedroom, quiet, airy house with high ceilings and white tile floors. I rode my mountain bike to and from work, went to Bali on holiday, and could start on a hike through green hills and rice paddies by walking out my backdoor. Could I live like that in the West?'

In 1995 she moved to another Bell-affiliate school in Bangkok, and after a year there, joined The British Council in Bangkok. Asked to compare Bangkok and Bandung, she said,

'Of course the pace of life is much faster here, and riding a mountain-bike to work is just a happy memory. But I'm finding that Bangkok is a good place to reflect on my experience in Asia because of the availability of books, magazines, journals; because of the libraries, theaters, art exhibits. For better or worse, in this urban environment I feel more in touch with the modern world than I did in Bandung.'

Appendix 2. Useful Indonesian words and phrases

Indonesian is very similar to Malay and most of the words and phrases listed below are almost identical to those listed in the Chapter 8 – Malaysia, Appendix 2.

Numbers

1	*satu*	9	*sembelan*	40	*empat puluh*		
2	*dua*	10	*sepuluh*	60	*enam puluh*		
3	*tiga*	11	*se-belas*	50	*lima puluh*		
4	*empat*	12	*dua-belas*	70	*tujuh puluh*		
5	*lima*	13	*tiga-belas*	80	*delapan puluh*		
6	*enam*	20	*dua puluh*	90	*sembelan puluh*		
7	*tujuh*	21	*dua puluh satu*	100			
8	*delapan*	30	*tiga puluh*				

Days

Monday	*Hari Senin*	Friday	*Hari Jumat*
Tuesday	*Hari Selesa*	Saturday	*Hari Sabtu*
Wednesday	*Hari Rabu*	Sunday	*Hari Minggu*
Thursday	*Hari Kamis*		

Months

January	*Januari*	July	*Juli*
February	*Pebruari*	August	*Ogos*
March	*Maret*	September	*September*
April	*April*	October	*Oktober*
May	*Mai*	November	*November*
June	*Juni*	December	*Disember*

Times and dates

Today	*Hari ini*
Tonight	*Malam ini*
Yesterday	*Kemaren*
Tomorrow	*Besok*
Next week	*Minggu depan*
What time is it?	*Jam berapa?*
When?	*Kepan?*

Greetings and small talk

Good morning	*Selamat pagi*
Good afternoon (early)	*Selamat tengahari*
Good afternoon (late)	*Selamat petang*
Good night	*Selamat malam*
Good-bye (said by the person going)	*Selamat tinggal*
Good-bye (said by the person staying)	*Selamat jalan*
How are you?	*Apa Kabar?*
I'm fine	*Baik*

I am sorry	*Minta maaf*
Excuse me	*Permisi*
It doesn't matter	*Tidak apa-apa*
Can you speak Indonesia?	*Kamu bisa bicara Bahasa Indonesia?*
Yes	*Si*
No	*Tidak/Bukan*
Can you speak English?	*Kamu bisa bicara Bahasa Inggris?*
I'm sorry I don't speak Indonesian.	*Maaf, saya tidak bicara Bahasa Indonesia*
I don't understand.	*Saya tidak mengerti*
Please	*Tolong*
Thank you	*Terima kasih*

Shopping

Where can I buy...?	*Dimana saya membeli...?*
How much does it cost?	*Berapa harganya?*
Do you have...?	*Ada...?*
Where is the...?	*Dimana...?*
Open	*Buka*
Closed	*Tutup*

Appendix 3. Public holidays

It is difficult to state the exact date of many Indonesian public holidays as the Islamic ones, and many of the Christian ones, are based on the moon's cycles of 354 days, and the Hindu ones are based on the Balinese calendar of a 210 day year. Fluctuating dates are marked with an asterisk *.

1 January	New Year's Day
* Early January	Ascension Day of Prophet Muhammad SAW
* Early April	Nyepi, Balinese New Year
* Early April	Good Friday
* Early May	*Idul Futri*
* Early May	Ascension of Jesus Christ
* Late May	Idul Adha
* Late May	Waisak Day, Buddha's birthday
* Mid June	Muslim New Year
17 August	Independence Day
* Mid August	Maulid of Prophet Muhammad SAW
25 December	Christmas Day

Appendix 4. Embassies and consulates

Selected Indonesian embassies abroad

Australia: 8 Darwin Avenue, Canberra, ACT, 2600. Tel: (06) 2 733 222.

Canada: 28 Maclaren Street, Ottawa, Ontario, K2P OL9.

New Zealand: 70 Glen Road, Kelburn, Wellington. Tel: (04)75 895.

UK: 38 Grosvenor Square, London W1X 9AS. Tel: (0171) 499 7661.

USA: 2020 Massachusetts Avenue, Washington, DC 20036. Tel: (202) 775 5200; 5 East 68th Street, New York, NY 10021. Tel: (212) 879 0600;

3457 Wilshire Boulevard, Los Angeles, CA 90010. Tel: (213) 383 5126; 1111 Columbus Avenue, San Francisco, CA 94133. Tel: (415) 474 9571; 233 North Michigan Avenue, Chicago, IL 60601. Tel: (312) 938 0101.

Appendix 5. Suggested reading

Almeister, A. M., *How to Master the Indonesian Language*, Sapdodadi, Jakarta.

Blare, Lawrence, *Ring of Fire*, Bantam Books, New York, 1988.

Indonesia, Footprint Handbooks, Bath/NTC, Chicago, 1997.

Ketut, Tantri, *Revolt in Paradise*, Crown, New York, 1989.

Koch, Christopher, *The Year of Living Dangerously*, New York, Penguin 1978.

McDonald Hamish, *Suharto's Indonesia*, Fontanel Books, Australia, 1980.

Mochtar, Lubis, *Twilight in Jakarta*, Oxford University Press.

Teach Yourself Indonesian, Hodder-Headline, London.

Turner, Peter, *Lonely Planet City Guide Jakarta*, Lonely Planet Publications.

Storey, R., D. Spitzer, R. Nebesky, and A. Wheeler, *Lonely Planet Travel Survival Kit Indonesia*, Lonely Planet Publications.

Lonely Planet Language Survival Kit Indonesian phrasebook, Lonely Planet.

Appendix 6. Suggested videos

The Year of Living Dangerously

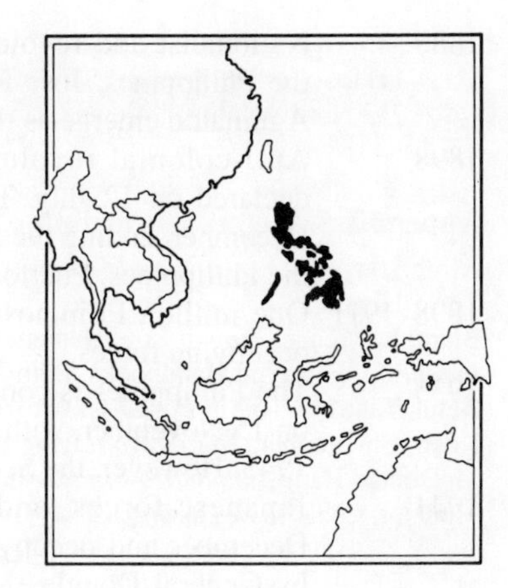

12

The Philippines

FACTFILE

History

The earliest evidence of human habitation in the Philippines was discovered in 1962 in Tabon Cave, in Palawan. Human bones, flake tools, and fossilized bat and bird bones have been carbon-dated at 22 000 BC.

3 000 BC	Austronesians arrive in canoes bringing pottery, woodcarving, and the art of tattooing.
1 000 AD	Chinese, Indian, Arab and Indonesian traders arrive bringing textiles, iron weapons, and jewelry to barter for pearls, gold, and coral.
14th century	Traders introduce Islam to the Philippines.
1521	Ferdinand Magellan from Spain, trying to find a westward route across the Pacific to India, arrives on Samar Island. Magellan is killed shortly after by a chieftain of Mactan Island.
1565	After four more Spanish attempts, Miguel Lopez de Legazpi, sailing from Mexico, claims the islands for King Philip II of Spain, naming them *Filipinas.* Mexicans establish themselves as lords of estates and Catholic missionary monks convert the islanders.
Late 18th/ early 19th century	Political, social and economic reforms are introduced allowing some Filipino participation in government. Cash crops are introduced ending the Manila Galleon monopoly on foreign commerce. A Nationalist movement is formed by some liberal clergy, professionals and students in Spain.

1880	Nationalist and revolutionary movements are formed in the Philippines. Jose Rizal, Andres Bonifacio and Emilio Aguinaldo emerge as the leaders.
1898	Anti-colonial revolution erupts and independence is declared on 12 July. The Treaty of Paris is signed on 10 December, ending the Spanish-American war. Spain cedes the Philippines, Puerto Rico and Guam to America.
1898–1911	One million Filipinos die fighting against the American occupying forces.
1935	The Philippines is constituted as a Commonwealth nation on 15 November, with the promise of full independence in 1945. However, the Second World War intervenes.
1941	Japanese forces land on the Bataan Peninsula on 10 December and occupy Manila. The American forces, led by General Douglas MacArthur, retreat from Corregidor leaving 80 000 prisoners of war. 10 000 prisoners die of starvation, torture and beating during the five-day Bataan Death March.
1944	General MacArthur returns to fight the Japanese who retreat to the historic city of Intramuros and refuse to surrender. Over 100 000 Filipino civilians die and Intramuros is almost completely destroyed.
1946	On 4 July Manuel Roxas, the first president, proclaims Filipino independence.
1965	Ferdinand Marcos becomes president.
1972	Martial law is declared. Marcos dissolves congress and rewrites the constitution to allow him to be president for more than the previously legally established three terms. Political opponents are jailed, including Benigno Aquino, who was considered his biggest political threat had the 1973 elections gone ahead.
1980	45 political and trade union organizations boycott the fraudulent and unconstitutional elections that allow Marcos to stay in power.
1981	In September thousands of people demonstrate against Marcos and demand the withdrawal of the US army bases in the Philippines.
1983	Opposition leader Benigno Aquino returns from exile in the USA and is murdered at Manila airport. Marcos is blamed for the murder. More than 500 000 people attend Aquino's funeral and demand that Marcos leave the Philippines.
1984	Opposition parties make substantial gains in the by-elections in May but fail to topple Marcos.
1986	Elections are held in February. Widespread corruption prevents Cory Aquino (Benigno Aquino's widow) from

winning. Aquino calls for civil disobedience (People Power), which eventually results in Marcos fleeing the country and Aquino assuming the presidency.

1992 A new president is elected: Fidel Ramos, a former military leader, who was endorsed during the election campaign by Aquino.

Geography

The Philippines is made up of more than 7 000 islands and lies off the north-east coast of the Malaysian state of Sabah. The islands stretch 1 770 kilometres from north to south and 1 102 kilometres across at their widest, although the total land area of the islands is only about the size of Italy. More than 90% of the population live on only about 10 of the islands, and of these, Luzon and Mindanao are the most important.

There are 12 active and many more dormant volcanoes on the islands, as well as primary forests with ferns and orchids, and wild animals similar to those found in Borneo, such as the mouse deer, porcupine, anteater, and mongoose.

Climate

Like the other countries in the South-east Asia region, the Philippines lies in the tropical zone and has two seasons – wet and hot, and dry and hot. The dry, slightly cooler season is from December to May, the monsoon season is July to October, and the hot, dry season is from November to late January. Humidity is high.

Time

The Philippines, like Singapore and Malaysia, is 8 hours ahead of Greenwich Mean Time, 13 hours ahead of New York, 16 hours ahead of San Francisco and 2 hours behind Sydney.

The people

There are over 60 million people in the Philippines. Filipinos are racially related to the Malaysians and the Indonesians. Over the centuries Chinese, Indian, Spanish, and American people have mixed with the original inhabitants, producing Filipino-Spanish, Filipino-Chinese and Filipino-American *mestizos.*

Politics

Today the Philippines is a constitutional republic with an elected president. It has a National Assembly made up of a House of

Representatives and a Senate. The present ruling party is Lakas ng Bansa and the President and Head of State is Fidel Ramos.

Languages

Tagalog or *Filipino* is the official language in the Philippines, although there are more than 80 languages and 110 dialects spoken on the islands. Most Filipinos can speak English as well as Spanish, in fact the Philippines is the third largest English-speaking country in the world. As in Brunei, this means you can easily make yourself understood, but severely limits your chances of making a good living as an EFL teacher.

Religions

The Philippines is in the unique position of being the only Christian majority country in South-east Asia (the main religion being Catholicism). 83% of the population is Catholic, 9% is Protestant, 5% Muslim, and 3% Animist. The minority Muslims and animists groups are in many ways quite separate from the rest of the country. The Muslims have a long history of resisting the assimilation of the Spanish, Americans or the Filipinos and today they mainly live on the island of Mindanao.

Cultural considerations

Asian, Spanish and American cultures have all left their marks on the Philippines. In many respects the Philippines seems much more Westernized than the rest of South-east Asia, but, despite the outward signs of Americanization, it is still a part of Asia and like other countries in the region, smiling, losing and saving face, and family loyalty are just as important.

Utan Na Loob (reciprocal favours)

An important and distinctive aspect of Filipino life is *utan na loob*. This is the custom of returning favours with interest. So you should make sure that you are ready to reciprocate if you ask a favour here.

TEACHING POSSIBILITIES

Private language schools

Although the British Council does not run a Direct Teaching Operation here, you can contact them in Manila and they will be able to give you advice about the teaching opportunities, if any, that are available.

The British Council, 10th Floor, Taipan Place, Emerald Avenue Ortigas Business Centre, Pasig City, Metro Manila. Tel: (02) 914 1011. Fax: (02) 914 1020.

International schools

Finding casual teaching work is difficult in the Philippines, as most of the population speak very good English. Probably your best bet for finding work is to contact the International Schools which might have vacancies for qualified primary, high school or EFL teachers.

Baguio City

Brent International School, PO Box 35, Baguio City 2600. Tel: (074) 442 2260. Fax: (74) 442 3638.

Cebu City

Cebu International School, Banilad, Cebu City. Tel: (032) 972 68. Fax: (032) 311 556.

Manila

International School, Manila, MCPO Box 323, Makati 1299. Tel: (02) 889 891. Fax: (02) 818 6127.

Brent International School, Manila, University of Life Complex, Meralco Avenue, Pasig, Metro-Manila. Tel: (02) 631 1265. Fax: (02) 633 8420.

The British School, Manila, PO Box 2079, MCPO 1260 Makati, Metro Manila. Tel: (02) 828 2261. Fax: (02) 828 1737.

Faith Academy, PO Box 2106 MCPO 0706, Makati. Tel: (02) 658 0151. Fax: (02) 658 0026.

BEFORE YOU GO

Insurance

Take out a travel and health insurance policy before you leave for the Philippines.

Vaccinations

See Chapter 1: Health about what health precautions you should take before and after arriving here.

ARRIVAL AND VISAS

Visas

Tourist visas. Visitors from countries which have diplomatic relations with the Philippines do not need a visa, provided they do not stay for more than 21 days. It is also quite simple to extend your visa for up to 58 days once you arrive here. Countries which have diplomatic relations with the Philippines include Australia, New Zealand, the UK and the USA.

Work visas. It is not possible to change your tourist visa into a work permit while you are in the Philippines, so you will have to take a short trip outside the country to the nearest Philippines Embassy in order to get a work visa.

Transport from the airport

Ordinary airport taxis to Ermita cost 80-90 pesos and white airport taxis cost 150 pesos. Ermita used to be the main budget accommodation area of Manila, but was recently 'cleaned up' by the Ramos government, removing many of the cheap places (see below for more details on budget accommodation).

ACCOMMODATION

Short-term accommodation

Expect to pay 200–500 pesos for accommodation in Metro Manila, but far less in remoter areas. In general, the cheaper the place you stay, the poorer the security, with plywood doors and flimsy padlocks passing as protection. Consider paying more for a hotel or guesthouse that offers better locks and a safety deposit box, for your own peace of mind.

Popular budget accommodation can be found in Ermita and Malate, which are actually two connecting areas in the tourist enclave in downtown Manila, about 12 kilometres from the airport.

Pensions are large, old houses which have been converted into small rooms and dormitories with communal bathrooms and dinning rooms. *Mansions* and *apertels* are small apartments with kitchens that are ideal for the long-term visitor or teachers who go to Manila to look for work. *Mansions* and *apertals* are usually cheaper than *pensions.*

Some popular *pensions, mansions* and *apertals* are:

Pensions

Carolina Pesion, 211 Carolina. Tel: (02) 522 3961.
Casa Dalco 1, 1318 Agoncillo. Tel: (02) 598 522.
Casa Dalco II, 1910 Mabini. Tel: (02) 508 855.

Mansions and apertals

Dakota Mansions, 555 Malvar. Tel: (02) 521 0701.
Pearl Garden, 1700 Adriatico. Tel: (02) 575 911.
Southern Cross Inn, 476 United Nations. Tel: (02) 581 6883.

EATING

Filipino food is simple but tasty; however it presents few culinary fireworks compared to some other countries in the region. The main influences in cooking are Spanish, Indonesian/Malay and Chinese. There is no identifiable national cuisine, but local dishes using fish, chicken, and pork provide good basic food.

Filipino specialties include *adobo* (pork or chicken stew which is marinated in soy sauce, vinegar, garlic and sugar); and *kare kare* (oxtail, beef or pig knuckles with a peanut sauce served with vegetables and rice).

TRANSPORT

Safety

First a warning about safety on transport: be especially careful of your belongings on buses. Pickpockets abound, and on long-distance buses many people have had their bags stolen while they were in the toilet at rest stops. The usual guidebook tip about not accepting food and drinks from friendly strangers is the case here too, but perhaps even more caution than usual is required because of the prevalence of armed kidnappings and general lawlessness. Towns and cities are generally not very safe at night.

Bus

For travel around the country, buses range from comfortable, air-conditioned, non-stop affairs with country music on the stereo, to cramped *'ordinario'* buses where you often have to share the ride with chickens. Long-distance buses are cheap and they leave frequently, but travel is tiring as the roads are very pot-holed. In Manila, buses leave from stations designated by the name of the bus company (Victory Liner, Rabbit, etc), not according to the various destinations. Just ask somebody if this proves confusing.

Jeepney

In Manila the local bus and jeepney rates are 1.50 pesos for the first four kilometres and 25 centavos for every kilometre after that. *Love bus* fares are a flat 10 pesos. Jeepneys are ubiquitous in towns and for short inter-town journeys. They are doorless, often gaudily personalized by the driver, and have their destination written on a sign in the front window. Prices start at 2 pesos. A jeepney journey is an essential Manila experience.

Taxi

There are two types of taxis in Manila – airconditioned and non-airconditioned. For aircon taxis, the flag down charge is 12.5 pesos and for non-air-con taxis the charge is 7.5 pesos. After that, both types of taxis charge 1 peso for every 250 metres.

Metrorail

Metrorail is a 10 kilometre overhead railway system in Manila. There is a flat rate fare of 3.5 pesos.

Tricycles

Tricycles are motorbikes with a side-car attached and are useful if you are going short distances down small sides streets. There is no set price for these and you should bargain and agree a price before you start.

SERVICES

Banks and financial matters

The currency of the Philippines is the peso (in Tagalog *piso*) and there are 100 centavos to the peso. Banks are open from Monday to Friday 9am to 4pm. It is difficult to change money anywhere but in banks, and the US dollar is the most readily accepted currency. Traveller's cheques are problematic to cash outside the larger towns.

RECREATION

Bars

Beer is very cheap for Asia at 12 pesos a bottle. Popular local brands are San Miguel, Red Horse, and Blue Ice. Bars which are popular with teachers and expats in Manila include:

Bistro RJ, Olympia Building, Makati Ave.
Hobbit House, 1801 Mabini Street.
My Father's Mustache, 2144 MH del Pilar St.

Sports

Scuba diving

One of the most popular sports here is scuba diving. The Philippines has 28 000 square kilometres of coral reefs to explore and plenty of scuba clubs and dive shops to choose from. For more information see *Philippines: A Divers' Paradise*, a leaflet available from the Philippine Convention and Visitors Corporation in Manila.

APPENDICES

Appendix 1. Useful Tagalog words and phrases

Numbers

1	*isa*	11	*labing isa*	21	*dalawampu isa*
2	*dalawa*	12	*labing dalawa*	30	*tatlumpu*
3	*tatlo*	13	*labing tatlo*	40	*apatnapu*
4	*apat*	14	*labing apat*	50	*limampu*
5	*lima*	15	*labing lima*	60	*anninapu*
6	*anim*	16	*labing anim*	70	*pitumpu*
7	*pito*	17	*labing pito*	80	*walumpu*
8	*walo*	18	*labing walo*	90	*siyamnapu*
9	*siyam*	19	*labing siyam*	100	*isang daan*
10	*sampu*	20	*dalawampu*		

Days

Monday	*Lunes*	Friday	*Biyernes*
Tuesday	*Martes*	Saturday	*Sabado*
Wednesday	*Miyerkules*	Sunday	*Linngo*
Thursday	*Huwebes*		

Months

January	*Enero*	July	*Hulyo*
February	*Pebrero*	August	*Agusto*
March	*Marso*	September	*Setyembre*
April	*Abril*	October	*Oktobre*
May	*Mayo*	November	*Nobyembre*
June	*Hunyo*	December	*Disyembre*

Times and dates

Today	*ngayon*
Tonight	*ngayon araw naito*
Yesterday	*kahopon*
Tomorrow	*bukas*
When?	*Kailan?*

Greetings and small talk

Good morning	*magandang umapa po*
Good evening	*magandang gabi po*

Good-bye	*paalam na po*
Please	*Paki*
Thank you	*Salamat*
I am sorry	*Pasensiya*
Yes (informal)	*Oo*
Yes (formal)	*Opo*
No (informal)	*Hindi*
No (formal)	*Hindi po*
Do you speak English?	*Marungong ka bang mag-Ingles?*
I'm sorry I don't speak Tagalog	*Pasensiya na hindi ako marung mag-Tagalog*
I don't understand.	*Hindi ko maintindihan*

Shopping

Where can I buy...?	*Saan ako makakabili..?*
How much does it cost?	*Magkano ito?*
Do you have...?	*Mayroon ba kayo ng?*
Where is the...?	*Saan ang?*
Open	*Bukas*
Closed	*Sarado*

Appendix 2. Public holidays

Fluctuating public holidays are marked with an asterisk *

1 January	New Year's Day
*27 and 28 March	Easter holidays
9 April	Bataan Day
1 May	Labour Day
12 June	Independence Day
24 June	Araw Nh Maynila – Manila Day (holiday only in Manila)
31 August	National Heroes Day
1 November	All Saints Day
30 November	Bonifacio Day
25 December	Christmas Day
30 December	Rizal Day
31 December	New Year's Eve

Appendix 3. Embassies and consulates

Selected embassies and consulates in the Philippines

Australia: Bank of the Philippines Islands Building, Ayala Avenue, cnr Paseo de Roxas, PO Box 1274, Makati, Metro Manila. Tel: (02) 817 7911. Fax: (02) 817 3603.

UK: LV Loscin Building, 6752 Ayala Avenue, cnr Makati Avenue, Makati, Metro Manila 3116. Tel: (02) 816 7116. Fax: (02) 819 7206.

USA: 1201 Roxas Boulevard, Manila. Tel: (02) 521 7116. Fax: (02) 522 4361.

Selected Filipino embassies abroad

Australia:	1 Moonah Place, Yarralumla, Canberra. Tel: (026) 732 535.
Canada:	130 Albert Street #106, Ottawa. Tel:(613) 233 1121.

UK: 9A Palace Green, London, W8. Tel: (0171) 937 1600.
USA: 1617 Massachusetts Avenue, Washington, DC 20036. Tel:(202) 483 1414; 447 Sutter Street, San Francisco, CA 94118. Tel: (415) 433 6666.

Appendix 4. Selected reading

Peters, Jens, *Lonely Planet Travel Survival Kit The Philippines*, Lonely Planet Publications.
Simons, Lewis M., *Worth Dying For*, William Morrow, New York, 1987.
Steinberg, David Joel, *The Philippines: A Singular and Plural Place,* Westview Press, Colorado, 1982.
Wolff, John, *Lonely Planet Language Survival Kit Pilipino Phrasebook*, Lonely Planet Publications.

Appendix 5. Suggested videos

Although there are no famous films available about the Philippines, the following movies were all made in the Philippines

Apocalypse Now
Born of the Fourth of July
Platoon
The Year of Living Dangerously

Index